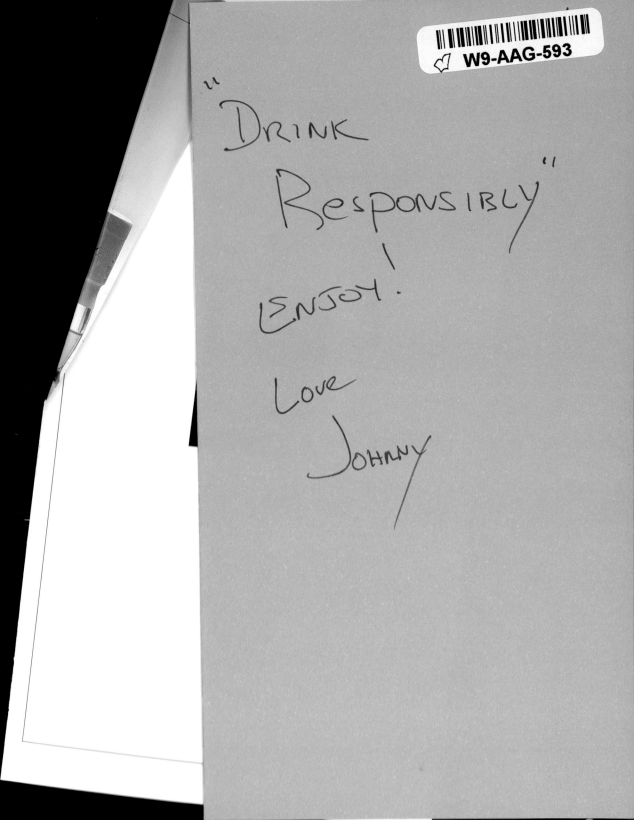

"DRINK RESPONSIBLY"

ENJOY!

Love

JOHNNY

A CONNOISSEUR'S GUIDE
TO THE SINGLE MALT
WHISKIES OF SCOTLAND

COMPREHENSIVELY REVISED
FIFTH EDITION

RUNNING PRESS
PHILADELPHIA • LONDON

MICHAEL JACKSON'S
COMPLETE GUIDE TO

SINGLE MALT
SCOTCH

A DORLING KINDERSLEY BOOK

Copyright © 1989, 1991, 1994, 1999, 2004 Dorling Kindersley Limited
Text copyright © 1989, 1991, 1994, 1999, 2004 Michael Jackson
First published in the United States in 1990
by Running Press Book Publishers
All rights reserved under the Pan-American and
International Copyright Conventions

Cover design by Bill Jones

Colour reproduced by Colourscan, Singapore
Printed and bound in China by Leo paper Group

9 8 7 6 5 4 3 2 1
Digit on the right indicates the number of this printing

Library of Congress Control Number: 2004090227

ISBN 0-7624-1313-1

Design   Nick Harris, Rebecca Painter, and Edward Kinsey
Editorial   Carla Masson and Elizabeth Stubbs
Research   Owen D. L. Barstow and Cathy Turner
Photography   Steve Gorton and Ian O'Leary

Additional material
Dave Broom, Jürgen Deibel, and Martine Nouet

FOR DORLING KINDERSLEY
Senior Editor   Simon Tuite
Senior Art Editors   Joanne Doran and Sue Metcalfe-Megginson
DTP Designer   Louise Waller
Production Controllers   Sarah Sherlock and Heather Hughes
Managing Editor   Deirdre Headon
Art Director   Peter Luff

MD 159
Fifth Edition first published in Great Britain as
Malt Whisky Companion by Dorling Kindersley Limited, London

PENGUIN GROUP

This book may be ordered by mail from the publisher.
Please include $2.50 for postage and handling.
But try your bookstore first!

Running Press Book Publishers
125 South Twenty-second Street
Philadelphia, Pennsylvania 19103-4399

Visit us on the web!
www.runningpress.com

CONTENTS

*Before dinner or after?
With coffee, chocolate, or a
cigar? These are just some
of the moments for malt.
There are suggestions with
every entry ...*

INTRODUCTION

A SECRET NO LONGER

IN MY LATE TEENS, I was introduced to malt whisky by a fellow journalist in Edinburgh. I was young to have discovered spirits, especially one thought to be for adults only. My first malt was Glen Grant 12-year-old, flowery and seductively sweet. An older colleague warned that the kiss of spirits led to moral decline, but it was too late. I had lost my virginity to a single malt.

The sensuous pleasures are still being delivered with every dram, but a good four decades later, I have spent more time in the ascendant: clambering up the granite slopes of the Grampians in search of water sources; high in the Spey Valley, bracing myself as Macallan tries to sow barley against a headwind; feeling the salt stinging my face as high seas break against the rocky shores of Islay. Even the southerly climes of Spain and Missouri offered snowy hillsides when I went prospecting for the resiny European oak and the sweeter American variety, which are required to make casks for Macallan and Glenmorangie respectively. There was a welcome warmth in the flames, smoke, and steam as the coopers of Andalusia and Kentucky wrestled 100-year-old oaks into roundness. A cooperage can be Dante-esque, but that is as close as I have been to the *Inferno*. The disposition of gods and angels are important too, as I have been reminded on the sites of abbeys in Scotland and temples in Japan. All of these influences make themselves felt in its aromas and flavours; the spirit of earth, wind, and fire reaches the glass. But where to raise the glass? A soft morning in Cork or Antrim is one pleasure, a foggy evening in Nova Scotia or Northern California quite another; the rituals of Kyoto's old town something else.

It is the experience offered by the whisky itself that has always been my greatest interest. In trying better to understand this, I began 30 years ago by reading authors such as Barnard, Bruce Lockhart, Daiches, Gunn, and McDowell. They told me about the process of whisky making, its lore, history, and geography, but little about aroma or taste.

At that time, malt whisky was very much a local drink in the Highlands. Even in Edinburgh many pubs were innocent of malts. Those that did stock this most rooted of Scottish drinks rarely had more than one example. Glens Fiddich, Farclas, and Morangie were to be seen here and there, but not much else. Scotland's great national drink was almost a secret.

I had written the odd short piece on the subject in the 1970s, but started more serious research in the 1980s. In those earliest days, my questions about single malts were not welcomed by some of the more conservative souls in the industry. Malt whisky, in their view, belonged only in blends. Their myopia was perhaps forgivable: blended Scotch whisky was the world's most popular drink, and its sales were built on brand loyalty. Attempts to describe aromas and flavours and explore connoisseurship might unsettle such loyalties. This was whisky, not wine or food.

Writing on whisky was a lonely business, but I was given great encouragement by Wallace Milroy and Derek Cooper. My first book on the subject was *The World Guide to Whisky*, published in 1987, and this was quickly followed by malt whisky book in 1989.

No other writer had attempted so thoroughly to describe the taste of individual whiskies, discussed so many, or taken the controversial step of scoring them. In that first edition, there were fewer than 250 tasting notes. By the fourth edition, the tally had gone past 750. In this new, fifth edition, I have exceeded 1000. Keeping up is ever more difficult, not only because of the numbers, but also due to the many bottlings that bear a vintage date or celebrate a special occasion. They flirt for a moment, and then are gone. While I am forever keen to include new bottlings, I hesitate to exclude old ones. This is not just to boost the numbers. It is also to recognize that, while the distillery, merchant, importer, or distributor may long have sold out, the consumer might still find the bottling in one of America's huge drinks supermarkets or in a stylish malts bar in Tokyo or Sapporo. Where a bottling is now hard to find, I have indicated that.

The diversity of malts has greatly increased consumers' interest in whiskies of all types. Their questions are being answered by a growing number of writers. In the United States, the magazine *Malt Advocate* was established in 1987 to cover both beer and whisky, but has increasingly concentrated on the latter. *Whisky Magazine*, founded in 1998 in Britain, has an international audience. Malt whisky can no longer be regarded as a minor interest reserved for Caledonophiles.

Michael Jackson

WHAT'S NEW?
TRENDS IN MALTS

MALT WHISKY IS BLOSSOMING AS NEVER BEFORE: new distilleries, new styles, new stars. New products line the shelves in airport shops and specialist wine merchants. How can whisky be simultaneously deeply rooted and dynamic? There are trends and fashions, but they arise from passion and individuality.

MICRODISTILLERIES

The term "micro" is more commonly applied to the very small breweries that have blossomed in the United States, especially during the 1980s and 1990s. In San Francisco, the Anchor Steam Beer brewery, a survivor from the California Gold Rush, has been an inspiration for the micro movement. Steam Beer has a fermentation system traditional to the West Coast, and in the 1990s, the company launched a traditional interpretation of rye whiskey. The rye is malted, and no other grain is used. Distillation takes place in a pot still. The brewery and distillery are in the same premises, on Potrero Hill, a rehabbed neighbourhood of design studios and art galleries. Several versions of a single malt rye have been produced and marketed. Old Potrero was first reviewed in the fourth edition of this book. At that time, several other small enterprises, some of them based in beer breweries, others originally established to make grape brandies or fruit *eaux-de-vie*, were beginning to produce malt whiskies. Like the first microbreweries, the new small distilleries began in the wine regions of the west, but have now spread further afield (*see pp. 434–38*).

Rye revivalist
A single malt rye is just one revival from Fritz Maytag, of Anchor Brewing. In addition, he also makes gin, wine, and cheese.

On Cape Breton Island, in the province of Nova Scotia (meaning "New Scotland"), Canada, the Glenora distillery seems finally to be on a firm footing, after 10 years of intermittent production and sporadic bottlings. It is a handsome distillery, with a restaurant and

Born-again Bladnoch
Small is beautiful in this typical distillery hamlet. Instead of a church tower, a pagoda. Buddhists in Bladnoch? No, it is the vent on the retired maltings.

hotel, in a dramatically beautiful location in an area noted for its festivals of Scottish music.

In a wintry location across the Atlantic, the world's northernmost whisky distillery ran its first spirit at the end of 1999, at Gavle, on the Baltic coast of Sweden. The Mackmyra distillery has been established on a site that made vodka in the 1800s.

In a region known for the cultivation of malting barley, the town of Lahti, Finland, has for eight years enjoyed beer brewed at the Teerenpeli bar ("the flirt"). Publican Anssi Pyysing and wife Marianne began to buy malt whisky from Scotland and finish it in sherry, brandy, and rum casks. In 2002, they installed a small still and began to produce single malt.

In Ireland, plans have been announced to open a new distillery in Kilbeggan, County Westmeath. This venture is not connected with the former Locke's distillery, which matures whisky from Cooley.

The Gwalia Distillery, near Aberdare, in Wales, released its first whisky on 1 March 2004, St David's Day. The nation's patron saint surely enjoyed the meaty, spicy, minty, Penderyn Single Malt. The whisky bears the name of the village where it is distilled, in the Brecon Beacons National Park.

In the Scottish county of Fife, work is proceeding on a distillery to be called Ladybank. The plan is to use barley from identified local farms. Meanwhile, a nearby farm, called Daft Mill (sic), has obtained planning permission for a distillery. At the opposite end of Scotland, plans were also announced for the Shetland Isles' first legal distillery, Blackwood. They aim to start distilling late in 2004.

While the term "microdistillery" is not widely used in Scotland, it could be applied to these projects, and perhaps to several others. The common feature is that these are not owned by national or international groups, and are not in the business of building "brands".

The use of barley contracted from local farms to produce identified bottlings has also been a feature at the old-established Springbank distillery of Campbeltown. In 2001, its owners began work on the refitting of the Glengyle distillery, which had been silent for 75 years.

In the Lowlands, the Bladnoch distillery, which had been closed for 10 years, reopened as a "micro". The aim is to operate part-time, producing whisky primarily for bottling as a single malt, with an emphasis on local sales.

The notion of "down-sizing" an existent distillery to make it viable has also been pursued by the renowned merchant Gordon & MacPhail, which bought the silent Benromach distillery on Speyside. This has been completely re-equipped for smaller-scale production.

Pending the opening of the various planned distilleries, Scotland's smallest distillery was Edradour. This was returned to private ownership in 2002, when it was acquired by Andrew Symington of the independent bottlers Signatory. Thus was endorsed the notion that small is beautiful.

RECOGNIZING JAPANESE MALTS

It was not quite as dramatic as the 1976 "Judgment of Paris", in which some of the great French châteaux were outscored by Californian vineyards, but *Whisky Magazine's* 2001 "Best of the Best" judging had a similar significance for Japanese malt whisky.

Each edition of the magazine carries a blindfold judging of new releases, usually a dozen or 20. There is also always a tasting of a similar proportion based on a region, country, or style. After the first two or three years of the magazine, all the whisky regions, countries, and styles had been sampled, so it was decided to compare the highest scorers from those tastings with the "winners" from each flight of new releases. Prior to the inception of this new "contest", a total of around 300 whiskies had been reviewed by the magazine's two regular critics, who had awarded metaphorical "medals" to about 50 of the best of them.

These "best" whiskies were now judged blindfold in Edinburgh, Kentucky, and Tokyo, by panels whose membership read like a *Who's Who?* of the whisky world. The samples were kept within categories, albeit broader, so that the whiskies were judged more or less like with like. A Lowland Scotch did not find itself being compared with a bourbon, nor a Canadian with a Japanese. Nonetheless, there was still a highest scorer in the entire tasting. It was a 10-year-old, single cask malt whisky from the Nikka Distillery of Yoichi in Hokkaido, Japan.

Soon afterwards, a 1986 vintage of this malt was made available to members of the Scotch Malt Whisky Society as a monthly selection. That such a body

Winning whisky
The most Scottish-looking distillery in Japan makes the most Scottish-tasting whisky. This distillery was built in the 1930s in the fishing village of Yoichi, north of Sapporo, Hokkaido.

should select a Japanese whisky was deemed worthy of a celebratory dinner at the society's headquarters, which are in an historic wine cellar in Leith. The guest of honour was Takeshi Taketsuru, son of Masakata Taketsuru, who founded Nikka and was the original consultant on whisky to Suntory. At the dinner, the digestif was the Nikka 1986. It is a complex, wintry whisky: smoky, peaty, leafy, and resiny, with a suggestion of garden mint.

It was decided to hold the "Best of the Best" every alternate year. In 2002, another single cask ten-year-old from Nikka was among the high scorers, but it was beaten by Suntory's Hibiki 21-year-old, a minty, spicy, creamy whisky, described by one Scottish whisky maker as being "unspeakably good".

THE FASHIONABILITY OF ISLAY

The openings and reopenings that excited malt lovers at the end of the 1990s and beginning of the 2000s have a westerly bias. The most exciting reopenings have been on the western whisky island of Islay, which is renowned for the intensity of its malts.

The Ardbeg distillery reopened under new ownership just before the last edition of this book was published in 2000, and has released about 20 bottlings since (*see pp. 97–101*). Then when, in 2001, Bruichladdich reopened, also under new ownership, there was a sense of confirmation: Islay really was experiencing a revival. Bruichladdich has since released a dozen bottlings (*see pp. 149–57*).

Soon afterwards, Bunnahabhain, which had been experiencing a lengthy silent season, also went back into production. This meant that all the workable distilleries on the island were in operation. At the time, Port Ellen, which closed in 1983, still had its full complement of

Bruichladdich's back
Opening day, and Jim McEwan, one of the principals, introduces past managers of the distillery.

distillery buildings, but no equipment. Plans to retain the 19th-century former kilns but demolish a pagoda and the still-house building were disclosed in 2002. An "official" bottling of Port Ellen had been released earlier, with a recommended price of £110/$170. It was believed that two or three further bottlings might be released, the last by the middle of the current decade. Port Ellen has become something of a cult whisky. It is by no means the only malt from a dismantled distillery, nor is its product the rarest, but the combination of location and quality seals its status (*see* "Regional Variations", *pp. 54–63*).

MULTIPLE MALTS

A single malt, by definition, emanates from just one distillery, but the converse does not apply. A single distillery can make more than one malt: either by using a different configuration of stills or different levels of peating. Only a handful of distilleries have done this in the past (*see, for example, Glenburgie and its Lomond stills, p. 246*). The most interesting example is the Springbank distillery, which combines both approaches. The original Springbank whisky is distilled in an odd configuration, described as two-and-a-half times, from medium-peated malt. A second whisky, Longrow, is double distilled, from heavily peated malt. A third, Hazelburn, is triple distilled, from unpeated malt. The first Hazelburn is expected to be bottled in 2006. The use of different peating levels was one of the first innovations from the new owners at Bruichladdich. The original Bruichladdich is lightly peated, but two more assertive spirits are now distilled, under the names Port Charlotte and Octomore. When Shetland's proposed Blackwood distillery was announced, the principals indicated that both unpeated and heavily peated whiskies would be produced.

Singles shop
It looks like an ordinary corner shop, but Eaglesome's in Campbeltown is a shrine to malt whisky. It was bought by the owners of the Springbank distillery and the bottlers Cadenhead. Together, they line its shelves with rare whiskies.

IDENTIFYING THE CASK

By definition, a bottle of single malt contains whisky from just one distillery, but it is usually a marriage (or "vatting") of several production runs, drawn from a variety of casks. The most traditional types of cask are hogsheads, butts, or puncheons that formerly contained sherry. These may be made from either European (usually Spanish) or American oak. The type of sherry might be anything from from the delicate fino to the rich Pedro Ximénez. Sherry casks are expensive, and Scottish distillers today more commonly use barrels that formerly contained Kentucky bourbon or Tennessee whisky. These casks are made from American oak.

Some Scottish distillers have begun to itemize (on labels, boxes, or accompanying booklets) the type of casks used in the maturation of a particular whisky. The information supplied might include the type of sherry formerly contained in the casks, and the number of times they have been filled with whisky. Some connoisseurs like to have this information for its own sake, but it also helps the potential buyer to understand what to expect from the whisky. For example, "first-fill" casks impart much more aroma and flavour than "refill" casks.

WOOD FINISHES

This trend, reviewed in the fourth edition of this book, has proven to be more than a fad. The Glenmorangie distillery, which pioneered the technique in the mid-1990s, has stepped up the frequency and diversity of its wood finishes, which now number about 20. Some prized examples have included Côte de Nuits (launched in 2000), Côte de Beaune (2001), and Sauternes (2002). Perhaps feeling it had been on too rich a diet, Glenmorangie put down its wine glass for a moment at the end of 2002. But although the year was finished, the last whisky wasn't. Missouri Oak Reserve was matured throughout in new American barrels.

Some of the most innovative essays have emerged from William Grant & Sons. First came a version of the honey-tasting Balvenie finished in casks that had previously matured an Islay malt (believed to be Laphroaig). This was followed by Glenfiddich Caoran, its Gaelic name referring to the embers of a peat fire. Caoran achieves its peaty character by spending time in Islay casks. A further version is Glenfiddich Havana Reserve, which is finished in rum casks.

While the industry still sometimes perceives malt whiskies as being rarefied, the counter argument is that their individuality and colour attract attention to whisky as a whole. Techniques from the world of malts, such as wood finishes, are also beginning to influence blends.

The finishing touch

Glenmorangie was a pioneer of distillery bottlings at cask strength and of wood finishes. Dr Bill Lumsden, one of the new generation of whisky makers, has a special interest in wood. While a wide variety of cooperage from the wine industry is used in "finishing", the principal maturation of Glenmorangie is usually in American white oak from the Ozark mountains.

The first two examples were The Famous Grouse Islay Wood Finish and Port Wood Finish. William Grant's own blend, bearing the company's name, is even more innovative, with a version finished in casks that previously contained a strong, typically malty Scottish ale, from the Caledonian Brewery of Edinburgh. This is labelled William Grant's Ale Cask Reserve.

The term "wood finish" implies that the whisky first had its normal maturation, usually in either bourbon or sherry wood, and has then been reracked into a wine barrique, port pipe, madeira drum, or whatever, for the finishing touch. This often only lasts for six months, but may occasionally last for a year or two.

The technique is controversial on several counts. The finishing of Speyside whiskies in Islay woods raised a difficult question: if there is any residual Islay whisky in the "empty" cask when it is filled, isn't the result a vatted malt rather than a single? It would follow that, if there were any residual port, sherry, or madeira, the end result would not be a pure whisky of any kind.

Some traditionalists object in principle, on the grounds that "finishing" is a marketing device, and not traditional. While such vigilance has protected the integrity of Scotch whisky, it assumes that nothing has ever changed. The likelihood is that the first Scottish distillers had used herbs in their whisky, and that they did not mature it. Were they "traditional"?

Today, the contribution of wood to aroma and flavour is increasingly appreciated, not only in respect of finishes. An interesting regime reviewed in the fourth edition of this book was that applied to the 16-year-old version of Bushmills Malt: equal proportions of whiskey (the Irish spelling) are matured in sherry butts and first-fill bourbon barrels, then married in port pipes. Bushmills has produced a number of wood finishes but, like several other distilleries, has also released malt whiskies matured throughout in woods other than the traditional sherry or bourbon. Bushmills' owners, Irish Distillers Limited, have records showing that their predecessor company was buying marsala, malaga, and madeira casks in the late 1800s and continued to do so until the eve of the First World War.

CASK STRENGTH

Cask strength whiskies were a novelty a decade ago. The extent to which this has now changed is illustrated by the number of recent bottlings in this style from United Distillers (now Diageo). The company's rare malts, for example, were an early recognition of connoisseur interest in whisky at "full" strength. Diageo later added a selection of limited bottlings under the rubric "cask strength". In the 2000s, the company introduced versions of more than 30 malts sub-titled "natural cask strength".

As the term "cask strength" implies, the spirit enjoys a variety of potencies on its way to the bottle. It is usually collected from the still at an average strength between the mid- or lower 70s and upper 60s. It is sometimes reduced with water to the mid-60s before being filled into casks. The water is felt to "open up" the spirit and help it to mature.

During ageing, a substantial volume of spirit is lost through evaporation. The size of this "angels' share" varies considerably, and is influenced by many factors. Among them are the height at which the casks are stacked, the style of construction of the warehouse, the ambient temperature, the age and size of the cask, the weather during its years of maturation, and the duration of the storage. Customs and excise allows the angels to take a maximum of 2.5 per cent of the volume per year.

Depending on these factors, a sample drawn from the cask could still be in the 60s, or may have dropped into the 50s or lower. So the term "cask strength" does suggest something more potent than usual.

The appeal to the consumer might diminish if evaporation had taken the alcohol below the levels at which malts are conventionally sold: 42 per cent (for "De Luxe" or "Export" bottlings) or 40 per cent. The industry has taken action to make the latter an international minimum.

Unless a whisky is very old indeed, it is unlikely to have reached either of these levels by evaporation. In conventional bottlings, the strength is normally reduced by dilution with water.

The only distilleries with bottling lines are Springbank (which also produces Longrow and Hazelburn); Bruichladdich (whose new owners installed the equipment); and Glenfiddich (with sisters Balvenie and Kininvie). These are therefore the only distilleries that can reduce their whiskies with the same water as they use in distillation. They therefore regard their whiskies as being "château-bottled". All the others use central bottling plants and reduce with de-natured water.

Similar standard or minimum strengths are applied to spirits in many countries, and are widely enshrined in laws, duties, and taxes. Many of these measures have their origins in legislation passed at around the time of the First World War. Concern about levels of drinking during this period gave rise to Britain's laws on pub hours, and Prohibition in the US and several other countries. During this period, whisky was sold at 37.2 per cent in Britain.

Whisky has always in a small way been available at cask strength, in that it was once supplied in the wood to country houses, farms, shops, and even bars. The very independent family distillers of Glenfarclas notably carried on the cask strength ideal in some of its bottlings. They were one of the inspirations behind the founding in 1983 of the Scotch Malt Whisky Society, which grew from a group of friends who formed a syndicate to buy at cask strength.

The independent bottler Cadenhead and some of its competitors have since become protagonists of cask strength. In 1990, Glenmorangie commercially pioneered the rediscovery of this notion with its "Native Ross-shire" bottlings. Explaining the appeal of such

It's a steal

When Glenmorangie first bottled its whisky at cask strength in 1990, it sported a mock-rustic label design. Had the consumer stolen the whisky?

editions, a marketing man at Glenmorangie said: "This is as near as you can get to sneaking up to the distillery in the middle of the night and tapping a cask. It is whisky as at source."

The term "cask strength" indicates that the whisky has not been reduced, but it could be a vatting of several production runs, from several casks. The person in charge of the vatting will choose his casks to achieve a desired character in the end result. He may also aim for what is considered to be a desirable alcohol content. Consumers may still wish to add water but, in the case of a cask strength whisky, they (rather than the bottler) choose how great the dilution.

Despite the potential of the alcohol to anaesthetize the palate, some whisky drinkers do like to drink their malt at cask strength. Some whiskies matured in sherry casks can "fall apart" if substantial amounts of water are added; and it might be argued more generally that a whisky which is rich, malty, and creamy in style should, indeed, be allowed to show its texture without being watered.

VINTAGE EDITIONS

The grape may be far more temperamental than the grain, but barley has its moments. Weather over the growing season may produce a richer or more delicious barley in a particular year. The quality of the distiller's water may vary according to the weight of rainfall and the depth and speed of mountain streams. A cold winter may make for a more effective condensation of vapours, and therefore a cleaner, creamier spirit. Despite all of this, it has been argued that the spirit differs more from one batch to the next than it does between years. Whatever the quality of the spirit, the weather during maturation is almost certainly more important, simply because its influence is exerted over a number of years.

Changes in production methods over the years are also an influence. In general, most malt is today less heavily peated than it was, stills are run faster, and cuts of spirit are wider. Occasionally, some quirk of the moment, or even a particular distillery manager, reverses such "progress" for a year or two.

A vintage edition contains whisky from just one identified year. Some malts, such as Knockando, quote on their labels the dates of distillation and bottling, rather than simply the age. Others, such as Glenfiddich and Balvenie, have in recent years made it an annual ritual to delve into their stocks and select one or more casks of very old whisky to bottle as a vintage edition. The Glenlivet Vintage, a selection from the 1960s and 1970s, was the first such official bottling from a distillery company. It was reviewed in the fourth edition of this book. In 2002, Macallan made vintages from 1926 to 1972 available, and published *The Definitive Guide to Buying Vintage Macallan*. Since 1996, the distillery has also made vattings that attempt to match the character of rare bottlings from 1841, 1861, 1874, and 1876, with more to come. This unusual venture is known as "The Replica Range".

SINGLE CASK

Many "vintage" bottlings are from a single cask, hence the term "single cask", as are many "cask strength" bottlings. Each of the three terms makes a slightly different promise, but they can overlap or coincide. Their growing popularity reflects the desire of discerning consumers to be better informed about the products they buy, to be able to exercise choice, and sometimes to prefer individuality to consistency.

UNCHILLFILTERED

Conventional malts are usually chilled before being despatched. The drop in temperature causes them to become cloudy. The haze comprises protein and other elements, which have dropped out of suspension. These are then removed by filtration. This pre-empts a protein haze forming if the purchaser of the whisky keeps it in the fridge, or adds ice to his drink.

As true whisky lovers do neither, they do not require such mollycoddling. In removing the haze, chill filtration also strips out some flavour elements, notably including fatty acids. "Unchillfiltered" is a clumsy term to find on a label, but it should be welcomed nonetheless. It indicates a whisky for people who like their meat on the bone or their bread crusty.

High society
The tasting panel at the Scotch Malt Whisky Society chooses treats for its members. The avoidance of chill filtration was part of the society's raison d'être.

WHY MALTS?

AN INSTANT GUIDE TO THE PLEASURES OF THE PURSUIT

AT ITS SIMPLEST, MALT WHISKY HAS A STARTLING PURITY. The snow melts on the mountains, filters through rock for decades, perhaps even centuries, bubbles out of a spring, then tumbles down a hillside, until it finds land flat enough and warm enough to grow barley. The water irrigates the barley in the field; persuades it to germinate in the maltings; infuses its natural sugars in the mash tun; becomes beer when the yeast is added; vaporizes in the still; becomes liquid once more in the condenser; enters the cask as spirit, and leaves it as whisky.

THE FLAVOUR of malted barley is always present to a degree, clean, sweet, and restorative, but there are many other elements. The rock from which the water rises will influence the character of the whisky. The vegetation over which it flows can also be an influence. In the process of malting, the partially germinated grain is dried, sometimes over a peat fire, and this will impart smokiness. The yeasts used in fermentation can create fruity, spicy flavours. Similar characteristics can be influenced by the size and shape of the stills, which also affect the richness and weight of the spirit. Further aromas and flavours are assumed during maturation in the cask, from the wood used, its previous contents, and the atmosphere it breathes (*see pp. 72–3*).

For people who enjoy a spirit with flavour, malt whisky at its most robust is a world champion. The flavours in a blended Scotch are usually more restrained, as they might be in a cognac. Those who suffer from fear of flavour might feel safer with white rums or vodkas.

THE INDIVIDUALITY of malts is what makes each so different. Naturally enough, they appeal to people who are individualists. A smoky, earthy, seaweedy, medicinal malt from the coasts or islands of Scotland is a spirit of unrivalled power on the palate. A Speysider may be sherryish, honeyed, flowery, and often very complex. Lowlanders are few, but they can be appetizingly grassy and herbal.

Glass of 2004?
Tasting glasses after a master class at Bruichladdich. Malt lovers like to learn classes, tastings, and whisky festivals are popular. Finding flavours and aromas is a sensuous activity.

THE MOMENT for a malt may simply be the occasion for a sociable drink, but some pleasures are more particular: the restorative after a walk in the country or a game of golf; the aperitif; even, occasionally, the malt with a meal; the digestif; the malt with a cigar, or with a book at bedtime.

Martine's cuisine
In Paris, writer Martine Nouet conducts classes in cooking with whisky. She drinks whisky with her meals.

THE MEAL Although malt whiskies are more commonly served before or after a meal, they very happily accompany some dishes, most obviously sushi. Some malt-loving chefs also like to use their favourite spirit as an ingredient (*see p. 441*).

THE EXPLORATION Malt drinkers rarely stick to one distillery. They enjoy comparing malts from different regions, and familiarizing themselves with the aromas and flavours of each. To do this is to explore Scotland by nosing-glass. This armchair exploration often leads on to the real thing.

THE DISTILLERIES are often in beautiful locations. Some have their own distinctive architecture. Most are quite small, and it is not unknown for visiting malt lovers to strike up long-term friendships with distillery managers or workers.

THE VISIT Malt lovers often become passionate about Scotland itself. Whisky tourism extends beyond visits to distilleries. The principal whisky regions (the Highlands, especially Speyside; and the Islands, especially Islay) are set in countryside offering outstanding opportunities for walking, climbing, bird-watching, and fishing. Islay has a festival of whisky and folk music in late May; Speyside has festivals in spring and autumn; and the distilling town of Pitlochry has a summer theatre festival.

THE CONNOISSEUR Just as wine enthusiasts progress from comparing vineyards or châteaux to assessing vintages, so malt lovers develop their own connoisseurship. A single distillery may offer malts of different ages, vintage-dated malts, a variety of strengths, and a diversity of wood finishes. As new bottlings are constantly being released, there is no end to this pleasure.

THE COLLECTOR Every lover of malt whiskies sooner or later becomes to some extent a collector. It may not be a conscious decision. It can just happen. A few casual purchases, the odd gift. For the collector's friends, birthdays and Christmas are suddenly easy. Some collectors have backgrounds in the trade. Some buy two of every bottle: one to drink, the other to keep. Such collectors pour scorn on those who do not drink any of their whisky. The most serious collections are often found in countries with a nostalgia for the Britain of gentlemen's clubs, leather-upholstered Bentleys, and rugby union. There are famous collectors in Brazil, Italy, and Japan.

Sukinder's stash
In London, Sukhinder Singh started with miniatures. Now he has 2500 bottles in his private collection, and is a whisky merchant.

THE INVESTOR 1 — AUCTIONS Even if it was not bought for that purpose, a collection soon begins to represent a valuable asset. Collections that began after the Second World War started to come up for sale in the 1980s. In 1986, the Scottish branch of the famous auction house Christie's began to include whiskies once a year in its sales of fine wines. Within two or three years, whisky had been separated from wine. Christie's Scotland then closed, and its whisky expert, Martin Green, moved to Scottish auctioneers McTear's.

Some single malts have appreciated fivefold or even tenfold (although some bottles have proven to be fakes, so care should be exercised). In 2002, a well-authenticated single bottle of 62-year-old Dalmore fetched £25,000 (about $38,000). In the 1990s, importer and distributor Norman Shelley bought 76 bottles of Macallan, ranging from current 30-year-olds to 1856 bottlings, for an undisclosed price. Within two or three years, his collection was valued at £231,500 (about $360,000).

THE INVESTOR 2 — EN PRIMEUR Some distillers have at times sold newly filled casks "en primeur", but this has not been a great success. The cost of storage during maturation, and the payment of duties and taxes, complicates the calculations. No one can be certain how well the cask will age, nor how saleable a single cask of whisky will be when it is mature. While the distillers involved have been perfectly respectable, some investment companies have behaved less scrupulously. Care is advised.

THE ORIGINS OF
MALT WHISKY

W HILE GRAPE VINES HAVE their roots in prehistory, barley staked out the beginning of civilization. As hunter-gatherers, human beings picked wild fruits such as grapes, but this source of refreshment and nutrition had a short season and a propensity to rot (or spontaneously ferment) into wines. Fruits take up rainfall from the soil and turn it into highly fermentable, sugary juice. Wild yeasts trigger fermentation, and this process creates alcohol. Perhaps the hunter-gatherers enjoyed the effect, but wine did not provide them with any much needed protein.

When human beings ceased to be nomadic and settled in organized societies they did so in order to cultivate crops. The earliest evidence of this, between 13,000 and 8000 years ago, occurs at several sites in the fertile crescent of the Middle East. The first crop was a prototype barley, and the first explanation of its use is a depiction in Sumerian clay tablets of beer making. This is sometimes described as the world's first recipe of any kind.

HALF-WAY TO WHISKY

To grow barley, transform it into malt and then into beer, is half-way towards the making of whisky. While it is easy to obtain the sugars from fruit – peel me a grape, take a bite from an apple – grain is less yielding. The first step toward the unlocking of the sugars in barley and several other grains is the process of malting. This means that the grain is steeped in water, partially germinated, and then dried. The Sumerian civilization was on land that is today Iraq. It may be that malting occurred naturally while the barley was still in the field, as the water rose and fell in the flood plains of this land. This is described poetically on clay tablets in "A Hymn to Ninkasi" *(see p. 26)*.

It seems likely that at this stage the Sumerians had no more precise aim than to make grain edible. They did so in the form of beer, though pictograms and relics suggest a grainy, porridgey beverage consumed through straws. This depiction bears a startling resemblance to the "traditional" beer still brewed in villages in some parts of Africa.

Road to the Isles
A few miles from the Bushmills distillery in Ireland, this remarkable rock formation heads for Fingal's Cave, Staffa, and Mull. The first whisky road ... or the first whisky legend?

WHEN YOU POUR OUT THE FILTERED
BEER OF THE COLLECTOR VAT,
IT IS [LIKE] THE ONRUSH OF TIGRIS AND EUPHRATES.
NINKASI, YOU ARE THE ONE WHO POURS OUT THE
FILTERED BEER OF THE COLLECTOR VAT,
IT IS [LIKE] THE ONRUSH OF TIGRIS AND EUPHRATES.

Grain and water meet ...

... in the "Hymn to Ninkasi" (c. 1800BC), found on tablets at several sites in Iraq.
Translated in 1964, by Miguel Civil, of the Oriental Institute of the University of Chicago.
The first evidence of malting?

If the cultivation of grain originally radiated from the first civilization of the Ancient World, the crop itself varied from place to place. To the east, the Chinese and Japanese grow rice, which is fermented to produce saké. To the north, the Russians use rye to make kvass. To the west, barley is brewed. The words "brewed" and "bread" have the same etymology, and, in Germany, beer is sometimes known as "liquid bread".

The soft, sensuous, delicate, capricious grape and the tall, spiky, resilient grain compete to make the world's greatest drinks: fermented and distilled. The weather divides temperate Europe into wine and beer belts. Wine is made in the grape-growing south: Greece, Italy, France, Iberia. Beer belongs to the grainy north: the Czech Republic, Germany, Belgium, and the British Isles. All of these countries also produce distilled counterparts, but the real emphasis on spirits is in the colder countries. The spirits belt links Russia, Poland, the Baltic and Nordic states, and Scotland.

Modern-day Iraq is due south of Armenia, and the Greek historian Herodotus tells us that the Armenians made "barley water". So perhaps the brewing of barley malt spread by way of Armenia, Georgia, and the Ukraine. The Greeks also called all "strangers" Celts. The Romans called them Gallic people, and a part of Turkey is known as Galatia. The term "Galatian" was also used by the Roman author Columella to describe the two-row "race" of barley, preferred today by many brewers.

Sites that were Celtic settlements are even today known for the brewing of beer, notably sites in Bohemia, Bavaria, and Belgium. Many of these sites later gave rise to abbeys, with breweries. Most of the early brewing sites in England, Scotland, and Ireland are on the locations of former abbeys. So are the distilling towns of Cork and Midleton in Ireland. The northeast of Ireland and the western isles of Scotland have associations with St Columba, who urged his community of Iona to grow barley. In 1494, Friar Cor, of Lindores Abbey in Fife, placed on record in the rolls of the Scottish Exchequer the purchase of malt "to make *aqua vitae*". He probably wasn't the first malt distiller, but he left us the first evidence.

THE ART OF DISTILLATION

It is easy to see how spontaneous fermentation provides a natural model for the first brewers. Evaporation and condensation occur in nature, too, but it is not clear when, or where, distillation was first practised. To distil is to boil the water, wine, or beer, collect the steam, and condense it back into liquid. This drives off certain substances (for example, the salt in water) and concentrates others (such as the alcohol in wine or beer). The process was used by Phoenician sailors to render sea water drinkable, by alchemists, by makers of perfumes and, eventually, in the production of medicines and alcoholic drinks.

One theory has the Phoenicians bringing distillation to Western Europe, via the Mediterranean and Spain, whence it crossed the sea again to Ireland. Another theory has the art spreading by way of Russia and the Nordic countries to Scotland.

The fermented raw material — wine or beer — is boiled to make steam, which, being wraith-like, may have given rise to the English word "spirit" or to the German "*Geist*" (ghost), especially since condensation brings it back to life in a restored (and restorative) form. The "water of life" they call it: vodka, a diminutive form, in Slavic countries; aquavit, in various spellings, in Nordic lands; *eau-de-vie* in French; and *usquebaugh*, in various spellings, in Gaelic. This last became *usky*, then whisky, in English. All of these terms at first simply indicated a distillate, made from whatever was local.

All spirit drinks were originally made in a batch process in a vessel that superficially resembles a kettle or cooking pot, and malt whisky is still made in this way today. But this "pot still" was an inefficient purification vessel, and, in the early days, if the spirit emerged with flavours that were considered disagreeable, they were masked with spices, berries, and fruits.

"PLAIN MALT"

In the mid-1700s, a distinction was made in Scotland between flavoured spirits and "plain malt". As the first industrial nation, Britain shaped its beer and whisky with the early technologies of the Industrial Revolution: England's "bright beer" was a copper-coloured pale ale, rather than the more "evolved" golden lager of Continental Europe, which was made using more advanced techniques. Scotland's whisky remained a pot-still product, with its own inherent flavours, turned to an attractive complexity.

Most of the northern European countries use a generic term such as "schnapps" for a spirit, and offer both plain and flavoured examples. More specific flavourings include caraway and dill, traditional in the aquavit of Scandinavia; and juniper, together with botanical flavourings such as iris root and citrus peel, in the gins of northern Germany, the Low Countries, northern France, and England. Flavoured or not, many grain-based spirits outside Britain employ a column still, and most are not aged.

The elements that go to make up a Scottish malt whisky are the local water; a grist comprising malted barley only; traditionally, a degree of peat; pot stills, usually designed and built in Scotland; and ageing in oak casks. The last of these elements gradually became more significant from the late 1700s onwards.

BLENDED SCOTCH

Like most drinks production, the distilling of malt whisky in Scotland was originally a sideline for farmers. In the coastal coves and Highland glens, illicit distillation was rife. Legislation in 1824 to regulate this activity began the shaping of today's industry. That process was largely finished by the legislation of 1909–15, which initially arose from a trading standards case in the London borough of Islington.

For the farmer-distiller, a few casks of malt whisky might be a hedge against a rainy day. A farm distillery would not have a bottling line. The casks could be sold directly to wealthy householders, to hotels or pubs, or to a licensed grocer, a Scottish institution similar to an

Blending the bottles
The "medicine bottles" on Richard Patterson's workbench contain the latest samples taken from casks of malt whiskies normally included in Whyte and Mackay's blended Scotch. Every cask is slightly different. Patterson checks colour, nose, palate – and adjusts accordingly.

American country store. (The outstanding example of such a shop, and still active, is Gordon & MacPhail of Elgin.) One or two renowned distillers might sell their whisky to a wine merchant, sometimes as far away as Edinburgh or London.

Each farmer's whisky would vary from one year to the next, and supply would be irregular. So rather than run out of farmer McSporran's fine dram, the licensed grocers would vat the malts and sell the result under their own label. Some became famous: names such as Chivas Brothers, Johnnie Walker, and George Ballantine. Among the wine merchants known for their bottlings, two in London are still active: Justerini & Brooks and Berry Brothers & Rudd.

Vatting turned to blending when, in the mid-1800s, the column-shaped continuous still was patented. This type of still, operated on an industrial scale, can produce whisky that is lighter in flavour and body. It can also produce whisky more quickly, at a lower cost, and in larger quantities than a pot still. Column-still whisky provides the bulk of a blend, while a combination of pot-still malt whiskies add character and individuality. The volume afforded by blended Scotches, and their less challenging style, helped them become the world's most popular spirits at a time when much of the globe was embraced by the British Empire.

Mountainous Scotland, with its long coastline, had provided mariners, explorers, engineers, teachers, soldiers, and administrators for the empire. Each turned out also to be a propagandist for the virtues of his country's greatest product.

BORN-AGAIN MALTS

More than 90 per cent of malt whisky still goes into blends. Scotland has about 100 malt distilleries, of which about two thirds are working at any one time. All but a handful are owned by international drinks companies whose products include blended Scotches. A blend can contain anything from six or seven malts to 30 or 40. The drinks companies like to own the distilleries whose malt whiskies are vital to their blends. They also exchange malts with one another.

The big drinks companies have been growing through mergers since the 1920s. A round of mergers after the Second World War left the handful of remaining independent distillers feeling vulnerable. William Grant & Sons, producers of Glenfiddich and Balvenie, decided they no longer wished to rely on supplying blenders, but to actively market their whisky as a single malt. The industry view was that single malts belonged to the past, and that the dominant position of the blends could not be challenged. Happily, Grant's were not dissuaded.

ABERLOUR

ESTD 1879

WAREHOUSE Nº1
SINGLE CASK SELECTION

SPEYSIDE MALT SCOTCH WHISKY

AGED 11 YEARS

BOURBON CASK MATURED

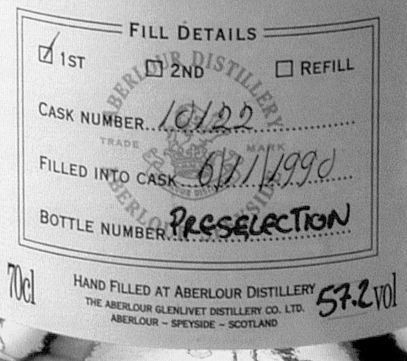

FILL DETAILS

☑ 1ST   ☐ 2ND   ☐ REFILL

CASK NUMBER...10122..............

FILLED INTO CASK...6/1/1990.....

BOTTLE NUMBER...PRESELECTION

70cl   HAND FILLED AT ABERLOUR DISTILLERY   57.2 vol
THE ABERLOUR GLENLIVET DISTILLERY CO. LTD.
ABERLOUR ~ SPEYSIDE ~ SCOTLAND

THE WORDS USED ON
THE LABEL

CONTROVERSY was aroused in 2003 when Cardhu single malt was relaunched as a pure malt. What is the difference, and why did it matter? This book is primarily concerned with malt whisky, but also looks briefly at grain whisky. The main body of the book, the A–Z section, is devoted only to single malt Scotches, but a section at the back deals with products from other countries – these are malt whiskies, but not Scotches. All of these overlapping terms are employed in labelling. What do they say about the liquid in the bottle?

MALT Cereal grain that has been partially sprouted – in preparation for the release of its fermentable sugars – then dried in a kiln. The grains look drier and slightly darker after being malted for distillation. The grain is always barley if the end result is to be malt whisky in the Scottish or Irish style. Other grains can be malted and used in other whiskies, as in the case of Old Potrero rye.

For the beer brewer or whisky distiller, the process of malting in part parallels the crush in wine making or brandy distilling. The premises in which it takes place is called a maltings. The grains are first steeped in water, to encourage their sprouting (or partial germination). Traditionally, the sprouting continues with the grains spread on a stone floor. They are constantly raked, or turned with a shovel, to keep them aerated. Floor malting requires a lot of space and is labour-intensive, but is felt by many to produce the most delicious result. There are several other methods, including ventilated boxes and rotating drums.

Just as grapes are also eaten or used to provide juice, so malted barley is used, either as whole grains or milled, in breads, cakes, and milk shakes. A syrupy, water-based extract of malt sugars is sold as a tonic. An ever-evolving series of barley varieties is used for malting. These are required to produce plump kernels and clean, sweet malt sugars. The farmer distinguishes between malting barley and feed barley for cattle.

Almost all types of whisky employ a proportion of malt. Those that employ no other grain are known as malt whisky. Single malt whiskies are often referred to simply as "malts".

Detailed dram
Malt lovers like to know what they are drinking, and Aberlour provides every last detail when you make your own vatting and bottling at the distillery's visitor centre.

Mountain men?
These pot-bellied creatures are the whisky stills at Ben Nevis. The pot-still shape is more evident when the whole vessel is visible.

WHISK(E)Y A spirit drink originating from Scotland and Ireland – but produced in a variety of styles in other countries – distilled from malted barley and other grains, and matured in oak. Its complex aromas and flavours originate from the raw materials, manufacturing process, and maturation. These distinguish whiskies from the more neutral grain spirits in the schnapps and vodka families.

There is a misunderstanding that there are British and American spellings of this term. However, it is not the nationality of the writer, or the country of publication, that should determine the spelling. It is the type of whisk(e)y: thus Scottish and Canadian "whisky", but Irish "whiskey". American styles, such as Kentucky Bourbon and Tennessee whiskey, generally favour the "e", but some labels dissent.

MALT WHISKY Whisky made only from malted barley. Typically distilled in a batch process, in a copper vessel resembling a kettle or cooking pot.

SINGLE MALT WHISKY Malt whisky produced in a single distillery, not vatted or blended with whisky made in any other distillery. Scotland has by far the most malt distilleries: just under a hundred, of which between 80 and 90 per cent are operating at any one time. Ireland has one distillery that can produce only malt whiskey, namely Bushmills. Malt whiskies are also distilled on a more limited scale at Cooley and Midleton in Ireland, though both of these also produce a range of other styles. Some very serious malt whiskies are made in Japan, and a scattering elsewhere in the world.

SCOTCH WHISKY This term can be applied only to a whisky made in Scotland, and matured for at least three years. No other nation can call a product "Scotch", although any nation can call a product whisky. Scotland's status is not widely understood beyond its borders. It is not a region but a nation, and has been for almost 1000 years. For the past 300 years, it has been part of a union, and this was not altered by the recent restoration of the Scottish Parliament. Scotland, England, and Wales share an island called Great Britain. These three nations and Northern Ireland (a six-county province) form the United Kingdom.

SINGLE MALT SCOTCH WHISKY Single malt whisky made in Scotland.

SINGLE CASK A bottling made from just one cask.

VATTED MALT If malt whiskies from different distilleries are combined, the result will be called a vatted malt. This might be done to create a desired character, perhaps the flavour of a region. This term assumes that all the whiskies in the vatting are malts.

PURE MALT A term that is likely to fall out of use because its meaning is insufficiently clear. It has been employed in some cases to indicate a single malt and in others to signify a vatted malt. When Cardhu switched from the former category to the latter, the term "pure malt" was used. Other distillers protested, arguing that the consumer was being misled – or, at best, confused – and that the integrity of malt whisky was being put at risk.

BLENDED SCOTCH WHISKY A stroke of Scottish genius, devised in the Victorian era. Craft producers, mainly in the Highlands and Islands, make small quantities of flavoursome malt whisky. Much larger, more industrial distilleries, mainly in the Midlands and the south, produce large quantities of more neutral grain whiskies to add volume to the malt. The result is a blended Scotch.

GRAIN WHISKY These may be produced from corn (maize), wheat, or raw barley. A small amount of malted barley is required to provide the enzymes needed in fermentation, in a continuous process, in a column-shaped still. Grain whiskies are light in body and flavour, but not neutral, and are matured for a minimum of three years in oak.

SINGLE GRAIN WHISKY There have been attempts to market single grain whisky as a more interesting alternative to vodka, or perhaps as a Scottish "grappa"? Occasional independent bottlings are also of interest to collectors.

FURTHER LABEL TERMS

PEATING When maltsters kilned their grains over open fires, the fuel was whatever could easily be found. In Poland, a style of beer was made from oak-smoked malt. In Franconia, Germany, beechwood was favoured. In Scotland, whisky malt was kilned over peat fires. The peat gave an especially distinct smokiness to Scotch whisky, and has to varying degrees been retained. Serious whisky lovers have come to cherish peatiness, and demand more, as many of the popular malts have become less smoky to appease consumers who fear flavour. Within the industry, the peat-smoke character is measured in parts per million (ppm) of phenol. The most heavily peated spirit currently being distilled is Octomore, at 80 ppm, but this will not be ready to bottle for some years. Neither will Port Charlotte, at 40 ppm (the same level as Laphroaig). Both are being distilled at Bruichladdich. The level for the whisky called simply Bruichladdich is 2–5 ppm. These figures do not tell the whole story, as the smokiness can be accentuated or softened by the design, shape, and configuration of the stills, the woods used in ageing and so on.

Burning at Bowmore
Stoking the firebox: the smoke rises through the mesh floor of the kiln, upon which the grains of sprouting barley are spread. The heat arrests germination, and the smoke imparts flavour.

DOUBLE/TRIPLE DISTILLATION Most Scottish malt whisky is run through a pair of stills, but a handful of distilleries have over the years used a system of three linked stills (*see* Springbank). Triple distillation was once traditional in the Lowlands of Scotland (*see* Auchentoshan). It is also favoured in Ireland. In theory, the more thorough the distillation, the lighter and cleaner the spirit. Triple should be more exhaustive than double. While this is broadly true, the still's influence on flavour is not completely understood.

BOURBON AGEING Why the name bourbon? The French helped the Americans in the War of Independence, and the Americans acknowledged this by naming towns and counties after the French royal family. Bourbon County, in Kentucky, was known for shipping whiskey down the Ohio and Mississippi rivers to New Orleans and other big cities. (Whiskey had been introduced to the United States by Northern Irish immigrants of Scottish origin.)

Local corn is always used to make bourbon, along with rye or wheat, and the bourbon is then matured in a fresh oak barrel. The inside of the barrel is charred to help the whiskey permeate the wood. After only one use in Kentucky, the barrel may be sent to Scotland and used to mature Scottish whisky. It will still retain enough of its typical vanilla-like flavours to impart some of these to the first fill of this whisky; and along with the vanilla, there may be caramel-toffee flavours, dessert apple, and a touch of tannin. There will still be some lively flavour contributuion in a second fill. By the third fill the barrel may be relatively neutral. Some barrels are recharred in Scotland.

SHERRY AGEING The word "sherry" derives from English attempts to pronounce the Spanish place name Jerez. The wine makers of the Jerez area, in the southwest, near Cadiz and Seville, have a long relationship with the British Isles. Large quantities of their fortified Jerez wines were for a long time shipped to Cork, Bristol (the nearest English port), and Leith (the port that adjoins Edinburgh). Instead of being shipped empty back to Spain, the drained butts and hogsheads were snapped up by whisky distillers. Today, this wine is bottled in Spain, and sherry wood is expensive. Nonetheless some distillers feel that its influence is important. They make the investment (*see pp. 70–1*), and are precise in their requirements. Most sherry is made from the Palomino grape. There are several styles – fino: dry, delicate and fresh; manzanilla: a saltier coastal cousin; amontillado: darker and nuttier; palo cortado: aromatic, complex, and cookie-like; oloroso: rich, creamy, and fruity; Pedro Ximénez (made with the grape of the same name, and not the Palomino): intensely raisiny, treacly and dark. *See also* "Cask Strength" (*pp. 16–17*), "Vintage Editions" (*pp. 18–19*); "Single Cask" (*p. 19*), "Unchillfiltered" (*p. 19*); as well as "Regional Variations" (*pp. 54–65*).

The Spanish connection
The tradition of sherry ageing brings an added dimension to Scotch whisky. The diversity of sherry itself is evident in the museum at the Gonzalez Byass bodega, in Jerez.

FLAVOURS

THE INFLUENCE OF THE LANDSCAPE

T HE UNIVERSE OF SPIRITS BEGAN to change when the word "designer", having become an adjective, attached itself to the word "vodka". Then, some of the most famous names in the world of distillation became better known for their "ready-to-drink" confections, misleadingly known in the United States as "malternatives". Now a new generation of consumers faces a choice between drinks that come from nowhere, taste of nothing much, and have a logo for a name; and drinks that come from somewhere, have complex aromas and flavours, and may have a name that is hard to pronounce.

Such drinks reflect their place of origin. They have evolved. They have a story to tell. They are good company, and they require something of the drinker in return: that he or she experiences the pleasure of learning to drink. Real, evolved drinks begin as the gift of God. They are grown, whether from grapes, grain, sugar cane, or, for example, the agave plant. They arise from their own *terroir*: geology, soil, vegetation, topography, weather, water, and air. To what extent they are influenced by each of these elements is a matter for debate, often passionate. People care about real drinks.

The most sophisticated of real drinks are the brandies of France and the whiskies of the British Isles. The most complex brandies are the cognacs and armagnacs. The most complex whiskies are those of Scotland and Ireland.

Within these two duopolies, cognac and Scotch are the best known. In Cognac, the regions of production are contiguous, stretch about 144 kilometres (90 miles) from one end to the other, and are all in flat countryside. The whisky distilleries of Scotland are spread over an area of about 448 kilometres (280 miles) from one end of the country to the other, from the Lowlands to the northern Highlands, from mountain to shore, and from the Hebrides in the west to Orkney (and by now Shetland?) in the north. Theirs is surely the greater complexity.

Under the volcano

Scotland's landscape can be silent and still, yet the evidence of eruptions, glaciations, and rocky collisions is everywhere. The dews and frosts, the marine plants and mountain forests — each valley or island has its own flavour. Arran, left, has extinct volcanoes and a newish distillery.

Whisky is a real drink. A single malt is as real as it gets. There are many potential influences on its character, and much dispute as to the relative importance – if any – of each. The Macallan distillery receives what might seem disproportionate attention in the following pages because it takes what might aptly be termed single-minded positions on almost every issue: the variety of barley; the strains of yeast; the size of still; and the provenance of the casks.

On these and other issues ever more research is carried out, but an apparent insight into one stage of the whisky-making process may raise new questions about the next. In production, if a procedure is changed, the result may not be apparent until the whisky is mature, perhaps 10 years hence.

THE WHISKY COUNTRIES

Scotland and Ireland can be cool and rainy, but their climates are temperate. The conditions are very favourable for the growing of barley, though excessive damp and wind can occasionally be a problem.

The windy main island of the Orkney islands still cultivates bere, a precursor to barley, but grown today for local bakers rather than distillers. It was used in whisky making in the past, and its importance was such that a dispute over taxes on bere even threatened the Act of Union in 1707.

Today, just as different wine regions champion their own grapes, so there are debates in Europe as to the merits of "continental" barleys, such as those grown in Moravia, Bohemia, and Bavaria, versus the "maritime" examples of Denmark, Scotland, England, and Ireland.

The blood of ...

... John Barleycorn was spilled by Robert Burns, a Lowlander but from the West. This field of barley is in the East, near the Lowland distillery, Glenkinchie.

Supporters of the continental barleys say they provide a sweeter, nuttier flavour. Protagonists for the maritime varieties argue that they have a clean, "sea-breeze" character.

Naturally, the Scots prefer their own barley. Depending upon the harvest, and their own needs, they have on occasion exported, but in other periods they have augmented their own malt with "imports" from England. Their second choice would be Denmark, and then elsewhere. Purists would prefer that the Scots used only their own barley. The Scots could argue that they are simply victims of their own success in selling so much of their whisky.

It is because barley is more resilient that it has a broader belt of cultivation, and can be more easily transported, than the grapes that make wine and brandy. Scotland's main growing regions are on the more sheltered eastern side of the country: on the shores of the Moray firth (The Black Isle and The Laich of Moray), Aberdeenshire, and the Borders. Ireland's are in the southeast, behind an imaginary line on the map, which runs from the border city of Dundalk (with a history of brewing) in County Louth, to the sailing (and gastronomic) resort of Kinsale, County Cork. Both countries might wish for more cultivable land; Scotland is mountainous, and Ireland boggy.

TASTING THE *TERROIR*

Scotland seems like a machine for the making of whisky: a nation on a small island, awaiting the vapours of the sea; providing summits to unlock their precipitation, which then filters through a diversity of rock, via springs and mountain streams, over peat and heather, to the fields of barley and the distilleries.

Scotland's heather-clad hillsides, its peaty moorlands, and its seaweed-fringed islands all contribute to the character of its national drink. To sample some of the more pungent malts is to taste the *terroir*. But to what extent are the aromas and flavours carried by the mountain streams or burns that feed the distilleries? Is the greater influence in the peat that is used to dry the malt? Then there is the question of the atmosphere in the damp, earth-floored warehouses, and its influence on the whisky.

Heather, peat, and seaweed are not unique to Scotland, but the country is unusually rich in all three. Their local variations, their proportion, their juxtaposition, and their relationship with the rest of the landscape are unique. Every landscape is. The colour of a person's hair or eyes, or the shape of a nose or jawline, are not unique, but the face is, and it derives from them all.

On the map, Scotland presents a weatherbeaten face. The outline – the coast – is penetrated by endless inlets from the sea. These inlets are variously known as "sea lochs" or "firths"; the latter word has the same roots as the Norwegian "fjord".

"SCANDINAVIAN SCOTLAND"

In its topography, its use of Viking words, its Protestant rigour (with some ambivalence toward alcohol), Scotland can resemble Norway, the nearest of the Scandinavian countries. Scotland seems to reach northwards, higher into the spirits belt, while its Celtic cousin Ireland (more especially the Republic) appears to lean south, toward the Roman Catholic countries of mainland Europe.

Scotland is bigger in both land area and population than Ireland. It also has 20 or 30 times as many distilleries. At one stage, for a brief period, the numbers of stills in each of the countries were close, but Ireland's industry spent decades in decline before rediscovering itself in recent years. Whichever country "discovered" the barley distillate, and this is contentious, Scotland is today's pre-eminent "Land of Whisky".

Only whisky made there can be called Scotch. For many years, the industry repeated this without making clear its meaning. Were their spokesmen simply repeating an appellation? Or did they mean that no other country could make a comparable product? Scotch whiskies all taste of their homeland to varying degrees, but in many the taste is so subtle as to be scarcely evident, while in others the aromas of peat and seaweed, for example, are wonderfully shocking.

The handful of malt whiskies (as opposed to the "pot-still Irish" type) made at Bushmills and Cooley in Ireland are similar in style to their Scottish counterparts; as are the handful of Japanese malts, though some have distinct local features. But a whisky cannot taste of Scotland if it is made in Ireland or Japan, however similar the *terroir*. The most characterful whiskies taste of the *terroir*, wherever it is. They are real drinks.

ROCK

Geology as a discipline began in Scotland – with the book *Theory of the Earth*, published in 1788. The author, Dr James Hutton, was a Scot, inspired in part by the natural landscape of his homeland. The geology of Scotland is more varied than that of any country of a similar size. Much of this diversity arises from a spectacular collision 400–500 million years ago. The part of the earth's crust that is now Scotland was at that time attached to North America. It was in

Rosebank

Roses once bloomed at Rosebank. Now rosebay willowherb has taken over. The whisky tastes of camomile ... or carboniferous rock.

collision with a European plate that included England, Wales, and Ireland. The fault line where the two plates met was more or less followed a few million years later by Hadrian's Wall, and the border between England and Scotland has rarely strayed more than a few kilometres from this line since. The geological turbulence continued, with everything from volcanoes to glaciers, until 20,000 years ago.

Thus not only did geology begin with Scotland, but Scotland began with geology: with the thrusts, intrusions, eruptions, and glaciations. It came to rest, semantically, as a Gaelic-language landscape, with "corries" (hollows in the mountainside); "lochans" (small lakes) and "lochs" in a wide range of sizes (sometimes stretching for many miles, and possibly with a small opening to the sea); "straths" (broad valleys); and the "glens" (or narrower valleys) that appear on every other label. *This* is the whisky-making machine.

In 1990, geologists Stephen Cribb and Julie Davison made a study of rock formations in Scotland's whisky regions, and compared them with tasting notes in books on the drink, including this one. Their findings suggested that the similar tastes in certain whiskies produced near each other might in part be due to the similar rock from which the water rose. For example, in the Lowlands, the crisp, dry Glenkinchie and Rosebank share the same carboniferous rock. The oldest rock is that which supplies water to the Bowmore and Bruichladdich distilleries on Islay, off the west coast of Scotland; it was formed about 600–800 million years ago, and seems to contribute an iron-like flavour.

For many years, whisky makers always spoke of granite. Being so hard, granite does not donate minerals to the water. Thus hard rock means soft water, and vice versa. Granite is the principal rock of the

Grampians, the group of mountains and sub-ranges that dominates the Highlands, and from which the River Spey flows. Every Speyside distiller seemed to claim that he had soft water, "rising from granite and flowing over peat". In looking at the Grampians, the Cribbs' book *Whisky on the Rocks* identified Ben Rinnes and the Conval Hills as sources of the typical Speyside water, feeding distilleries such as Glenfarclas, Aberlour, and Craigellachie. The study went on to point out that the region's geology is diverse, embracing substantial areas of limestone and sandstone. One distillery that has, sensibly, made a virtue of its sandstone water source is Glenmorangie, located in the northern Highlands.

Mineral flavours – and textures – are familiar from bottled waters, and also seem evident in some malt whiskies. Water is used to steep the grain at maltings (though only a handful of these are attached to distilleries). It is employed in the mash tun at every distillery to extract the sugars from the malted barley. It is used to reduce the strength of spirit in the cask to aid maturation. It is also used to reduce mature whisky to bottling strength. For this last stage the local water is influential only in the handful of distilleries that bottle on site, and in those cases, it is very influential indeed.

SNOW

Vodka marketeers love to promote their products with suggestions of snowy purity, whether they are distilled in St Petersburg, Poznan, or in Peoria, Illinois. Some vodkas are distilled in one place and rectified in another. Others have Slavic origins, but are produced under licence in North America or elsewhere.

Snow on the Spey

The river Spey rises south of the Dalwhinnie distillery, one of Scotland's highest. Clearly whisky made from snowmelt, but also with some peaty complexity. Absolut Scotland ...

Snow-melt is more reliably found in Scottish malt whisky. There is typically snow on Scotland's highest mountain, Ben Nevis (measuring 1344 metres or 4410 feet high), for six to seven months of the year, and occasionally for longer: perhaps from September to May, or even all year. The same can be true in the Grampians, though three or four months is more common.

At sea level, especially in the drier east, Scotland may have less than 800 millimetres (32 inches) of rain and snow a year. In the mountains, that figure can more than triple. Once the snow melts, it descends by a variety of routes, filtering through fissures in the rock, emerging from springs, swelling streams or burns, or gushing into rivers like the Spey, Livet, and Fiddich.

High in the hills, distilleries like Dalwhinnie or Braeval might regard their water as snow-melt. By the time it has swollen the Spey, then been tapped by Tamdhu, it is regarded as river water. If it filters through the Conval Hills in search of Glenfiddich, Balvenie, or Kininvie, it emerges as the spring water of Robbie Dubh. Every distillery knows where it collects its water, and protects its source as a critical asset. Distillers know where their water arrives, but it may be impossible to say whence it came, or how long its journey was, except that it was once rain or snow.

WATER

The worry over water concerns not only quality, but also quantity. A great deal is required, not only for the steeps at the maltings and the mash tun at the distillery, but also to cool the condensers or worm tubs, to wash vessels, and to reduce the strength of the spirit in the cask or the mature whisky at bottling.

Unlike brewers of beer, the distillers of whisky do not add or remove salts to change the composition of their water. Not only must water for malting and mashing be available in volume, it must also be consistent in character. If a source threatens to run dry in the summer, the distillery may stop production and devote a few weeks' "silent season" to annual maintenance and vacations. If the water runs unusually slowly, or quickly, it may become muddy or sandy. If the water source is endangered by a project in the next county upstream, that could be a critical problem. And it is certainly critical if the distillery's production is outstripping the water source. Even the most sophisticated of distillery companies has been known to hire a water diviner to find an additional nearby source. Every effort will be made to match the character of the principal water used.

The issue of soft water versus hard goes beyond the flavour of any salts naturally occurring in the water. Calcium, for example, increases the extract of malt sugars in the mash tun, and may also make for a cleaner, drier whisky. Whether it does – whether, indeed, such influences could survive distillation – is hotly debated.

Visitors to distilleries are sometimes invited to sample the water. It can taste intensely peaty. Yet the whisky may be barely peaty at all. This is the case at the famous Speyside distillery, Glen Grant. The explanation would seem to be that the peaty taste does not survive distillation. Speyside is also rich in heather. Is that why its whiskies are so floral? The circumstantial evidence is strong, but some distillers might argue that the flowery character actually results from reactions during maturation.

On the island of Islay, even the tap water can be tinged a peaty brown or ironstone red. Perhaps the water flowed over peat for a longer distance. Did it linger, and take up more peatiness? Or flow faster and dig up its peaty bed? The bed may also have contributed some ironstone, or some green, ferny, vegetal character. This time, the flavours do seem to carry over into the whisky. Perhaps the flavours were absorbed when the peaty water was used to steep the barley at the beginning of the malting process. Unlike the maltings on the mainland, those on Islay highlight the intensity of local peat. It is the use of peat fires in the drying of the grains that imparts the greatest degree of smokiness and "Islay character" to the malt. The peat in the kiln is the smoking gun. The Islay distiller has the soul of an outlaw.

Tasting the *terroir*
The basis of terroir *is the earth. Here, it is sliced, and placed on a fire, so that its smoke pervades the malt. Some peat cutting on Islay is still done by hand.*

PEAT

Not only is aroma the bigger part of taste – the drinks and foods that arouse the appetite and the imagination are often fragrant – but these same foods are in fact frequently grilled, barbecued, roasted, toasted, or smoked: the breakfast kippers, bacon, toast, and coffee; the steak sizzling on a charcoal grill; the chestnuts roasting on an open fire. Of all the techniques historically used to kiln malt in different parts of Europe, the peat fires of Scotland surely produce the most evocative aromas. While some devotees of single malts have a catholic view, many take sides: will it be the peaty, briny whiskies of the islands and coasts; or the flowery, honeyed, sometimes sherried Speysiders?

The partisans for peat lust for its intensity (and love quoting ppm), but it also imparts a number of complex flavours and aromas. At least 80 aroma compounds have been found in peated malt.

While peatiness excites connoisseurs, it can alienate first-time tasters. When people say they "don't like" Scotch whisky, they often refer to a "funny taste", which turns out to mean peat. To take exception to such a fundamental element of the drink may seem odd, but distinctive, powerful flavours, especially if they are dry, can be challenging. Very hoppy beers are a perfect parallel. At a pinch, heavily oaked wines might also be drawn into the discussion.

In whisky, the dryness of peat provides a foil for the sweetness of barley malt, but that is a bonus, as is peat's rich content of anti-oxidants, the enemy of free radicals.

Peat was used in the first place because it is a convenient and plentiful fuel. Ninety per cent of the world's peat bogs are in temperate-to-cold parts of the northern hemisphere. Two-thirds of Britain's bogland is in Scotland, which in land area is half the size of England. Scotland's northern Highlands has Europe's largest expanse of blanket bogs. These bogs, in the counties of Caithness and Sutherland, are said to set a standard in the worldwide study of the phenomenon.

The peat that seduces whisky lovers is on the distillery islands of Orkney and Islay. In both cases, the sea air and high winds add salty flavours to the peat. The coast of Islay is heavily fringed with seaweed, which adds an iodine, medicinal character to the atmosphere. This, too, penetrates the peat. The Orcadian peat is younger, more heathery, and incorporates a wide range of salt-tolerant maritime plants. In the western islands, especially Islay, the peat is rich in bog myrtle (*Myrica gale*), also known as sweet gale, which has a sweet, cypress-like aroma and bitter flavour. Bog myrtle was one of the flavourings used in beer before the hop plant was adopted, and clearly influences the flavours imparted by the peat.

When peat is being cut by hand, the spade digs out a cube with surfaces as shiny and dark as a bar of "black" chocolate. It sometimes looks as edible as Mississippi mud pie. A closer look at the muddy block sometimes reveals the fossil-like remains of mosses. The principal component is sphagnum, a spongy moss that intertwines with other plants to form a fibrous soil, which, under pressure, will eventually become coal. The peatbogs of Scotland began to grow between 7000 and 3000 years ago, and are up to 7 metres (23 feet) deep.

Ireland is also famously boggy, and no doubt its rural whiskey makers burned peat, but distilling quickly moved to an industrial scale, concentrated in the few big cities, and the lack of peat became a defining characteristic of the "smooth" Irish whiskies. The large, urban distillers used coke to fire smokeless maltings. Having been overtaken in volume long ago by the country next door, the Irish are now rediscovering the merit of variety. A peated single malt called Connemara was launched in 1995–96 by the Cooley distillery, and has gone on to win several judgings.

HEATHER

In the unofficial national anthem, the "Flower of Scotland" is Robert the Bruce; in heraldry, it is the thistle; in the world of drinks, it is surely heather. While the thistle is Scotland (prickly, defensive, and looking for a fight), heather is attractive and lucky. In Scotland, especially Orkney, it was traditionally the flavouring for an ale. When a whisky has a floral aroma, the flower is frequently heather. Often, it is not the flower itself but heather honey.

These characteristics are especially notable on Speyside and Aberdeenshire, where the hills are dense with heather. Glen Elgin and Balvenie are two whiskies with a notably heather-honey character. In

The colour purple
Heather is a distinctive feature of the Scottish landscape. Its colour does not affect the whisky, but the floral and honey aromas often seem to have jumped into the glass.

Aberdeenshire, Glendronach and Glen Garioch have an enjoyable touch of heather, balancing their dry maltiness.

Heather is a significant component of much peat in Scotland. At some distilleries, notably Highland Park, lore has it that sprigs of heather were thrown on to the peat fire in the maltings. Water flows over heather to several distilleries. Besoms, or brooms, made of heather twigs were once commonplace in Scotland, and were typically used to clean wooden washbacks (fermenting vessels). Whether their effect was to sanitize or inadvertently to inoculate with micro-organisms is a piquant question. Wild yeast activity is at its height in summer, when bees are pollinating, and heather is a favourite source of nectar.

The Greek for the word "brush" gives us the botanical name *Calluna vulgaris* for the purple ling heather, which carpets the hillsides from mid-August into September. The brighter, redder bell heather (*Erica cinerea*) and the pinker, cross-leafed variety (*Erica tetralix*) flower about a month earlier. The English name for this group of small evergreen shrubs derives from their liking of heaths, but they also grow in bogs and on mountainsides. All three occur in Scotland, where heather covers between 1.6 and 2 million hectares (4 to 5 million acres).

Some varieties are found throughout northern Europe, others are native to Scotland, which has the greatest abundance of the plants. Scottish settlers introduced heather to North America.

BARLEY

Everyone knows that wines and brandies are made from grapes, but what about beer or whisky? Many consumers are unsure. Beer is often thought, mistakenly, to be made from hops. And whisky?

In explaining, and therefore promoting, its natural qualities, the grape does rather better than the grain. Wine makers often indicate on their labels which varieties of grape they have used. They may do this even if the wine is not a varietal. They might even discuss their choice of grape varieties on a back label or hang tag, and in their public relations and advertising.

Whisky makers do not in general do this. Why not? Are they using poor-quality barley? No. Malting requires barley of good quality. The argument for reticence is threefold: barley's contribution to flavour in whisky is less than it would be in beer, and even less than that of the grapes in wine. Second, perhaps simply as a reflection of the above, the difference between varieties is less obvious when it comes to flavour. Third, perhaps explaining this, the act of distillation removes some characteristics, and others are masked by the flavours gained during maturation. All of this is true up to a point, but what the distiller puts into his vessels must be a factor in the liquid that issues from them.

Almost all whisky distillers buy their barley according to a set of technical criteria (corn size, nitrogen, moisture content, etc.), rather than by variety. Some varieties bred or selected in the period of innovation after the Second World War are still legends. The last of that line, Golden Promise, represented 95 per cent of the harvest at its peak. Its short straw stands up to the wind; it ripens early (in August); and it produces nutty, rich flavours.

As the industry has grown, farmers have switched to varieties that give them more grain per acre, and therefore increase their profitability, while distillers have sought varieties that yield more fermentable sugars. These, however, do not necessarily produce delicious flavours, any more than do bigger, redder strawberries out of season. Nor do the varieties last much more than four or five seasons before being overtaken by something "better".

In 1994, the author was asked by Macallan to taste blindfold two samples of spirit, fresh from the still ("new make"). What was the purpose of the comparison? What was being sought? No explanation was offered. Nor were there any give-away clues such as colour; the spirit had not yet acquired any, not having begun its maturation. One sample seemed rich, malty, sweet, and Macallan-like. It turned out to have been distilled from Golden Promise, a variety that Macallan regards as being an essential component of its malt grist. The other tasted thin, metallic, and dusty. It had been distilled from a more recent, high-yield variety.

At the time, only one or two farmers were still cultivating Golden Promise, but Macallan had set about persuading others. The distillery stands on an estate, and its farm has now been leased and turned over to Golden Promise. A single farm can contribute only a fraction of the barley required, but the gesture is worth much more. Perhaps one day soon whisky lovers will be offered a single estate malt.

SEAWEED

The medicinal note in most Islay malts, especially Laphroaig, surely derives from seaweed, a source of iodine. The sea washes against the walls at all the distilleries, except Bruichladdich, and the coast is enwrapped with seaweed. How do the seaweedy, iron-like aromas get into the spirit? It seems likely that they are carried ashore by the winds and the rain, and permeate the peaty surface of the island. Then, when the rivers and burns flow over the peat to the distilleries, they

Whisky and water

The village and distillery of Bowmore face the sea loch around which Islay wraps itself. Some of the distillery's warehouses are below sea level. Even on a calm day, the atmosphere is rich in the aromas of seaweed.

pick up these flavours and impart them in the steep or the mash tun. If the boggy surface is, indeed, impregnated with the seaweedy rain, then a further opportunity will arise when the peat is cut and burned in the distillery's maltings.

The greatest scepticism concerns the belief that the casks in the warehouses "breathe in" the atmosphere. Distillers who use centralized warehouses, away from the distillery, especially favour this argument. Some age on site spirit which is destined to be bottled as single malt, but send to centralized warehouses spirit that is destined for blending.

Seaweed has been described as one of Scotland's most abundant natural resources. The harvesting of seaweed was once a significant industry in Scotland. There is some circumstantial evidence that the practice was introduced by monks on the islands of the west. This is the part of Scotland with the most seaweed. Skye has especially dense kelp forests, sometimes stretching 5 kilometres (3 miles) offshore and more than 20 metres (65 feet) deep. In the islands, kelp was traditionally used as a fertilizer. It was also collected as a source of iodine. More recently, it was used to provide alginates to clarify beer and set jellies and desserts.

The infusion
Like coffee in a filter, the ground grains of malted barley are soaked in warm water, in a vessel with a sieve-like base. The stirring mechanism rotates and can be lowered so that its blades prevent the mixture from solidifying.

FLAVOURS SHAPED AT THE DISTILLERY

In the balance of influences, much more importance has been accorded in recent years to the way in which the distillery works. Twenty-seven malt distilleries, (about a third of the industry's working total) are owned by Diageo, the world's biggest drinks group; and Diageo argues strongly that the most important influences on flavour come from within the distillery itself.

The basic process of making malt whisky is the same throughout Scotland, but there are endless small but significant areas of variation. The degree of peating in the malt is one, similar to the choice of roasts in coffee. Another example is the density (or original gravity) of the malt-and-water mixture that goes into the mash tun (the "coffee filter"). The time the mixture spends in the mash tun, the temperatures to which it is raised, and the duration of each stage, all vary slightly from one distillery to the next. Inside a traditional mash tun is a system of revolving rakes to stir the mixture. In the more modern lauter system, developed in the German brewing industry, a system of knives is used. The German word "lauter" means pure or transparent, and refers to the solution of malt sugars that emerges from the vessel.

As in cooking, every variation affects everything that follows, so that the permutations are infinite. It can be very difficult to determine which aspect of procedure has what effect. Despite that, the industry in general has over the years adopted a rather casual attitude towards yeast's use in fermentation. The view taken was that yeast's influence on flavour would largely be lost in distillation, and that its job was simply to produce as much alcohol as possible.

For years, almost all of Scotland's malt distillers employed the same two yeast cultures. An ale yeast from one of the big brewers was used because it started quickly. Then there was a second pitching with a whisky yeast from Distillers' Company Limited (now long subsumed into a component of Diageo). This had less speed but more staying power. Mergers and changes in ownership resulted in different yeasts coming into the industry. Many distilleries now use only one culture; even Macallan, who insisted on three, have retreated to two.

The action of yeast in fermentation creates flavour compounds called "esters", which are variously fruity, nutty, and spicy. It is difficult to accept that none of these would survive distillation. Diageo believes that the amount of time spent in the fermenter is critical to the individuality of each distillate. The effect of a new yeast culture can be tasted in new make, but the final result will not be determined until the whisky is mature.

Fermentation vessels in Scottish malt distilleries are known as "washbacks". Some are closed vessels made of metal, usually stainless steel. These are easy to clean and relatively safe from contaminants. Despite this, some distilleries prefer wooden washbacks, usually made from larch or Oregon pine. These are open, with a movable lid. Although they are cleaned thoroughly, it is hard to believe that they accommodate no resident microflora. Perhaps these contribute to the house character of some of the more interesting whiskies. Meanwhile, whether the microclimate in and around the distillery has an influence is hotly debated.

Anyone who cooks will know that a recipe, however rigidly followed, will produce different results every time, depending upon the source of heat, the utensils, the cook, and so forth. The design of the stills is a factor increasingly emphasized by Diageo, but even this has an element of location. Some farmhouse distilleries clearly had stills designed to fit their limited space. Elsewhere, several distilleries in the same valley will have the same shape of still (in much the same way that railway stations on the same line may look alike). Obviously, the local coppersmith had his own way of doing things. Distilleries are reluctant to change the shape or size of their stills when wear and tear demands replacement, or when an expansion is planned. The

legend is that if a worn-out still has been dented at some time, the coppersmith will beat a similar blemish into its replacement, in order to ensure that the same whisky emerges.

Illegal distillers used just one small (and therefore portable), copper pot. Since then stills have grown, and are typically run in pairs (or occasionally threesomes), but the principles have not changed. It is clear that design has been largely empirical, with experiments and innovations introduced by individuals. It is often hard to imagine how a bit of extra piping here or there can make a difference. The ratio of surface areas to heat, liquid, vapour, and condensate have infinite effects that are not fully understood.

Water music?

Not a French horn, or any musical instrument, but the unromantically named worm tub. This one is at Edradour. The coil is 24.5 metres (80 feet) long. The diameter starts at 20 cm (8 inches) and finishes at 5 cm (2 inches).

It is argued that in a tall, narrow still, much of the vapour will condense before it can escape. The condensate will fall back into the still and be redistilled. This is known as reflux. The result is a more thorough distillation and a more delicate spirit. Because there is far less reflux in a short, fat still, the spirit will be oilier, creamier, and richer. This is just the simplest example of the shape influencing the character of the whisky.

Stills vary enormously in size and shapes range from "lantern" or "lamp" to "onion" or "pear". Some have a mini-column above the shoulders or, more often, a "boil ball". Others have pipes known as "purifiers" in order to create reflux. The pipe that carries the vapour to the condenser is sometimes at an upward angle, or it can be straight, or point downward. The first will create the most reflux and the last little or none.

The traditional method of condensing is in a worm tub. The vapours pass through a worm-like coil of copper piping in a tub of cold water. This tends to produce a more pungent, characterful spirit, with a heavier, maltier, cereal-grain character.

The more modern system has the opposite relationship between vapour and water. It involves a single large tube, inside which are packed smaller tubes. The small tubes are circulated with cold water,

Still life

The creaminess of Macallan is attributed in part to its short, fat stills. In this picture, the stillman provides a sense of scale. The stills at Glenmorangie are twice as tall, and produce a spirit of legendary delicacy.

while the vapour passes through the large tube. This is called a shell-and-tube condenser. It is more efficient, and is said to produce lighter, grassier, fruitier spirits.

At a time when the industry was moving from worm tubs to shell-and-tube, Diageo made this change at its Dalwhinnie distillery. It was subsequently decided that the spirit had changed character to an unacceptable degree, and the distillery reverted to worm tubs.

One of the most important judgments in influencing flavour is deciding the speed at which the stills are run. Equally important is the decision about when the process has arrived at an acceptable spirit.

In maturation, most distillery managers prefer a stone-built, earth-floored, cool, damp warehouse. Such an atmosphere is felt to encourage the casks to breathe. In this type of structure, known as a dunnage warehouse, the casks are normally stacked only three high, usually with planks between them as supports. The more modern type of warehouse has a concrete floor and fixed racking. As is often the case, the old, inefficient system, more vulnerable to the vagaries of nature, produces the more characterful result.

REGIONAL VARIATIONS

LIKE WINES – AND MANY OTHER DRINKS – the single malts of Scotland usually identify in their labelling not only their country of origin but also the region within it. To know where in Scotland a whisky was produced is to have a very general idea of its likely character. The differences arise from *terroir* and tradition; there are no regional regulations regarding production methods. In their aroma and palate, some whiskies speak of their region more clearly than others, as is the case with wines. Within Bordeaux, a particular Pomerol, for example, might have a richness more reminiscent of Burgundy; similar comparisons can be made in Scotland.

THE LOWLANDS

These are the most accessible whiskies, in both palate and geography, but sadly few in number. From the border town of Carlisle, it is less than 160 kilometres (100 miles) to the southernmost Scottish distillery, Bladnoch, which has been back in production since December 2000, albeit on a limited scale. It is distilling twice a week for half the year. Spirit tasted at 18 months as work in progress was malty, oily, dry, and very flowery. Mature whisky is not expected until 2008–10. Meanwhile, in the shop, distillery rescuer Raymond Armstrong offers a Flora and Fauna edition of Bladnoch, and various independent bottlings produced by former owners Diageo/UDV (*see* Bladnoch).

Only two Lowlanders are in constant production. One of these is Auchentoshan, sometimes billed as "Glasgow's only working distillery". It is on the edge of the city, at Dalmuir, across the Dunbartonshire county line. In Lowland tradition, the whisky is light in both flavour and body, but surprisingly complex and herbal. Auchentoshan is now the sole practitioner of the Lowland tradition of triple distillation. The distillery does not have a visitor centre, but professional tours are possible by arrangement. With its galleried mash house and uncluttered still-house, it is very visitor-friendly.

Maritime malt
Rivetted, not welded, this pot still has a marine appearance befitting its region. Campbeltown's heyday was the era of coastal steamers. Fat stills make oily, muscular whiskies.

The other thriving Lowlander, at the opposite side of the country, is Glenkinchie, "The Edinburgh Malt". This pretty distillery is about 25 kilometres (15 miles) southeast of the city, in the direction of the border. Its spicy whisky has a popular following, and the distillery has a visitor centre.

In the last couple of years, hope has faded for the reopening of the Lowland distilleries Littlemill and Rosebank, although various bottlings of both are still available (see pp. 393–96 and 333–34). Rosebank, which triple distilled, was widely regarded as a classic, and its whisky is collectible. Half a dozen further whiskies are still to be found from Lowland distilleries, some of which closed as long ago as the 1970s. There are even new bottlings, such as those from Glen Flagler and Killyloch (see pp. 267–68). These may be esoteric malts, but the region will not quibble.

There were never a great many Lowland malts, but to have only three active distilleries is perilously few. The delicacy of the Lowlanders makes its own contribution to the world of single malts. This style can be very attractive, especially to people who find the Highlanders and Islanders too robust.

The Lowlanders' problem has been that the Highlanders and Islanders have the romance. Many consumers like a gentle, sweetish malt such as is typical in the Lowlands, but they want the label to say it came from the Highlands. This is analogous with the wine industry, where consumers who like sweetish Chardonnays nevertheless insist that they are drinking a "dry white".

The notion of the Lowlands as a whisky region would be reinforced if it could annex two distilleries that are barely across the Highland line: Glengoyne and Loch Lomond. The first is very pretty, can be visited, and is barely outside Glasgow. Its malty whisky would be perfectly acceptable as a Lowlander. The second is a more industrial site, but a much more attractive distillery than it once was, and it makes a variety of whiskies. Pressed to "defect", both would probably cling to the Highland designation.

THE HIGHLANDS

The border between the Lowland and Highland distilleries is surprisingly southerly, following old county boundaries, stretching across the country between the rivers Clyde and Tay. Some commentators talk of a "southern Highlands", embracing the Tullibardine distillery, which is currently mothballed, and Deanston, which is fully active. Beyond these two, the spread is clearly eastern.

The border

It is neither the Berlin Wall nor Hadrian's, but it is Border country. The outer wall of a warehouse is turned to brash advertisement at the otherwise discreet Bladnoch distillery. Several distilleries identify themselves with such bold wall paintings.

THE EASTERN HIGHLANDS includes, among others, the newly independent Edradour, the smallest distillery in Scotland. Another tiny, farm-style distillery, Glenturret, now finds itself greeting visitors as "The Famous Grouse Experience". The much larger but handsome Aberfeldy distillery has a similar role as "Dewar's World of Whisky". All of these, together with Blair Athol, are in Perthshire. Any of them could comfortably be visited in a day trip from Edinburgh (about 112 kilometres, or 70 miles, away), and all are on or near the main road north to Speyside. Perhaps for reasons of geology, several distilleries in this region have notably fresh, fruity whiskies. Farther north, in barley-growing Aberdeenshire, some heftier whiskies emerge from handsome distilleries such as Royal Lochnagar, Glen Garioch, and Glendronach, with its coal-fired stills burning once more.

SPEYSIDE is not precisely defined, but it embraces between a half and two-thirds of Scotland's distilleries, including the most widely recognized whisky names. A generous definition of Speyside is assumed in this book. Strictly speaking, the long-gone distilleries of Inverness were regarded as Highlanders, not Speysiders. The same might be argued of Aberdeenshire distilleries like Glendronach, but it is easier for the visitor to regard this stretch of the Highlands as a contiguous region.

Again for the convenience of the visitor, this book divides the region into a series of river valleys. In some of these valleys, there do seem to be similarities between the whiskies of neighbouring distilleries.

The River Spey itself is lined with distilleries on both banks, but a number of tributaries and adjoining rivers frame the region. Speyside's ascendancy rested not only on the Grampian mountain snow-melt and the malting barley of Banff and Moray, but also on the railway era. Trains on a rustic branch alongside the Spey took workers and barley

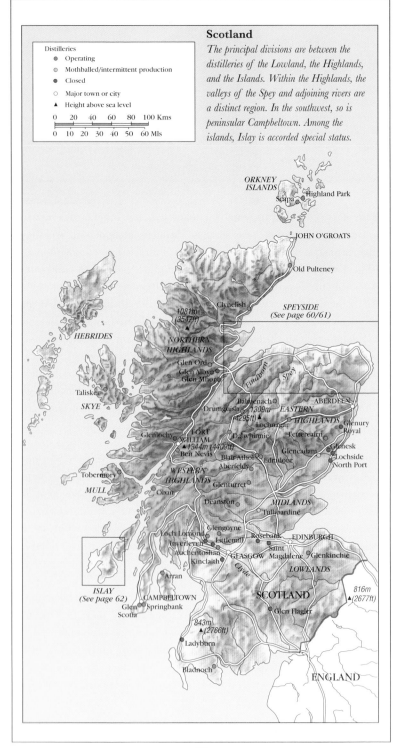

Scotland

The principal divisions are between the distilleries of the Lowland, the Highlands, and the Islands. Within the Highlands, the valleys of the Spey and adjoining rivers are a distinct region. In the southwest, so is peninsular Campbeltown. Among the islands, Islay is accorded special status.

Distilleries

- ● Operating
- ◉ Mothballed/intermittent production
- ● Closed
- ○ Major town or city
- ▲ Height above sea level

0   20   40   60   80   100 Kms

0   10   20   30   40   50   60 Mls

ORKNEY
ISLANDS
Scapa Highland Park

JOHN O'GROATS

Old Pulteney

Clynelish

1081m
(3547ft)

SPEYSIDE
(See page 60/61)

HEBRIDES

NORTHERN
HIGHLANDS

Glen Ord
Glen Albyn
Glen Mhor

Findhorn   Spey

Talisker

SKYE

Balmenach
1309m
(4295ft)   EASTERN   ABERDEEN
Drumguish   HIGHLANDS   Glenury
Lochnagar   Royal
Fettercairn
Glenlochy   FORT
WILLIAM   Dalwhinnie
Glencadam   Glenesk
▲1344m (4409ft)   Blair Athol   Edradour   Lochside
Ben Nevis   North Port
Aberfeldy

WESTERN
HIGHLANDS

Tobermory

MULL   Oban   Glenturret

Deanston   MIDLANDS
Tullibardine

Loch Lomond   Glengoyne
Inverleven   Littlemill   Rosebank   EDINBURGH
Auchentoshan   Saint
Kinclaith   GLASGOW   Magdalene   Glenkinchie

Arran   Clyde   LOWLANDS

SCOTLAND

816m
(2677ft)

ISLAY
(See page 62)   CAMPBELTOWN
Glen   Springbank   Glen Flagler
Scotia

843m
(2766ft)

Ladyburn

Bladnoch   ENGLAND

or malt to the distilleries, and returned with whisky for the main line to Edinburgh, Glasgow, and London. Only vestiges of the Speyside railway survive today, though it is a popular walk. The active line from Aberdeen to Inverness (just over 160 kilometres or 100 miles) follows the main road. The rivers are crossed as follows:

DEVERON: This valley has Glendronach distillery and Glen Deveron. There are five or six distilleries in the general area, but these are quite widely dispersed. Most produce firm, malty whiskies.

ISLA: This has nothing to do with island (it has a different spelling; there's no "y"). Dominican monks brewed here in the 1200s, and there is mention of heather ale in the records. The oldest distillery on Speyside is Strathisla (founded in 1786), showpiece of Chivas Brothers, in the town of Keith in the Isla Valley. There are four or five distilleries in this area, and some of its whiskies have a cedary dryness.

FIDDICH AND DULLAN: These rivers meet at Dufftown, one of the claimants to be the whisky capital of Scotland. There are still six working distilleries in the area, despite the loss of Pittyvaich in 2002. A couple more are currently silent. Some classically rounded, malty Speysiders are produced here, including the secret star, Mortlach.

LIVET: The most famous distillery is called after the river valley itself, and there are three others in the area, all producing light, soft, delicate whiskies. The Livet appellation was once widely copied, but has been increasingly protected. The hill town, Tomintoul, is a base for exploration.

SPEY: Macallan, Aberlour, and Glenfarclas, three of the heavier interpretations of Speyside malts, are all to be found on the most heavily whiskied stretch of the Spey. There are about 12 distilleries, none more than a kilometre from the next, immediately upstream of the village of Craigellachie, home to a famous hotel and whisky bar.

ROTHES BURN: Actually no more than a stream, this river is one of several that reach the Spey at Rothes, another whisky "capital". This one-street town has five distilleries, producing some very nutty whiskies. Speyburn, usually shot through the trees, is the most photographed distillery in Scotland, while Glen Grant has a spectacular "tropical" garden, a coppersmith's, and a "dark grains" plant, which turns residual malt into cattle feed.

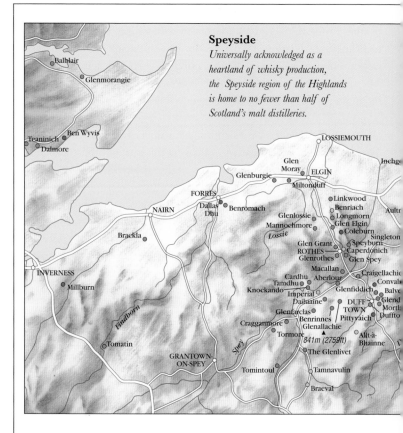

Speyside
*Universally acknowledged as a
heartland of whisky production,
the Speyside region of the Highlands
is home to no fewer than half of
Scotland's malt distilleries.*

LOSSIE: Was it the water that first attracted the Benedictines of Pluscarden to this region? They no longer brew there, but they still have a priory next door to the Miltonduff distillery. Two secret stars, Longmorn and Linkwood, are among the eight distilleries just south of Elgin. The world's most famous whisky shop, Gordon & MacPhail, is in Elgin itself. This sometimes ornate Victorian town is the undisputed commercial capital of Speyside and the county seat of Moray. The Lossie whiskies are sweetish and malty.

FINDHORN: Born-again Benromach is near the town Forres. Production restarted in 1998: the new make tasted creamy and flowery. The museum distillery of Dallas Dhu is nearby, and in the distance is Tomatin.

THE NORTHERN HIGHLANDS is a geographically clear-cut region, which runs from Inverness, straight up the last stretch of the east coast. The region's water commonly runs over sandstone, and there is a gentle maritime influence. There are four or five distilleries in short

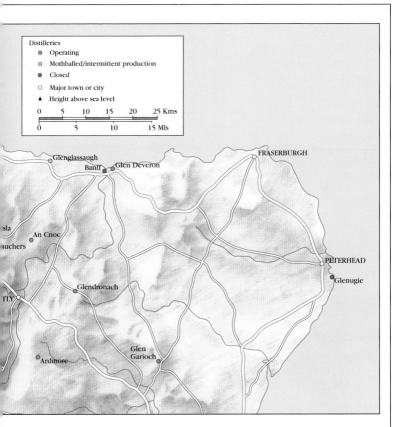

order; including the energetic Glenmorangie and the rich Dalmore. Then there is a gap before the connoisseurs' favourite, Clynelish, and an even bigger gap before the famously salty Old Pulteney in Wick. As its distilleries have become more active, the northern Highlands has gained more recognition as a region. Its whiskies tend toward firm, crisp dryness and a light saltiness.

WESTERN HIGHLANDS The far northwest is the only sizeable stretch of the country with no legal whisky makers. It is just too rugged and rocky. Even the centre cut has only two distilleries. On the foothills of Scotland's (and Britain's) highest mountain, Ben Nevis, the eponymous distillery can be regarded as being "coastal", according to its manager, Colin Ross. Why? Because it is on a sea loch. The Oban distillery certainly does face the sea, and has the flavours to prove it.

The other active mainland distilleries, Loch Lomond and Glengoyne, are so close to Glasgow that they might attract more attention reclassified as Lowlanders. In 2003, Glengoyne was acquired by Ian Macleod Ltd.

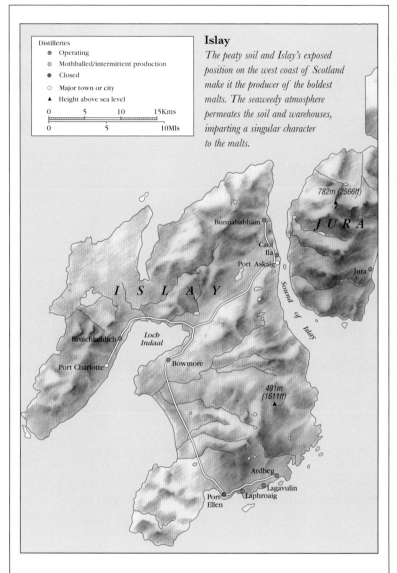

Distilleries
- ● Operating
- ◉ Mothballed/intermittent production
- ● Closed
- ○ Major town or city
- ▲ Height above sea level

0   5   10   15Kms

0   5   10Mls

Islay

The peaty soil and Islay's exposed position on the west coast of Scotland make it the producer of the boldest malts. The seaweedy atmosphere permeates the soil and warehouses, imparting a singular character to the malts.

THE ISLANDS

The greatest whisky island by far is Islay (above), with its seven distilleries. The others have one apiece, except for Orkney, which has two distilleries.

ORKNEY For the moment, Highland Park is Scotland's northernmost distillery. Its whisky is one of the greats, peaty and smoky, but a superb all-rounder. Saltier whiskies from the Scapa distillery have a strong following, but are not in production at the moment.

SHETLAND The first ever legal distillery in Shetland is promised for 2004 – it will be Scotland's most northerly.

SKYE Talisker whisky from Skye is a classic – volcanic, explosive, and peppery. The taste reflects the wild, looming *terroir*.

MULL Tobermory is a restrained islander, but the distillery also produces the peatier, smokier Ledaig. It is to be hoped that Tobermory does not suffer from its parent's acquisition of Bunnahabhain.

JURA The decidedly piney Isle of Jura whisky has appeared in more expressions and has been better promoted since the owning group, Whyte and Mackay, seceded from its American parent, Jim Beam.

ISLAY The 2003 takeover of Bunnahabhain by Burn Stewart makes this distillery look more secure. All seven of the island's workable distilleries are operating, and the Islay Festival in late May is establishing itself as an annual favourite.

ARRAN The newest distillery in Scotland, Arran ran its first spirit in 1995. Its small stills produce a creamy spirit with only faint touches of island character: a touch of flowery pine in the finish.

CAMPBELTOWN

The announcement in 2001 that Springbank's owners planned to restore the Glengyle distillery was quickly followed by the start of work. The distillery, which has been closed for 75 years, is due to reopen in 2004.

The Springbank distillery itself produces three whiskies, using entirely its own malt – the Springbank maltings was restored a decade ago. This distillery has on occasion also assisted with the management of the other Campbeltown distillery, Glen Scotia, which is currently also in production.

Springbank, the independent bottlers Cadenhead, and the Eaglesome shop are all related businesses. The whisky veteran behind them all, Hedley Wright, has been determined to keep Campbeltown on the whisky map. Its remarkable history is evidenced by fragments of about 20 distilleries converted to other uses. There are said to have been 32 distilleries here in 1759. The town's location at the foot of the Kintyre peninsula provides not only a harbour, but also a location surrounded by the sea and often shrouded in mist.

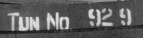

Tun No. 92 9

Rotation No. 0

Bulk Ltrs. 2130/1 2115/2

G/F 12 Y.O SPECIAL RESERVE

WHAT IS THE PERFECT
AGE?

I N 2000, THE WORLD'S BIGGEST SELLING single malt, the principal version of Glenfiddich, changed its mind about age, for the second time. Like some of its immediate competitors, it had for much of its life carried no age statement. At one stage, it was bottled as an 8-year-old. Now it became a 12-year-old.

In announcing the change, Glenfiddich observed that malt drinkers looked for an age statement as a reassurance of authenticity and quality. This is not true of the more experienced malt drinker, who does not necessarily accept the inference that older is always better.

The extra years worked well for Glenfiddich. The earlier versions were light and pleasantly fruity, but could be a little sharp and thin. The extra years have rounded out the spirit and introduced a touch of the "white chocolate" found in older bottlings.

Glenfiddich, the first malt whisky to be methodically marketed, had possibly become over-familiar. It was seen as an unchallenging whisky, overtaken by more robust neighbours. The 12-year-old was perhaps a response: the whisky catching up with the consumer.

THE IMPOSSIBLE DECISION

Upgrading the age is not easy. Most distilleries have some reserves of maturing whisky that is older than they strictly need, but these stocks would not be sufficient to support such a major change. Had sales been falling sharply, a backlog of stock would have built up, but this was not the case. The decision to increase the age would have required sufficient stock to be laid down 12 years earlier, probably with a view to the change.

The person who makes such decisions has an impossible job. However good their judgment, knowledge, and understanding of the industry; however thorough the company's market research; and however many futurologists it consults, it is simply impossible to predict how much whisky will be required in five, ten or fifteen years. When the time comes, there is always too little or too much. Across the industry this is why distilleries open, close, are mothballed, and so frequently change ownership.

Single but married
Glenfiddich Special Reserve is already 12 years old when it goes into this marrying tun for about four months. The object is to iron out natural differences and ensure a consistent product.

MAKING A VATTING

The components of a bottling may also embrace casks of various sizes and with different histories. Although the contents of the casks will be vatted according to a "recipe", adjustments will have to be made to account for the way in which the whisky has developed during maturation. No two casks, even with the same origin, are alike. Casks from the bottom of the warehouse will have matured at a different rate from those in the airier racks at the top. A warehouse nearer the sea may impart brinier characteristics. Some distilleries have only the classically damp, earth-floored, stone-built warehouses, with casks stacked three high, separated by planks of wood; others have fixed racking, with casks nine high; some have both. All of these factors may affect the distillers' choice of casks for a bottling.

Ages around six, seven, and eight years are commonly used in blends, but they could be used in a vatting for a single malt. If it carries an age statement, regulations demand that it be based on the youngest age, but as "6-year-old" might sound callow, the producer might prefer to manage without an age statement. When Glenfiddich was marketed as an 8-year-old, it probably included whiskies of nine and ten years or more. Now it is a 12-year-old and probably includes whiskies of up to 15 years old. Some of the lighter-bodied malts hit their stride at eight or ten years old, while 12 is so common as to be regarded by consumers in some markets as a standard for mature malt.

DEVELOPING A RANGE

If there were a "best" age for malt whisky, it would be universally adopted. In Italy, where the words "malt whisky" are potent, devotees are delighted with a 5-year-old. In Japan, where age is respected, a 30-year-old is appreciated. In recent years, distillers have offered not only a greater range of ages but also of strengths, types of cask, and finish. These have come to be known as different "expressions" of the same malt. For those consumers bored with consistency, there is the merit of greater individuality in some of the more unusual bottlings, particularly vintages, and especially those at cask strength.

To take Glenfiddich as an example, it also offers: a variation on the 12-year-old (involving casks from Islay); a 15-year-old (Solera Reserve); a 21-year-old (Millennium Reserve, with a variation employing Havana rum barrels); and several dated vintages (of which the 1961 was a single cask). A bottling from a single cask represents a very limited edition, with the merit of its own individuality. Such a bottling is made for malt lovers who wish to explore.

Vintage whiskies

While seeking consistency in its principal product, Glenfiddich offers diversity of character in its vintages. The barley harvest and climate differ slightly each year, but bigger differences develop in the cask.

Glenfiddich's Malt Master, David Stewart, creates daring whiskies that dance on the tongue with balletic elegance. His 12-year-old is a deft transformation, but he might well have preferred to approach the task from a wider angle: retaining some younger malts from the 8-year-old, but increasing the proportion of older malts (or increasing their ages). Young malts can inject liveliness to a vatting, while the older ones add complexity. This might have produced an even more complex whisky. Why did he not follow that course? Because it would have precluded the use of the age statement "12 years old".

Blenders like to use a wide range of ages within a vatting, but are constrained by the marketing men, with their reliance on bold statements of maturity.

In 1991, nine casks of a 50-year-old Glenfiddich were bottled. At such an age, whisky can be excessively woody (smelling like musty furniture in a derelict house), but that depends on the quality of the casks. Glenfiddich's semi-centenarian whisky had been in excellent oak. For its age, the whisky was surprisingly rounded and chocolatey, without excessive oakiness. The bottles were sold in London at around US$5000 (about £3,000) each, but one fetched US$70,000 (about £40,000) in an auction in Milan.

In 2003, for the Islay Festival, the Bunnahabhain distillery bottled seven hogsheads that had been filled in 1963. Evaporation had taken one or two to below 40 per cent alcohol, the legal minimum for whisky. When all had been checked, it was determined that a vatting of the seven would produce a bottling at 42.9 volume.

A whisky can be too woody at 21 years, or it can still be enjoyable at 50, but – like death and taxes – evaporation eventually takes its toll. Unlike a human being, a whisky that has over-stayed its time on earth is sure to meet the angels. Just as humans in ancient cultures revered trees, especially oaks, so *Quercus robur* and *Q. alba* are the greatest influences on the maturation of *aqua vitae*.

THE PERFECT WOOD

D ID THE FLAVOURS IN YOUR GLASS begin a dozen years ago, with the sowing of barley on the Black Isle? Or decades earlier, as a blizzard on the Grampians? If the malt was peated, you could be enjoying a few leaves of bog myrtle that have been waiting 7000 years for your rendezvous. Or did your favourite flavours emerge a century ago on a forest slope in Galicia, Spain? Or perhaps in the Ozark Mountains of Missouri?

The creation of alcoholic drinks in different parts of the world employs in various roles a whole alphabet of trees: for their fruits and berries; to make charcoal, to act as a filter; as a fuel in the kilning of malt; to provide vessels for fermentation or maturation, or simply to act as containers. Various drinks are stored in (or consumed from) cedar, juniper, and chestnut, but the wood most commonly used for all those purposes is oak. Its most attractive property is its pliability. It must bend to make a barrel, and the elegant curves of this traditional vessel strengthen it, just as an arch reinforces a building. Even in the most mechanized distillery, casks are rolled and occasionally dropped or bounced. They must be tough and not split or leak. They contain an increasingly precious product.

United States regulations insist that bourbon is matured in new oak, but the cask may subsequently cross the Atlantic and be filled three or four times with the spirit of Scotland. If each of those fillings is matured for only six or seven years, the cask will have seen two or three decades' service. If a cask is tapped at 25 years, then repeats the performance, it already has half a century under its belt. It must be tough, yet also able to breathe during the maturation of the whisky, and perhaps also have some flavours and aromas to donate.

OAK AND FLAVOUR

Wooden casks were originally regarded simply as containers. Whisky was sold in the cask to inns and country houses, and customers noted that it mellowed in the cellar. Over the years, it has increasingly been recognized that the character of the wood plays a big part in the

Tough but pliable

Oak does not break under torture, but it bends to provide the elegant, strengthening curves of the cask. This cooperage is in Andalusia. Charring to enhance flavour is more typical in Kentucky.

development of the whisky's aromas and flavours, but how big? The perceived importance of wood has greatly increased across the industry in recent years, yet opinions differ more widely than ever.

The issue was not much discussed while former sherry casks were readily available for the maturation of whisky. These casks seem to have been accepted without much question, though they must have imparted a variety of characteristics. Some had been used in fermentation, others in maturation, others for transport. They had contained different styles of sherry – and sometimes other fortified wines.

As sherry fell out of fashion, exports to the United Kingdom diminished. Meanwhile, the dictator Franco died in 1975, Spain became a democracy, and its trade unions insisted that the bottling of wines be carried out by local labour in Spain.

Distilleries anxious to continue sherry ageing now had to work directly with the bodegas in Jerez. Macallan has been the most consistently active proponent of this approach. So through several changes of control at Macallan, its top managers have each year swapped the granite and heather of Speyside for the orange trees and Moorish architecture of Jerez.

WHICH VARIETY OF OAK?

The Macallan is a full-bodied whisky, which as new make is rich in fruity esters reminiscent of flowering currant, apple, citrus, and even tropical fruits such as banana. These flavours are balanced by the tannins and acids found in European oak.

Setting aside those that grow as shrubs and bushes, there are more than half a dozen European species of oak tree. Two have traditionally been used in cooperage. The second choice is usually *Quercus petraea*, known as the sessile oak, for the way the acorns "sit" on the twigs. The first choice is *Quercus robur*, the pendunculate oak. The epithet refers to the way the acorns are suspended on stalks.

The *Q. robur* tolerates a wide range of growing conditions, and is typically found in England, France, and Iberia. In France, where region appellations are used, Limousin and Tronçais oaks are usually of the *Q. robur* variety.

The principal growing area in Spain is the northwest corner of the country, where the coast between the cities of Santander and Corunna faces the Bay of Biscay and the Atlantic. Behind the coast rise stony hills, the valleys between them dappled with oaks. These once fed shipyards making galleons; then Spanish oak was turned into barrels for wine; and now its final destination is Scotland.

The centre of the timber industry is the city of Lugo, in the province of the same name, in the region of Galicia. A sawmill there cuts staves for Macallan. The staves are air-dried for 12 to 15 months simply by being left outdoors. The weather washes out some of the tannins, moderating the intensity of the wood, and the staves then become casks at a cooperage in Jerez. They are filled with newly pressed cloudy grape juice, for between two weeks and six months, and then used a second time, to mature sherry, before being sent to Scotland. The casks are shipped whole, thus maintaining the sherryish character of the wood. This would diminish if they were knocked down into staves.

Iron lady
Torture continues … this machine forces the hoops to hold the staves in position.

Much as it is desired by Macallan, Spanish oak is less well supported in its own country. Spanish wine makers, including those of Jerez, increasingly prefer the sweeter, more vanilla-like character of American oak.

BUTTS, HOGSHEAD, OR BARRELS?

The casks used for the maturation of sherry are known as butts, and typically have a capacity of 500 litres (110 UK gallons or 132 US gallons). There is a beauty and an integrity to such vessels, but their size and weight make them difficult to handle.

The term "hogshead" refers to a traditional cask size of 250 litres (55 UK gallons or 66 US gallons). Sherry hogshead can be found, but the designation is more commonly applied to a Scottish adaptation of an American barrel. In this instance, the barrel is shipped as staves. It is then reassembled with new heads (barrel ends) to increase the size. The new heads also freshen up the wood influence. The term "American oak" is sometimes used to indicate a bourbon barrel, which typically has a capacity of around 200 litres (44 UK gallons or 53 US gallons). Many single malts are vatted from a combination of sherry butts and bourbon barrels, usually with the latter in the majority.

Many producers of lighter-bodied, more delicate-tasting whiskies feel that they express their aromas and flavours more successfully when matured in bourbon barrels. A long-time proponent of this approach is Glenmorangie. Its 10-year-old is wholly aged in bourbon, and this is the initial regime for other expressions, even though many are wood finishes.

The man in charge of distillation and maturation for Glenmorangie, Bill Lumsden, has worked with the Blue Grass Cooperage in Louisville to develop a bourbon barrel that perfectly suits both sides of the Atlantic. More than 360 kilometres (225 miles) southwest and 160 kilometres (100 miles) south of St Louis, Missouri, oak for the casks is grown around Altenburg, a town settled by immigrants from Saxony in Germany. The town sign still uses the word "*Stadt*" for "city".

This is an area of mixed deciduous woodland, with small, privately owned lots. The soils are very well drained. The part of the country has four definite seasons, but the winter cold has enough restraint not to damage the crop. The wood is clean, without knots, and with good pores. This is white oak, *Quercus alba*.

WHAT HAPPENS DURING AGEING

Several processes take place during maturation. While the new distillate may have some harsh, "spirity" flavours, these can be lost by evaporation. With the expansion and contraction of the wood, caused by seasonal changes in temperature, spirit flavours may be exhaled and the natural aromas of the environment taken into the cask: piney, seaweedy, and salty "sea-air" characteristics can all be acquired in this way. Flavours are also imparted by the cask: sherry wood may add the nutty note of the wine; and bourbon barrels can impart caramel flavours, vanillins, and tannins.

Perhaps the most important influence on the flavour is that of a very slow, gentle oxidation of the whisky. While oxygen is regarded as an "enemy" by brewers and some wine makers, because it can cause "stale" flavours, its influence is also a part of the character of other drinks such as Madeira wines. The importance of oxidation in the

Steam heat
*Scalded into submission …
after these sequences of
tortures, the casks can settle
down to a life of sipping
sherry, then whisky.*

maturation of whisky has been the subject of much recent work by Dr Jim Swan, originally at the Pentlands Scotch Whisky Research Institute, and more recently by his own company. Dr Swan argues that oxidation increases the complexity and intensity of pleasant flavours in whisky, especially fragrant, fruity, spicy, and minty notes.

As in the production of all alcoholic drinks, the flavours emerge from a complex series of actions and reactions. Traces of copper from the stills are the catalyst. They convert oxygen to hydrogen peroxide, which attacks the wood, releasing vanillin. This promotes oxidation, and additionally pulls together the various flavours present. These processes vary according to the region of origin of the wood, and its growth patterns. Vanillin is a component that occurs naturally in oak. As its name suggests, it imparts a vanilla-like flavour.

In Spain, trees from the most mountainous districts of Galicia are more resiny. In the US, growth is mainly in a belt across Ohio, Kentucky, Illinois, Missouri, and Arkansas. The western part of this contiguous region has the poorest soil and the most arid climate, and therefore the trees have to fight to survive. This optimizes spring growth, which has the most open texture and is the most active in the maturation process.

LIGHT, MEDIUM, OR ALLIGATOR?

Bourbon barrels are toasted or charred on the inside to enable the whiskey to permeate the wood. There are stories of this happy discovery having arisen from an accidental fire, but it seems more likely to have emerged from the technique of toasting the wood to make it pliable.

Charring gives the spirit access to positive properties and flavours in the wood, but also enables it better to expel undesirable flavours. American cooperages typically offer three degrees of char: light, medium, and alligator. The latter, the heaviest, leaves the wood looking like a log so heavily burned that it has formed a pattern of squares reminiscent of an alligator's skin.

A sherry butt or bourbon barrel will impart considerable aroma and flavour to its first fill of whisky. "First-fill sherry casks were used in the maturation of this whisky" is the type of claim that appears on the neck label of an especially voluptuous malt. Some distillers feel that the more restrained second fill provides a better balance. A third fill will impart little, but let the character of the spirit speak for itself. If there is a fourth fill, it is likely to go for blending after which, 30 or 40 years on, the inside of the cask might be recharred. The preferred word is "rejuvenated".

OWNERS, DISTILLERS, AND BOTTLERS

IN THE NEXT SECTION IS A REVIEW, in alphabetical order, of every Scottish malt distillery that has ever witnessed its product in a bottle. These are not "brands" (though their names may be registered); they are actual distilleries: premises at which malt is turned into whisky. Among today's distilleries, only the relatively new Kininvie has not seen its product, a deliciously creamy whisky, bottled. Some of the distilleries reviewed have long closed, but bottlings from their stocks are still being made, or were within recent memory – and therefore may still be on the odd shelf.

NAMES OF DISTILLERIES Some distilleries have been known over the years by several different names. They are listed here by the most recent name on the label of the principal bottlings, though reference may be made in the text to earlier names. If you have bought, or are considering buying, a malt that appears not to be in this book, check the index. If it is not listed there, its name is not that of a distillery. Importers, distributors, and supermarkets often buy malt whisky to bottle under invented names (for example, Glen Bagpipe, Loch Sporran). These products are not reviewed. The bottle will probably contain whisky supplied by a reputable distiller who happens to have a surplus, but the source could change at any time. The next bottle under the same name might contain an entirely different whisky.

WHO OWNS THE DISTILLERIES? The biggest changes ever seen in the ownership of distilleries have taken place in the first few years of this millennium. Although the overall effect has been to concentrate control of Scotland's distilleries yet further, it has also shaken loose a handful into various degrees of independence.

Ninety-odd distilleries are working or capable of being put into operation. Ninety per cent of them are owned by groups, about half of which are international drinks companies. Some of the world's biggest corporations own tiny, rustic distilleries.

THE INTERNATIONAL DRINKS COMPANIES

Diageo is the giant of the industry, and the least changed since the 4th edition of this book. It owns four maltings, twenty-seven malt distilleries, and two grain distilleries. Some elements of this business date from the 1700s, but its emergence as a group can be traced to the 1880s, when a portfolio of distilleries was assembled to produce whiskies to create blends. As the Distillers Company Limited (DCL), this group produced almost all the famous names in blended Scotch, and dominated the industry for 100 years. In the 1980s, DCL merged with Bell's to become United Distillers (UD).

The new company acknowledged the growing interest in malts by introducing bottlings from six distilleries, each highlighting a different region. These were dubbed The Classic Malts. The same whiskies have since been offered with wood finishes as The Distillers Edition. Although each malt in these two families has its own label design, the graphic genre is similar. This still left many UD distilleries without a bottled single malt to offer tourists in their region. A range with labels showing local flora and fauna was developed. This was purely for local sale, though it soon became more widely popular. UD then decided to bottle stocks they still held from distilleries that had closed or that had even been demolished. These were identified as The Rare Malts, and marketed at prices that reflected their scarcity value. As stocks diminished, this series then began to call upon rare vintages from distilleries still in operation. This was reflected in an extension of the series as Cask Strength Limited Editions. More recently, some whiskies that were appreciated by connoisseurs but not widely known have been released as Hidden Malts. Small, outstanding batches are bottled each year as Special Releases, though this rubric does not appear on the labels.

UD merged with Britain's other drinks giant, International Distillers and Vintners (IDV), in 1997 and coined the name Diageo, which is intended to speak of the daily pleasures of food and drink. The group owns Tanqueray gin, Smirnoff vodka, Cuervo tequila, Guinness stout, and many other drinks.

Chivas Brothers has 11 distilleries, all on Speyside, including famous names like The Glenlivet. This group began with two brothers from the Highlands and a wine and spirits shop established in Aberdeen in the mid-1800s. The business was acquired as a foothold in Scotland by Seagram, the Canadian whisky distillers. Taking advantage of the shutdown of US distilling during Prohibition, Seagram had become the world's biggest drinks company. It subsequently diversified into the entertainment industry, and withdrew from distilling. In one of the industry's biggest takeovers, its Scottish distilleries were acquired in 2001 by Pernod Ricard. This family-owned business, based on pastis, is now an international drinks company. Its subsidiaries include Irish Distillers Limited and Wild Turkey Kentucky Bourbon.

Allied Distillers also has roots in Canada's sales of whisky to the United States. Its original parent was Hiram Walker, producer of Canadian Club. Among its ten distilleries, Laphroaig, on Islay, is the only one to have been consistently promoted. Its coal-fired Highland distillery, Glendronach, reopened in 2002, and its products are readily available. The other distilleries in the group have bottlings primarily for sale to visitors. These are called Special Distillery Bottlings. Allied's distilleries have over the years produced whisky primarily for the internationally known Ballantine's blends. Allied-Domecq is today's parent, embracing sherry, brandy, and wine.

Three groups have five malt distilleries each:

The Edrington Group produces one of Britain's best selling blends, The Famous Grouse. Its malt distilleries include Macallan and Highland Park. The core of the group was known as Highland Distillers until a complex realignment in 1999/2000, involving several other old-established businesses in the Scottish whisky trade. It has links with Rémy-Cointreau, the French brandy and liqueur company.

Dewar's, the best-selling blend in the US, was owned by United Distillers until the merger that created Diageo. In approving the merger, the European Commission and the US Federal Trade Commission were both concerned about market domination. Diageo already owned Johnnie Walker and J&B. Dewar's principal distillery, Aberfeldy, and three others were sold to Bacardi, the rum producer. Bacardi already owned Glen Deveron, through Martini & Rossi, the vermouth producer.

Inver House has its origins in a long-gone American group, but was given its present shape by a management buy-out. During the 1990s, the company bought distilleries that were silent or surplus to the requirements of their owners. The Scottish management remains, but the company has since 2001 been owned by Pacific Spirits, a family-controlled drinks company in Thailand.

One company has four malt distilleries:

Whyte and Mackay is an old-established name that has been resurrected. The Whyte and Mackay distilleries were for a time owned by Jim Beam, but in 2001 there was a management buy-out, using the name Kyndal. In 2003, the original name was reinstated. The company also owns the Invergordon grain distillery. Some vintage bottlings bear the rubric Stillman's Dram.

Four companies each have a trio of malt distilleries. (The first is an international drinks group; the next three are only involved in whisky distilling):

Burn Stewart is now owned by Angostura Limited. Based in Trinidad, this company produces the well-known cocktail bitters. This piquant product may seem a drop in the ocean of drink, but it has given rise to its own international company, with a portfolio including rums and wines. In 2003, Angostura acquired Burn Stewart, owner of the Tobermory and Deanston distilleries. Later the same year, it added Bunnahabhain.

William Grant & Sons remains a family firm. The original William Grant was a distillery manager before he set up his own. He and his family built the Glenfiddich distillery in 1886, and Balvenie in 1892. Kininvie was added rather more recently, in 1990. William Grant also owns the Girvan grain distillery. The company's growth has been a well-earned reward for its vision in pioneering the marketing of single malts.

Glenmorangie is the biggest selling malt in Scotland and the fourth worldwide. Glenmorangie plc, formerly known as Macdonald & Muir, is still family controlled, but is quoted on the London Stock Exchange. Its distilleries are Glenmorangie, Glen Moray, and Ardbeg. A small stake is held by the company's American distributor, Brown Forman, owner of Jack Daniel's Tennessee whiskey.

Morrison Bowmore was a family business, built around the highly regarded maltings and distillery in the "capital" of Islay. The company also owns Auchentoshan, the last Lowlander to practise triple distillation. The third distillery in the group is Glen Garioch, in the Highlands. The Morrison family had a long co-operation with Suntory before the Japanese giant became the proud owner of this small but well-balanced business.

Two more distilleries are in Japanese ownership:-

Ben Nevis is owned by the Asahi subsidiary Nikka, old-established Japanese whisky distiller and competitor to Suntory.
Tomatin is owned by Takara Shuzo Co. Ltd, producers of the Japanese spirit shochu.

DEGREES OF INDEPENDENCE

Two companies own a couple of malt distilleries each:

Loch Lomond owns the long-established malt distillery of the same name (with additionally a grain distillery on the site), and has now added Glen Scotia. (It also owned Littlemill, but this distillery is no longer operating and has been partially demolished).

Angus Dundee is a small company bottling under the name MacKillop's Choice. In recent reshuffles, it acquired the Tomintoul distillery from Jim Beam and Glencadam from Allied.

Other links between bottlers and distilleries:

Cadenhead has long shared ownership with Springbank.
Scott's Selection is owned by the Christie family, and opened the Speyside (Drumguish) distillery in 1990.
Gordon & MacPhail bought Benromach from UD and reopened it in 1998.
Murray McDavid has some common ownership with Bruichladdich, acquired from Jim Beam in 2000.
Signatory has the same principal as Edradour, acquired in 2003 from Pernod Ricard.
Ian Macleod acquired Glengoyne in 2003.

NATURAL CASK STRENGTH

SINGLE MALT
SCOTCH WHISKY
FROM
BENROMACH
DISTILLERY

1982

59.7% VOL

70cl

PROPRIETORS: GORDON & MACPHAIL

SPECIALLY SELECTED, PRODUCED AND BOTTLED BY
GORDON & MACPHAIL
ELGIN · SCOTLAND

PRODUCT OF SCOTLAND

CASK Nos.
112, 114

REFILL SHERRY HOGSHEADS

DISTILLED
02/02/82

BOTTLED
24/10/01

Distilleries not linked to other businesses:

Tullibardine (mothballed), part of Jim Beam's sale to Kyndal, sold to a consortium proposing to run the distillery as part of a retail development.
Arran is a new distillery, established in 1995 as an independent business.
Bladnoch was bought by a private individual from UD and restarted production in 2001.
Glenfarclas is the last family-owned single distillery. Licensed as a farm distillery in 1836, it was acquired two years later by John Grant, and is still in the family. (There is no connection with William Grant & Sons or the Glen Grant Distillery.)

THE CONFUSING WORLD OF INDEPENDENT BOTTLERS

Newcomers to the world of single malts are often puzzled by the way in which whisky from the same distillery may appear under several different labels. Equally, whiskies from 20 or 30 different distilleries may all appear under labels which are almost identical. This is because, with three exceptions, distilleries do not carry out their own bottling. The original farm distilleries pre-dated mechanized bottling. They sold their whisky by the cask to wealthy householders, hotels, or licensed grocers or wine and spirit merchants.

Two merchants, dating from the 1800s, kept malts alive after the industry turned its attention almost entirely to blends. (*See* Gordon & MacPhail *and* Cadenhead, *below*.) As the practice of blending grew, the trade of whisky broker emerged. Brokers buy casks of whisky, often speculatively, and supply them to blenders, bottlers, or merchants. A great deal of whisky is in the hands of brokers. With the growing interest in single malts, the availability of this whisky is exciting the interest of a growing number of independent bottlers. As most distilleries still supply the bulk of their output for blending, some do not wish to be concerned with the business of single malt, and are happy to leave it to the independent bottlers.

At the opposite extreme, some famous distilleries have very definite ideas about the way their whisky is presented as a single malt (age, strength, type of cask). Some have controlled stock, and even bought back casks, to prevent independent bottlings. Others have taken legal action. This can be difficult when the brand name is also a place.

The terms "distillery bottling" or "official bottling" are occasionally used in this book. These terms imply a bottling that has been made on behalf of the distillery's owners. Distilleries that are owned by groups will usually have a central bottling line, typically within easy reach of Glasgow and Edinburgh.

Gordon & MacPhail is a family-owned shop in the Speyside heartland at Elgin, but its bottlings reach every corner of the world. Over the decades, it has acquired considerable stocks, which it has matured in its own warehouses. For this reason Gordon & MacPhail's bottlings of a particular malt have a consistency of style, often with a typical sherry-aged character, especially those in the Connoisseurs Choice Range.

Cadenhead has since the 1960s been owned by the proprietors of Springbank, in Campbeltown. The company is happy to buy small quantities of whiskies as they become available, so that bottling runs are short and the age or type of cask used may vary greatly. This makes for a great diversity of interesting bottlings. Cadenhead led the way in not chill filtering.

OTHER INDEPENDENTS

Adelphi Emphasizes cask strength. Tends toward full-flavoured whiskies. Founded in the early 1990s by Jamie Walker, whose forebears owned the Adelphi Distillery (1825–1902) in Glasgow.

Berry Brothers Seek whiskies that are good examples of the distillery's character (*see* Glenrothes).

Blackadder The jocular name is appropriate. Bottlings range from the noble to the downright eccentric. Raw Cask is a sub-range. Whiskies bottled "on lees". Founded in 1995 by whisky writer Robin Tucek.

Coopers Choice Good regional diversity. Part of The Vintage Malt Whisky Company. Founded in 1992 by a former sales director of Morrison Bowmore.

Douglas Laing Likes to offer contrasting expressions from the same distillery. Typically bottles at 50 volume. Independent bottlings (as Old Malt Cask) since 1998, but family has been in the whisky trade since 1949.

Duncan Taylor Shop in Huntly, Aberdeenshire. Bottler since 2002. Ranges include Peerless and Whisky Galore. Large portfolio, based on inventory (some dating from the 1960s). Bequeathed by pioneering American importer, Abe Rosenberg.

Hart Brothers Emphasizes wood finishes and good oak character. Bottling since 1989. Wine background since 1960s.

Ian Macleod Rare malts at unusual ages or with distinctive finishes. Smart packaging. Chieftain's and Dun Bheagan ranges since 2000. Blender and broker since 1930s.

James MacArthur "Small is Beautiful". Low-profile business, started as a hobby in 1982. Selects in the basis of best age for each whisky.

Lombard Sensitive to age. Buys whiskies and continues to mature. Bottling recent, but brokers since late 1960s.

MacKillop's Choice Selections By Lorne MacKillop, Master of Wine. Bottler since 1998.

Murray McDavid Has sought in each bottling (since 1996) "the truest expression of the distillery". The Mission range is selected by Jim McEwan, of Bruichladdich.

Scott's Selection Emphasizes silent stills and rare malts. Started in mid-1990s by blender Rob Scott (now retired). Linked to the warehousing, blending, and bottling business established by George Christie (*see* Drumguish).

Signatory Father of the new wave of bottlers. Established in 1988 and one of the few to have its own bottling line. Signatory pioneered single cask bottlings. Founder Andrew Symington previously worked in hotels.

Wilson & Morgan Has used Marsala barrels. Based in Italy. Bottling since 1992. Importing since 1960s.

Whiskies reviewed include some bottlings for retailers in the UK. These include:
The Whisky Shop (Glasgow and branches), Royal Mile Whiskies (Edinburgh and London),
The Wee Dram (Bakewell, England), The Vintage House and The Whisky Exchange
(both London), and Oddbins (UK chain).

A–Z
OF SINGLE MALTS

WHATEVER THE ARGUMENTS about their relative prices, no one denies that a Château Latour is more complex than a mass-market table wine. The fine wines of the whisky world are the single malts. Some malts are made to higher standards than others, and some are inherently more distinctive than their neighbours. This cannot be obscured by the producers' blustery arguments about "personal taste". A tasting note cannot be definitive, but it can be a useful guide, and will tell you, for example, if the whisky is a light, dry malt, or if it is rich and sherryish, or peaty and smoky.

The tasting notes start with a comment on the house style – a quick, first, general indication of what to expect from each distillery's products, before looking at the variations that emerge in different ages and bottlings. I also suggest the best moment for each distillery's whiskies (such as before dinner, or with a book at bedtime). These suggestions are meant as an encouragement to try each in a congenial situation. They are not meant to be taken with excessive seriousness.

Tasting note example:

AUCHENTOSHAN 1973, 29-year-old, Sherry Butt No 793, 55.8 vol

COLOUR Pinkish red. Almost rhubarb-like.
NOSE Jammy. Australian Shiraz. Red apples. Peaches.
BODY Textured. Fluffy.
PALATE An extraordinarily fruity whisky, with peach dominant. Peach-stone flavours, too. Underneath all that, it is hard to divine any Auchentoshan character. Severely marked down for those reasons.
FINISH Nutty dryness. With the cheese? After dinner?

SCORE **69**

COLOUR The natural colour of a malt matured in plain wood is a very pale yellow. Darker shades, ranging from amber to ruby to deep brown, can be imparted by sherry wood. Some distilleries use casks

A character-forming home
Skye forms a natural crucible, in which the flavours of a great whisky are fused. Living in the mountains and surrounded by sea, the whisky assumes a gusty salt-and-pepper house character.

that have been treated with concentrated sherry, and this can cause a caramel-like appearance and palate. Some add caramel to balance the colour. I do not suggest that one colour is in itself better than another, though a particular subtle hue can heighten the pleasure of a fine malt. We enjoy food and drink with our eyes as well as our nose and palate.

NOSE Anyone sampling any food or drink experiences much of the flavour through the sense of smell. Whisky is highly aromatic, and the aromas of malts include peat, flowers, honey, toasty maltiness, coastal brine, and seaweed, for example.

BODY Lightness, smoothness, or richness might refresh, soothe, or satisfy. Body and texture (sometimes known as "mouth feel") are distinct features of each malt.

PALATE In the enjoyment of any complex drink, each sip will offer new aspects of the taste. Even one sip will gradually unfold a number of taste characteristics in different parts of the mouth over a period of, say, a minute. This is notably true of single malts. Some present a very extensive development of palate. A taster working with an unfamiliar malt may go back to it several times over a period of days, in search of its full character. I have adopted this technique in my tastings for this book.

FINISH In all types of alcoholic drink, the "finish" is a further stage of the pleasure. In most single malts, it is more than a simple aftertaste, however important that may be. It is a crescendo, followed by a series of echoes. When I leave the bottle, I like to be whistling the tune. When the music of the malt fades, there is recollection in tranquillity.

SCORE The pleasures described above cannot be measured with precision, if at all. The scoring system is intended merely as a guide to the status of the malts. Each tasting note is given a score out of 100. This is inspired by the system of scoring wines devised by the American writer Robert Parker. In this book, a rating in the 50s indicates a malt that in my view lacks balance or character, and which – in fairness – was probably never meant to be bottled as a single. The 60s suggest an enjoyable but unexceptional malt. Anything in the 70s is worth tasting, especially above 75. The 80s are, in my view, distinctive and exceptional. The 90s are the greats.

A modest score should not dissuade anyone from trying a malt. Perhaps I was less than enthusiastic; you might love it.

ABERFELDY

PRODUCER John Dewar & Sons Ltd
REGION Highlands DISTRICT Eastern Highlands
ADDRESS Aberfeldy, Perthshire, PH15 2EB
TEL 01887 822010 WEBSITE www.dewarswow.com
EMAIL worldofwhisky@dewars.com VC (Visitor Centre)

DEWAR'S WORLD OF WHISKY, which opened in 2000, uses aromas, flavours, music, interactive games, and entire room settings to celebrate one of Scotland's great whisky families. The buccaneering style that made Dewar's White Label a bestseller typified the commercial energy that made blended Scotch the world's most popular spirit, and is well captured in some of the early advertising.

The original John Dewar was born on a croft near Aberfeldy in 1806, and was introduced to the wine trade at the age of 22 by a distant cousin. The family blended whisky and in 1896–98 established their own distillery at Aberfeldy. Its job was to provide the heart of the malt whisky content of the Dewar's blends, and it continued to do so in recent years under the ownership of United Distillers. Perhaps it is the Aberfeldy malt that imparts to Dewar's that fresh, lively crispness.

The hard water used at the distillery rises from whinstone flecked with iron and gold, and runs through pine, spruce, birch, and bracken. It is piped from the ruins of Pitilie, an earlier distillery. Aberfeldy still has its pagoda, though malting stopped in 1972. The owners at the time, DCL, were closing distillery maltings in favour of centralized sites. Some of the space liberated at the distilleries was then used to expand still-houses, at a time when production was being increased. The upgraded still-house at Aberfeldy is in the classic design of the period. The stills themselves are tall, with a gentle contour. The distillery also has a small steam locomotive, no longer in operation.

When UD merged with IDV in 1998, it had an embarrassment of distilleries. Then Aberfeldy, Aultmore, Craigellachie, and Royal Brackla were sold to become John Dewar & Sons, under the ownership of Bacardi.

The UD Flora and Fauna 15-year-old has now been replaced by a Dewar's bottling at 12 years old. This younger whisky is lighter in body, fruitier, and in a more refreshing style. The 25-year-old has deeper aromas and flavours, and more of everything.

HOUSE STYLE Oily, cleanly fruity, vigorous. Sociable, with dessert, or book-at-bedtime, depending upon ascending age.

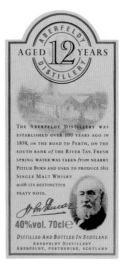

THE ABERFELDY DISTILLERY WAS
ESTABLISHED OVER 100 YEARS AGO *in*
1898, ON THE ROAD TO PERTH, ON THE
SOUTH BANK *of* THE RIVER TAY. FRESH
SPRING WATER WAS TAKEN *from* NEARBY
PITILIE BURN AND USED TO PRODUCE *this*
SINGLE MALT WHISKY
with ITS DISTINCTIVE
PEATY NOSE.

40%vol. 70cl℮

DISTILLED AND BOTTLED IN SCOTLAND
ABERFELDY DISTILLERY
ABERFELDY, PERTHSHIRE, SCOTLAND

ABERFELDY 12-year-old, 40 vol

COLOUR Warm gold to bronze.

NOSE Lively. Orange zest. A hint of smokiness. Warm.

BODY Light on the tongue. Oily.

PALATE Emphatically clean fruitiness. Tangerines. Trifle sponges.

FINISH Like biting into a kumquat. Dusty. Spicy. Gently warming.

SCORE **76**

ABERFELDY 25-year-old, 40 vol

COLOUR Bronze.

NOSE A hint of sherry. Warm. Malty sweetness.

BODY Syrupy but not cloying.

PALATE Even maltier. Shortbread, topped with
glazed almonds and orange peel.

FINISH More complex. Spicier. Warming. A touch of oily, perfumy peat.

SCORE **77**

SOME INDEPENDENT BOTTLINGS
ABERFELDY 1978, Connoisseurs Choice, 40 vol

COLOUR Full gold.

NOSE More aromatic. Drier. Toasted marshmallows.

BODY Oilier.

PALATE More expressive. Very citrusy. Sweeter. Scenty.
A beautifully complex, elegant whisky.

FINISH Appetizing. Lemony. Very dry.

SCORE **78**

ABERFELDY 1978, Signatory, 43 vol

COLOUR Greeny gold. White wine.

NOSE Lightly dry. Incense. Flowery.

BODY Oily.

PALATE Orangey, but more creamy in style. Less complex.

FINISH Very sweet indeed, though there is a sudden
hit of peaty-smoke dryness in the finish. Very long.
Sweet enough to try with (or in) trifle.

SCORE 75

NOW HARD TO FIND
ABERFELDY 15-year-old, Flora and Fauna, 43 vol

COLOUR Amber.

NOSE Oil, incense, heather, lightly piney, and peaty
(especially after water is added).

BODY Medium, very firm.

PALATE Very full flavours. Light peat, barley. Fresh,
clean touches of Seville orange, rounded.

FINISH Sweetness moves to fruitiness, then to firm dryness.

SCORE 77

ABERFELDY 1980, Bottled 1997,
Cask Strength Limited Bottling, 62 vol

COLOUR Pale gold.

NOSE Restrained, fragrant, pine and heather. Drier.

BODY Medium, smooth, distinctly oily.

PALATE Creamier, nuttier. Hint of orange toffee. Still lively, but two or three
years in the cask has brought more tightly combined flavours.

FINISH Nutty, late pine. Leafy, peppery dryness.

SCORE 77

OTHER VERSIONS OF ABERFELDY

A 14-year-old from Adelphi (bottled 1997) had a deliciously fresh orange
toffee character, with a fruity, peppery finish. SCORE 77

A Scott's Selection 1978, at 59.3 vol, was powerfully fruity and piney,
with a bitter finish. SCORE 75

ABERLOUR

PRODUCER Chivas Brothers
REGION Highlands DISTRICT Speyside (Strathspey)
ADDRESS Aberlour, Banffshire, AB3 9PJ
TEL 01340 881249 WEBSITE www.aberlour.co.uk VC

HAVING ACQUIRED CHIVAS IN 2002, with its dazzling family of Speyside distilleries (The Glenlivet, Glen Grant, and Longmorn are but three), will French parents Pernod Ricard still love Aberlour? It was their Number One son; now it has siblings. The whisky is well respected in Scotland, but its greatest popularity, based on merit as much as on adoptive parentage, is in France. At the Speyside Festival in May, the distillery has hosted a series of whisky dinners created by spirited writer Martine Nouet.

Aberlour is at least a super-middleweight in body. With medals galore in recent years, it competes as a light-heavyweight, standing up well against bigger names, much as Georges Carpentier did. Aberlour rhymes with "power" in English, but most French-speakers make it sound more like "amour".

The regular range in Scotland and the rest of the United Kingdom comprises the 10-year-old, the a'bunadh, and the 15-year-old sherry wood finish, but there are larger selections in duty-free and in France. The overall range includes a great many minor variations.

Since 2002, visitors to the distillery have been able to hand-fill their own personally labelled bottle of Aberlour, from an identified single cask. A sherry butt and a bourbon barrel, each felt to provide a good example of its style, are set aside for this purpose. As each is exhausted, it is replaced by a similar cask. This personalized whisky is bottled at cask strength.

On the main road (A95) that follows the eastern bank of the Spey, an 1890s lodge signals the distillery, which is hidden a couple of hundred yards into the glen of the river Lour (little more than a burn). The Lour flows into the Spey. The site was known for a well associated with St Drostan, from the epoch of St Columba. The distilling water is soft. It rises from the granite of Ben Rinnes, by way of a spring in the glen of the Allachie, and is piped half a mile to the distillery.

HOUSE STYLE Soft texture, medium to full flavours, nutty, spicy (nutmeg?), sherry-accented. With dessert, or after dinner, depending upon maturity.

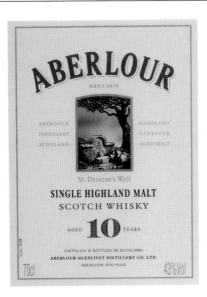

ABERLOUR 10-year-old, Principal Version, 43 vol

COLOUR Amber.

NOSE Malty, spicy, mint toffee.

BODY Remarkably soft and smooth. Medium to full.

PALATE Distinctively clinging mouth feel, with long-lasting flavour development. Both sweetness and spicy, peppery dryness in its malt character. Nutmeg and berry fruit.

FINISH Lingering, smooth, aromatic, clean.

SCORE **83**

ABERLOUR a'bunadh ("The Origin"), No Age Statement, 59.6 vol

A single malt comprising Aberlours from less than 10 to more than 15 years, vatted together. All sherry-ageing, with an emphasis on second-fill dry oloroso. No chill filtration. Mainly in duty-free and British Isles. In Victorian-style bottle.

COLOUR Dark orange.

NOSE Sherry, mint, pralines. Luxurious, powerful.

BODY Full, creamy, textured, layered.

PALATE Rich, luxurious, and creamy, with a hint of mint and cherries behind.

FINISH Nougat, cherry brandy, ginger, faint smoke. Definitely after dinner.

SCORE **86**

ABERLOUR a'bunadh Sterling Silver, 12-year-old, 58.7 vol

COLOUR Darker. Deep, shiny, chestnut.

NOSE Sherry, mint, pralines. Oakier and smokier than
the version above. Sherry. Black chocolate. Oil of peppermint.

BODY Big, firm.

PALATE Drier. Spicier. Ginger-and-plum preserve. More assertive.

FINISH Long. Lots of alcohol, but warming and soothing.
Prunes. Sappy, juicy fresh oak. Cedar. Cigar boxes.

SCORE 87

ABERLOUR 12-year-old, Sherry-matured, 43 vol

*Matured in first-fill dry oloroso. Originally marketed in France,
but now mainly found in duty-free.*

COLOUR Full amber.

NOSE Nutty, appetizing, relatively fresh, sherry aroma.

BODY Medium, soft.

PALATE Fresh, soft, malty. Soft liquorice, anis, hint of blackcurrant.

FINISH Silky, enwrapping, soothing.

SCORE 84

ABERLOUR 12-year-old, Double Cask Matured, 40 vol

Vatting of first-fill sherry and unspecified refill casks. Mainly for the French market.

COLOUR Bronze.

NOSE Earthy, fruity. Pears. Apples. Tarte tatin.

BODY Medium, firm.

PALATE Melty pastry. Caramel sauce. Custard (in this instance,
let's call it crème anglaise). Leaves of garden mint.

FINISH More of the mint. Now it has become spearmint.
Ends rather abruptly and sharply.

SCORE 82

ABERLOUR 16-year-old, Double Cask Matured, 43 vol

Same principle as the above. Also for the French market.

COLOUR Bronze red.

NOSE Seville oranges, lemons. Turkish delight. Rose-water.

BODY Gently rounded.

PALATE Smooth. Spun sugar. Caramel. Tightly combined flavours.
The extra years have made a big difference.

FINISH Cinnamon. Ground nutmeg. Nutty.

SCORE 84

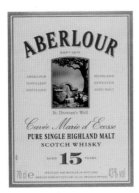

ABERLOUR Cuvée Marie d'Ecosse, 15-year-old, 43 vol

A marriage of bourbon- and sherry-aged Aberlour, for the French market.

COLOUR Amber.

NOSE Malty and toffeeish, developing flowering currant.

BODY Medium to full. Silky smooth.

PALATE Toffee, liquorice, anise, crème brûlée.

FINISH Late spiciness and ginger. Long, soothing.

SCORE **83**

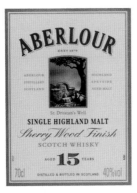

ABERLOUR 15-year-old, Sherry Wood Finish, 40 vol

A marriage of sherry and bourbon. Finished in sherry.

COLOUR Fuller reddish amber.

NOSE Roses, candyfloss (cotton candy), slightly buttery.

BODY Very firm. Smooth.

PALATE Rounded, tightly combined flavours. Beautiful balance of
sherryish nuttiness, anise, and emphatic orange flower.

FINISH Cookies, liquorice toffee. Rootiness, spiciness,
emphatic mint, late dryness.

SCORE **84**

LONG-MATURED EXPRESSIONS IDENTIFIED BY AGE
ABERLOUR 21-year-old, Limited Edition, Cask No 32, 43 vol

Mainly in duty-free and North America.

COLOUR Bright pale orange.

NOSE Sherry, oak, polished leather.

BODY Firm, smooth, lightly creamy.

PALATE Packed with lively flavours: malt, cookies, fruit, mint.

FINISH Spicy, rooty, dry, and very long.

SCORE 85

ABERLOUR 23-year-old, 40 vol

The intention is to create a position in the regular range for a vatting highlighting the oldest whiskies in the distillery's warehouses. Based on current stocks, this emerges at 23 years.

COLOUR Brassy. Pale for an Aberlour.

NOSE Fresh, pronounced mint toffee.

BODY Creamy. Shortbread.

PALATE Syrupy, fruity. Apricot.

FINISH Slightly tart, sharp. Dryish. Violets.

SCORE 84

A SELECTION OF VINTAGE-DATED BOTTLINGS
ABERLOUR 1980, 43 vol

Minimum age 22 years, in second-fill casks, mainly bourbon but with some sherry. Mainly for the French market.

COLOUR Iridescent greeny gold.

NOSE Delicately spicy. Develops in the glass. Vanilla. Cedar.

BODY Light but textured.

PALATE A sudden explosion of spicy flavours, especially nutmeg, but also cinnamon and pepper.

FINISH Curiously bittersweet. Briar-like. Very lively.

SCORE 84

ABERLOUR 30-year-old, Limited Edition, Bottle 852, 43 vol

Mainly in duty-free and North America, but now very hard to find.

COLOUR Amber.

NOSE Polished leather. Tobacco. Cigars.

BODY Firm, smooth.

PALATE Firmly malty, creamy, liquorice, rootiness, hint of smoky peat. Complex and sophisticated. Maturity and finesse.

FINISH Surprisingly fresh oak. Sappiness. Log fires. Warming.

SCORE 85

ABERLOUR Distiller's Selection, 1988, 40 vol

Mainly for the Spanish market.

COLOUR Amber.

NOSE Soft but expressive. Bourbon oak. Nuts. Fudge. Citrus.

BODY Medium to full. Smooth. Rich.

PALATE A dazzling display of fresh malty flavours. Sweetish, but beautifully balanced. Butterscotch, vanilla, orange and lemon, sambuca.

FINISH Sticky toffee pudding, balanced by a dryness like crystallized ginger.

SCORE **85**

ABERLOUR 1976, 21-year-old, Bottle 921 of 3000, 43 vol

Matured in first-fill bourbon casks.

COLOUR Bright amber.

NOSE Quick, assertive malt honey, then powerful berry fruit at back of nose. Blackberries?

BODY Medium, firm, almost crunchy.

PALATE Dryish, nutty, toffee, fruit, nutmeg. Lacking in roundness.

FINISH Restrained sappy oak. Gingery, warming.

SCORE **83**

ABERLOUR 1964, 25-year-old, Bottle 5664 of 10,000, 43 vol

COLOUR Full amber.

NOSE Richer oak.

BODY Medium to full. Firm, smooth, slippery.

PALATE Firm, smooth. Very good oaky extract. Hint of vanilla creaminess.

FINISH Firm, rounded dryness. Hint of perfuminess.

SCORE **84**

HARD TO FIND

ABERLOUR Antique, No Age Statement, 43 vol

Contains whiskies of 10 to 25 years. Bottled for duty-free stores.

COLOUR Full amber.

NOSE Oloroso sherry, treacle, raisins.

BODY Firmer.

PALATE More dryness, cookie-like malt notes, and spiciness.

FINISH More complex and spicy, with hints of peat. After dinner.

SCORE **84**

ABERLOUR 18-year-old, Sherry Wood Matured, 43 vol

100% sherry-aged. Mainly for the North American market.

COLOUR Bright orangey amber.

NOSE Sherryish but dry and slightly oaky. Burnt sugar.
Spicy, rounded, teasing.

BODY Smooth, nutty.

PALATE Well balanced. Spicy, flowery, nutmeg, nutty, fruity.
Light, delicate flavours for this distillery and age.

FINISH Fresh sherry and oak.

SCORE **84**

ABERLOUR 100° Proof, No Age Statement (Around 10 years), 57.1 vol

Mainly in duty-free.

COLOUR Bright orangey amber.

NOSE Fresh oak, giving way to light nuttiness and sherry.

BODY Firmer, crisper.

PALATE Dry oiliness. Delicious, soft fruitiness. (Apricots? Cherries?)
Much more spiciness. Some butterscotch, toffee, and cough-candy.
Both robust (tastes relatively young) and complex.

FINISH Big, firm, dry. This version is more of a winter warmer.

SCORE **84**

SOME INDEPENDENT BOTTLINGS

A 12-year-old, at 50 vol, distilled in 1988, in Douglas Laing's Old Malt
Cask series, had the colour of ripe limes; a blossoming fruitiness; a smooth,
sweet, perfumy palate; and a honeyed, distinctively aromatic, soothing
warmth in the finish. SCORE 84

An Aberlour distilled in 1990 was bottled in 2002, at 59.9 vol, by Blackadder,
in its Raw Cask series. It had a slightly darker colour, again with a greenish
tinge. It was very similar, but with a warming finish that was curiously
dry and medicinal. SCORE 79

A 1989 distillate, at 46 vol, bottled at 13 years old by Cadenhead,
had a very pale greenish colour; a lightly syrupy, intensely sweet,
scenty palate; and a soothing, dryish, but more rounded, finish. SCORE 82

A 1970, at 46 vol, from Lombard, had a full gold colour, with a bronze tinge.
The whisky had some more nutty toasty, notes in the palate, and a hint of
peat in the finish. SCORE 85

ALLT-A-BHAINNE

PRODUCER Chivas Brothers
REGION Highlands DISTRICT Speyside (Fiddich)
ADDRESS Glenrinnes, Dufftown, Banffshire, AB55 4DB

A FLURRY OF CONSTRUCTION enlivened Speyside in the mid-1970s, with four or five new distilleries built. It was one of those periods when the industry tries to catch up with underestimated demand. This distillery and the present Braeval were built by Seagrams. Their light, airy architecture is a happy marriage of traditional allusions and modern ideas, but they are lacking in humanity. Both are designed to operate with minimal staff, and their spirit is matured in central warehousing elsewhere.

In Gaelic, Allt-á-Bhainne means "the milk burn", and the distillery lies to the west of the River Fiddich in the foothills of Ben Rinnes, near Dufftown. Its malt whisky is a component of the Chivas blends. There have been no official bottlings, so malt lovers curious to taste the whisky have had to rely on independents. One of them, Cadenhead, has released two different casks from the same year.

HOUSE STYLE Light, slightly vegetal, flowery-spicy. Aperitif.

ALLT-A-BHAINNE 16-year-old, The Old Malt Cask, 50 vol

COLOUR Bright, pale, greeny gold.

NOSE Hint of peat. Seaweed (the edible kind). Soy sauce. Nutty. Sweaty.

BODY Light, flabby.

PALATE Bean curd. Protein-like. Oyster crackers.

FINISH Sweet. Biscuity.

SCORE 72

ALLT-A-BHAINNE 1992, 9-year-old, Cadenhead, 58.8 vol

COLOUR Pale greeny gold.

NOSE Faint hint of peat. Flowery. Slightly gummy.

BODY Lightly syrupy.

PALATE Intensely sweet. Lemon-sherbet. Surprisingly aggressive. Peppery.

FINISH Liquorice. Fennel. Soothing.

SCORE **73**

ALLT-A-BHAINNE 1992, 9-year-old, Cadenhead, 59.4 vol

COLOUR Very bright greeny gold.

NOSE Heathery. Ferny. Forest floor after rain.

BODY Lightly buttery.

PALATE Fiddlehead ferns with butter.

FINISH Green peppercorns. Quite assertive.

SCORE **75**

ALLT-A-BHAINNE 17-year-old, Sherry Wood, Dun Bheaghan, 43 vol

COLOUR Very bright greeny gold.

NOSE Cleaner. Hint of peat, earthy. Graphite?

BODY Light. Spring water.

PALATE Clean. Sweet. Malty. Marshmallow.

FINISH Minty. Silky.

SCORE **73**

OTHER VERSIONS OF ALLT-Á-BHAINNE

The flowery spiciness of this malt was typified by a 13-year-old bottled by The Whisky Castle, a shop in Tomintoul, in the late 1990s. SCORE 73
A 12-year-old bottled by James MacArthur in the mid-1990s seemed slightly bigger, no doubt as a result of the cask used. SCORE 74
A 1980 released by Oddbins in 1992 seemed to have enjoyed sherry, but was perhaps a little overwhelmed by the sappiness of the oak. SCORE 73

ARDBEG

PRODUCER Glenmorangie plc
REGION Islay DISTRICT South Shore
ADDRESS Port Ellen, Islay, Argyll, PA42 7EA
TEL 01496 302244 WEBSITE www.ardbeg.com
EMAIL oldkiln@ardbeg.com VC

A LREADY ONE OF THE WORLD'S GREAT DISTILLERIES in the days when single malts were a secret, and revived at a cost of millions (whether euros or dollars), Ardbeg shines ever more brightly. Its reopening was one of the first signs of the Islay revival, of which it has become both a principal element and a beneficiary. Its owners' ambitions for the distillery are being rewarded. So is their faith in young manager Stuart Thomson and his wife Jackie.

Her knowledge and energy "front of house" have consolidated the distillery's popularity with visitors. When Ardbeg reopened, one of the former kilns was turned into a shop, also offering tea, coffee, a dram, and a clootie (dumpling). The Old Kiln is also used by local people: it now serves meals, and has been the western venue for writer Martine Nouet's whisky dinners (*see p. 441*).

Ardbeg aficionados still cling to the hope that the second kiln may one day return to use. The maltings were unusual in that there were no fans, causing the peat smoke to permeate very heavily. This is evident in very old bottlings. The peaty origins of the water are also a big influence in the whisky's earthy, tar-like flavours. Some lovers of Ardbeg believe that an apple-wood, lemon-skin fruitiness derives from a recirculatory system in the spirit still.

The distillery traces its history to 1794. The maltings last worked in 1976–77, though supplies of their malted barley were no doubt eked out a little longer. Ardbeg closed in the early 1980s, but towards the end of that decade began to work again, albeit very sporadically, using malt from Port Ellen. Whisky produced at that time, but released by the new owners, is less tar-like than the old Ardbeg. Such heavily peated whisky as was inherited has been used in some vattings. The distillery is currently buying an especially heavily peated malt, the impact of which will be seen in bottlings in the course of the next six or seven years.

HOUSE STYLE Earthy, very peaty, smoky, salty, robust. A bedtime malt.

ARDBEG 10-year-old, 40 vol

COLOUR Fino sherry.

NOSE Smoke, brine, iodine dryness.

BODY Only medium to full, but very firm. A young light-heavyweight, not musclebound by age. Pound-for-pound, the hardest hitter in the Ardbeg team, though without the power conferred by the old maltings.

PALATE Skips sweetly along at first, then becomes mean and moody. Bottlings a little variable.

FINISH Hefty, lots of iodine.

SCORE 85

ARDBEG 17-year-old, 40 vol

COLOUR Full, shimmering, greeny gold.

NOSE Assertive, briney, seaweedy, tar-like. Hint of sulphur.

BODY Medium, oily. Very firm.

PALATE Peppery but also sweet. Cereal grains, oil, gorse. Tightly combined flavours. More mature and rounded, but still robust. Very appetizing.

FINISH Oily. Lemon skins. Freshly ground white pepper.

SCORE 86

ARDBEG 21-year-old, 56.3 vol

Slightly more assertive than an Adelphi bottling reviewed in the fourth edition of this book.

COLOUR Deeper. More refractive and oily. Greeny gold.

NOSE Firm, but aromas more tightly combined. As though the brine and iodine-like seaweed had permeated a stretch of hard, compacted sand.

BODY Firm, unyielding.

PALATE Instant hit of flavours. The maritime character overlaying pepper, lemons, fresh limes, bananas. (After that bracing walk on the beach, an afternoon of snoozy luxury with fruits and pastries?)

FINISH After the snooze, a hot shower with coal-tar soap. That characteristic tar-like smokiness and phenol.

SCORE 87

ARDBEG 1976, 46 vol

COLOUR Again, that oily green tinge.

NOSE Still showering with coal-tar soap.

BODY Lotion-like.

PALATE Fresh, perfumy, therapeutic.

FINISH Very smoky. Driftwood bonfires. Remarkably late suggestion of sherry.

SCORE **88**

ARDBEG 1977, 46 vol

Very similar, but less rounded in flavours.

COLOUR Slightly more oily than the vintage above.

NOSE Bonfires again. Sappy. Leafy.

BODY More oily. Clings to the tongue.

PALATE Sweet lemons.

FINISH Fragrant smokiness. Lingering warmth.

SCORE **87**

ARDBEG "Lord of the Isles " 25-year-old, 46 vol

"The supreme expression of Ardbeg", according to the label, but where is the smoke and clamour of battle? This whisky is named after the island rulers who fought the Vikings.

COLOUR Full gold.

NOSE Sea air. Distant smoke.

BODY Silky.

PALATE The Ardbeg fruitiness, usually lemony and fragrant, has become more assertive and complex with age. Here, there are flavours reminiscent of candied orange peel and, especially, cherries. Lots of flavour development. Walnuts, almonds. Marzipan. Bittersweet.The roundness of flavours masks the peat.

FINISH Long, haughty. Steely. Not as earthy as might have been hoped.

SCORE **89**

COMMITTEE RESERVE, 55.3 vol

More than 20,000 enthusiasts for Ardbeg have joined this "committee". This bottling, made in 2002, was vatted from whiskies distilled in the 1970s, 80s, and 90s.

COLOUR The Committee's whisky is marginally paler than the Lords'.

NOSE Very fresh. Herbal. Spicy. A suggestion of saffron.

BODY Textured. Tongue-coating.

PALATE Sweet, then sharp. Huge flavour development in the middle, becoming spicy (saffron again, salty, sandy).

FINISH Big, firm, gripping, long. Warming, soothing, appetizing. A *tour de force*.

SCORE **90**

ARDBEG Uigeadail, 54.2 vol

COLOUR Pale gold.

NOSE Intensely smoky. Dry, clean, tangy barbecue smoke.

BODY Light, firm.

PALATE Firm, very smooth, then explodes on the tongue.

FINISH Hot. Alcoholic. A shock to the system.

SCORE **92**

FOUR SINGLE-CASK BOTTLINGS FOR FOREIGN MARKETS

ARDBEG 1976, Cask No 2396, 53.5 vol *(For the Italian market.)*

COLOUR Dark orange satin.

NOSE Dusty. Earthy.

BODY Light to medium. Slightly chewy.

PALATE Chewy sweetness. Earthy. Bitter chocolate.

FINISH Powerful, long, warming. Woody. Menthol. Spearmint.

SCORE **88**

ARDBEG 1976, Cask No 2395, 54.4 vol *(For the Japanese market.)*

COLOUR Greeny orange.

NOSE More oily. Orange essence. Black chocolate. Coffee.

BODY Slightly bigger and smoother.

PALATE Expressive. Delicious. Lightly syrupy. Sweetish. Fruitier.
More obvious orange. Reminiscent of orange-liqueur chocolates.

FINISH Smoky, fragrant dryness. Some late, disappointing woodiness.

SCORE **91**

ARDBEG 1975, Cask No 4701, 54.4 vol *(For the French market.)*

COLOUR Golden plum. Greengage?

NOSE Iced buns. Spiced buns. Malt loaf.

BODY Fondant.

PALATE Ginger cake. Yorkshire Parkin. Treacle toffee.

FINISH Shredded root ginger. Bitter chocolate. Mid-afternoon in the patisserie.

SCORE **89**

ARDBEG 1975, Cask No 4716, 45 vol *(For the German market.)*

COLOUR Golden plum.

NOSE Sweetness and saltiness. Sandy beach. A hint of seaweed.

BODY Firm.

PALATE On the thin side, but firmer and drier than the rest of this group.

FINISH Cedary. Some woody bitterness.

SCORE **87**

THE ARDBEGGEDDON ARDBEG 1972,
29-year-old, Sherry Cask, 48.4 vol

Bottled by Douglas Laing for The Whisky Shop. An outstanding Ardbeg, lyrically, presenting the full range of the distillery's typical flavours.

COLOUR Bright pale gold.

NOSE Rich, soft, oily smokiness. Very appetizing.

BODY Seductively smooth.

PALATE Against a firm, steely background: a dexterous interplay of grassy peatiness; oiliness; just lurking suggestions of lemony fruitiness, sherry, and oak.

FINISH Lively, evocative, maritime flavours. A long walk on a sandy beach, with a vigorous, salty spray.

SCORE **92**

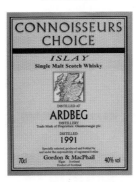

ARDBEG 1991, Connoisseurs Choice, 40 vol

COLOUR Pale, warm gold.

NOSE Light, dry. A hint of peat. Tobacco. Peppermint.

BODY Oily. Creamy.

PALATE Sweet, minty, developing a herbal, spicy dryness.

FINISH A gentle sting. What happened to the heavyweight embrace, the boxer still punching in the clinches?

SCORE **92**

ARDBEG Provenance, Distilled 1974, Bottled 1998, 55.8 vol

An intentional reminder of the old Ardbeg.

COLOUR Full gold to bronze.

NOSE Sea air. Seaweed. Oak, rope, leather.

BODY Rich and creamy, but dry on the tongue.

PALATE Huge flavour development. Malty, toffeeish, sweet, fruity. Barbecue wood. Mustard. Salt.

FINISH Distinctly sappy, smoky, and very warming.

SCORE **93**

ARDMORE

PRODUCER Allied Distillers Ltd
REGION Highlands DISTRICT Speyside (Bogie)
ADDRESS Kennethmont, by Huntly, Aberdeenshire, AB54 4NH
TEL 01464 831213 VC

HAD COAL-FIRED STILLS been disdained in favour of steam in the early days of Ardmore, that might have been seen as progress. To douse the flames as the distillery celebrated its recent centenary seemed perverse indeed. This sizeable distillery is at the eastern fringe of Speyside, where Aberdeenshire barley country begins. Will the switch to steam mean a less caramelish maltiness in Ardmore whisky and the blends of parent Teacher's (so to speak)? Probably.

HOUSE STYLE Malty, creamy, fruity. After dinner.

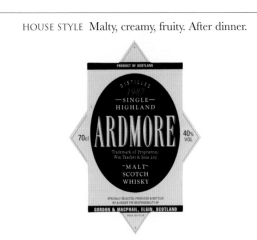

ARDMORE 12-year-old, Centenary Bottling, 40 vol

More elegant, but less robust, than the regular Gordon & MacPhail 12-year-old bottling.

COLOUR Warm primrose.

NOSE Fresh, clean, sweet. Flowery-fruity. Cream. Sherry trifle.

BODY Light, but very smooth. Slippery smooth.

PALATE Delicate, fruity (raspberry?) flavours reminiscent of blancmange.

FINISH Flowery. Nutty dryness. Toasted almonds.

SCORE **73**

EARLIER VERSIONS OF ARDMORE

The fruity flavours emerge much more strongly – sweet orange, red apple? – in a 21-year-old at 40 vol, also bottled for the centenary. This version is much more robust, complex, and expressive. SCORE 75

ARRAN

PRODUCER Isle of Arran Distillers Ltd
REGION Highlands   ISLAND Arran
ADDRESS Lochranza, Isle of Arran, Argyll, KA27 8HJ
TEL 01770 830264   WEBSITE www.arranwhisky.com
E-MAIL arran.distillers@arranwhisky.com   VC

SINCE IT OPENED IN 1995, and released its first whisky in 1998, the Isle of Arran distillery has inspired several similar projects elsewhere in Scotland. Until any of them is realized, Arran is still the country's newest distillery.

The island, a favourite with walkers and bird-watchers, is easily accessible. From Glasgow it is a short drive south to the Ayrshire port of Ardrossan, whence a frequent ferry runs to Brodick, on the east of the island. A narrow road then winds its way round the north coast to the distillery, in the village of Lochranza. There is accommodation in Lochranza, and a ferry to Kintyre, for those who wish to visit the Campbeltown distilleries. A couple more ferries extend the trip to Islay and Jura.

Arran has dramatic granite mountains, peaty land, and good water. The island was once known for its whisky, but spent a century and a half without a legal distillery. The inspiration for a new distillery came after a talk given at the Arran Society in 1992. Industry veteran Harold Currie, a retired managing director of Chivas, organized a scheme in which 2000 bonds were sold in exchange for whisky from the new distillery. As Arran has many visitors, the distillery was seen as an additional attraction for tourists. It has a shop and a restaurant with an excellent kitchen.

HOUSE STYLE Creamy, leafy. Restorative or with dessert.
No obvious island character.

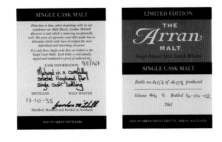

ARRAN **SINGLE MALT, 43 vol**

COLOUR Attractive pale yellow.

NOSE Fresh, creamy, vanilla-like. Flowery.

BODY Creamy.

PALATE Fresh cream. Flowery. Leafy. Vegetal. Angelica.

FINISH Children's sweets. Liquorice. Spicy.

SCORE 73

ARRAN **SINGLE MALT, Nonchillfiltered, 46 vol**

COLOUR Bright, pale, greeny gold.

NOSE Distinctly flowery sweetness. Appetizing.

BODY Creamy, dusty, substantial.

PALATE Flowery, almondy, fresh cream.

FINISH Perfumy. Sweet limes. Lightly vegetal dryness.

SCORE 74

SOME SINGLE CASK ARRANS

ARRAN **Single Cask, Cask No 95/173, Sherry Hogshead, 55.3 vol**

COLOUR Tamarind.

NOSE Nutty. Dates. Cinnamon.

BODY Syrupy.

PALATE Fruity. Gingery. Sappy. A curious inversion. As though the
whisky (rich and sweet, but without penetrating flavours) provides
the background, while the sherry and wood are the highlights.

FINISH Powerful. Spicy. Developing some oiliness.

SCORE 76

ARRAN **Single Cask, Bottle 332 of 347, Distilled 18 July 1997, Bottled 14 October 2002, 58.6 vol**

Exclusively for the wine and spirit merchant Hanseatic, of Bremen.
Matured in sherry. Also reracked to finish in sherry.

COLOUR Full, warm, gold.

NOSE Oily. Marshmallow. Seed cake.

BODY Soft, luxurious.

PALATE Dried fruits. Raisins. Sauternes. Chocolate.

FINISH Firm. Gripping. Winey.

SCORE 77

AUCHENTOSHAN

PRODUCER Morrison Bowmore Distillers Ltd
REGION Lowlands DISTRICT Western Lowlands
ADDRESS Dalmuir, Clydebank, Dunbartonshire, G81 4SJ
TEL 01389 878561 WEBSITE www.auchentoshan.com VC

THIS IS A CLASSIC LOWLAND DISTILLERY, not only in its location, but also in its adherence to triple distillation. Light-bodied whiskies result; light in flavour, too, but by no means bland. If you fancy single malts, but do not care for intensity, Auchentoshan offers the perfect answer: subtlety. Stan Getz rather than Sonny Rollins; Vivaldi, as opposed to Beethoven.

Auchentoshan ("corner of the field") is pronounced "och'n'tosh'n", as though it were an imprecation. The distillery is at the foot of the Kilpatrick Hills, just outside Glasgow. There are suggestions of a distillery on the site around 1800, but 1825 is the "official" foundation date. The distillery was rebuilt after the Second World War, re-equipped in 1974, and further overhauled ten years later, when it was acquired by Stanley P. Morrison. The acquisition provided a Lowland partner for their Islay and Highland distilleries, Bowmore and Glen Garioch. The company is now called Morrison Bowmore, and is controlled by Suntory. The Japanese cherish the distilleries, and the upkeep is superb. Much has been done to highlight the equipment at Auchentoshan and to show how the whisky is made.

HOUSE STYLE Light, lemon grassy, herbal, oily. Aperitif or restorative.

AUCHENTOSHAN Select, No Age Statement, 40 vol

COLOUR Shimmery gold.

NOSE Appetizing, clean, warm, cereal grain. Cookies fresh from the oven.

BODY Lightly oily.

PALATE Lemon-grass notes. Toasty maltiness –
definite, but light. Cleanly sweet.

FINISH Light, crisp. Hint of lemon-grass spiciness.

SCORE **79**

AUCHENTOSHAN 10-year-old, 40 vol

COLOUR Bright yellowy gold.

NOSE A warm embrace, with perfumes of vanilla,
lemon grass, and saddlery.

BODY Light but soft, oily.

PALATE Lemon zest, marshmallow, sweet but not cloying.

FINISH Longer. Lemon grass, faint ginger, vanilla, perfumy. Soft.

SCORE **83**

AUCHENTOSHAN Three Wood, No Age Statement, 43 vol

*This whisky has at least ten years in bourbon wood, a good year in oloroso and six months
in the hefty Pedro Ximénez. In addition to offering an unusual array of wood
characteristics, it fills a gap in Auchentoshan's age range.*

COLOUR Orange liqueur.

NOSE Soft. Orange zest, apricot, dates, marshmallow.

BODY Oily. Marshmallow-like.

PALATE Perfumy, lemon grass, cashews. A delicate interplay of flavours, but
the whisky struggles to make itself heard among the woods.
Better with little or no water.

FINISH Long. Creamy. Raisins. Aniseed. Fresh oak. Sappy dryness.

SCORE **85**

AUCHENTOSHAN Selected Cask Vatting,
18-year-old, Distilled 1978, 58.8 vol

This superb vatting further fills the previous gap in the age range.

COLOUR Full gold to bronze.

NOSE Linseed, saddlery, fresh leather.

BODY Smooth, layered, soft.

PALATE Linseed, fresh leather, perfumy. A very expressive Auchentoshan.

FINISH Clean, lemony, scenty.

SCORE **87**

AUCHENTOSHAN 21-year-old, 43 vol

COLOUR Full, deep gold.

NOSE Orange zest, date boxes, cedar, oil.

BODY Light to medium, oily, very smooth indeed.

PALATE Oily, citrusy, orange peel, lightly spicy, with lots of flavour development. Full of subtleties. More oak character than previous entry. Fresh, with no obtrusive woodiness.

FINISH Cedar, vanilla, beautifully rounded and aromatic.

SCORE **86**

AUCHENTOSHAN 22-year-old, 43 vol

COLOUR Deep gold to amber.

NOSE Rich fresh leather.

BODY Very firm, smooth, and oily.

PALATE Oily, cedary, spicy. Male cosmetics. If soap were edible.

FINISH Dry, cedary.

SCORE **86**

VINTAGE-DATED AUCHENTOSHANS

Logically, a Lowland whisky is too light in body and flavour to cope with much influence of wood. Despite this, Auchentoshan has retained its character in bottlings at considerable ages, for example, a 22-year-old and a 31-year-old each rated 86 points in the fourth edition of this book. The more recent bottlings, reviewed here, have proven less resilient. The 1973 is the more interesting drink, but says little of whisky, let alone of Auchentoshan. The 1965 is more whiskyish, but less rounded. Both are of more interest to the collector than the taster.

AUCHENTOSHAN 1973, 29-year-old, Sherry Butt No 793, 55.8 vol

COLOUR Pinkish red. Almost rhubarb-like.

NOSE Jammy. Australian Shiraz. Red apples. Peaches.

BODY Textured. Fluffy.

PALATE An extraordinarily fruity whisky, with peach dominant.
Peach-stone flavours, too. Underneath all that, it is hard to divine any
Auchentoshan character. Severely marked down for those reasons.

FINISH Nutty dryness. With the cheese? After dinner?

SCORE **69**

AUCHENTOSHAN 1965, 31-year-old, Cask No 2502, 49.3 vol

COLOUR Old gold.

NOSE Some candy-floss sweetness.

BODY Syrupy, then dusty. Icing sugar. Cocoa powder.

PALATE Spun sugar. Quickly becoming drier. Nutty. Flavours reminiscent
of peanut shells, coconut-fibre matting.

FINISH Dry, musty.

SCORE **72**

SOME INDEPENDENT BOTTLINGS

There was something of a flood of 1992 distillates, bottled at 10 years.
A Cadenhead bottling was creamy tasting but slightly aggressive. SCORE 81

A Murray McDavid edition was fresh with a deliciously clean,
marshmallowy maltiness, and an excellent balance of herbal,
yeasty dryness. SCORE 83

A James MacArthur bottling, at 64.2 vol, combined a flapjack sweetness,
oaty oiliness, and cleansing dryness. SCORE 82

The other three bottlings were at 46 vol. A Whisky Galore edition had a
garden mint aroma and a fresh, floral, apple-blossom palate. SCORE 84

AUCHROISK

PRODUCER Diageo
REGION Highlands DISTRICT Speyside
ADDRESS Auchroisk Distillery Mulben, Banffshire, AB55 6XS
TEL 01542 885000 WEBSITE www.malts.com VC

TOO YOUNG to make promises for eternity, but "Always Auchroisk" might be a wise text for the future. This distillery was established in 1974. Given that a distillery can survive two or three times as long as a human, Auchroisk is barely an adolescent. For several years, it has, in the hope of seducing foreigners, been calling itself The Singleton. That term is sometimes used to indicate a single cask (in this case, a sherry butt). It was therefore thought to be an appropriate substitute for the original Gaelic name, which means "ford on the red stream".

The distillery, between Rothes and Dufftown, is on a ridge by the Mulben Burn, which flows into the Spey. Nearby is a spring called Dorie's Well, which determined the site of the distillery. The soft water and large stills make whisky of a delicacy that deserves a chance to show itself without sherry, and under its own name.

Phonetic guides can always be provided, except that no one agrees. Auch Roysk, says the manager; Ach Rask (or Rusk), insist the locals. There is schism over the "ch" being pronounced as a "th". Can the foreigners cope with this? Funny how the simply delicious Singleton never hooked as many sales worldwide as some unpronounceably complex whiskies from the west.

HOUSE STYLE Very soft. Berry fruits. Aperitif. Or with fruit salad or similar desserts.

AUCHROISK 10-year-old, 43 vol

COLOUR Soft, burnished yellow.

NOSE Pronounced fruitiness. White grapes. Gooseberry. Berry fruits.

BODY Light, soft, seductive.

PALATE Lightly fruity, with a suggestion of figs. Becoming nuttier and drier. Shortbread.

FINISH Faint sun-scorched grass and peat.

SCORE **78**

A 27-year-old independent bottling from Old Malt Cask, 43.8 vol, had a suggestion of bananas and cream toffee. SCORE 77

AULTMORE

PRODUCER John Dewar & Sons Ltd
REGION Highlands DISTRICT Speyside (Isla)
ADDRESS Keith, Banffshire, AB55 6QY
TEL 01542 881800 VC

A FINE MALT IN THE OAKY STYLE that seems to characterize the whiskies made near the river Isla. This distillery, which is just north of Keith, was built in 1896, and reconstructed in 1971. In 1991, United Distillers, its owners at the time, introduced a bottling in their flora and fauna series. They issued a Rare Malts edition in 1996, and a Cask Strength Limited Bottling in 1997–98. These and other past bottlings were reviewed in the fourth edition of this book. In 1998, Aultmore was acquired by Bacardi, but no new bottlings have yet appeared.

HOUSE STYLE Fresh, dry, herbal, spicy, oaky. Reminiscent of a fino sherry, albeit a very big one. Before dinner.

SIGNATORY VINTAGE
Vintage 1989
Single Highland Malt Scotch Whisky
Distilled at Aultmore Distillery
on 30th May 1989
70CL Matured in a sherry butt for 12 years 43% VOL
Bottled on 28th September 2001 Natural Colour
Butt No. 2394 · Bottle No. of 712
This whisky has been selected, produced and bottled in Scotland for and under the sole responsibility of
Signatory Vintage Scotch Whisky Co. Ltd, Edinburgh EH8 9PY Scotland

AULTMORE 1989, Signatory, 43 vol

COLOUR Crystal-bright greeny gold.

NOSE Steely. Slightly smoky.

BODY Soft, rounded.

PALATE Lean, sweet and fruity, then nutty. Developing cereal-grain oiliness.
Flavours reminiscent of bread and butter pudding.

FINISH Gently spicy.

SCORE 75

AULTMORE 1987, 15-year-old, Whisky Galore, 46 vol

COLOUR White wine.

NOSE Fruity. Flowering currant.

BODY Distinctively firm, smooth, and oily.

PALATE Tightly combined flavours. Spicy, dry, appetizing.

FINISH Gentian bitterness, but gentle.

SCORE 76

BALBLAIR

PRODUCER Inver House Distillers Ltd
REGION Highlands DISTRICT Northern Highlands
ADDRESS Edderton, Tain, Ross-shire, IV19 1LB
EMAIL enquiries@inverhouse.com WEBSITE www.inverhouse.com

THE CHANGE OF CONTROL AT INVER HOUSE in 2001 has thus far had no dramatic effect on the company's portfolio of malt distilleries. They are all relatively small, long established, and generally traditional in design and process. None is a household name, but all are respected distilleries. This one and Speyburn are especially pretty, and are the most popular choices when an art director or photographer want to show a "typical" malt distillery in an attractive location.

The light spiciness and fresh dryness of the northern Highland malts are equally typical in the Balblair whiskies. These characteristics show best in young whiskies. So why the increase in older bottlings? Perhaps that is one small sign of the new broom: tidying the stock in the warehouses. There is a limit to the number of heirlooms that can be accommodated; whiskies can become woody; and evaporation can take them below the minimum permitted alcohol.

They are made using water that has flowed from the piney hillsides of Ben Dearg and over dry, crumbly peat towards the river Carron and the Dornoch firth. A burn near the distillery feeds Balblair, which is amid fields at Edderton, close to the firth and the sea. There is said to have been brewing and distilling in the vicinity in the mid-1700s. Balblair is among Scotland's oldest distilleries. It began in 1790, and the present building dates from the 1870s.

HOUSE STYLE Light, firm, dry. Aperitif when young.
Can be woody when older.

BALBLAIR "Elements", No Age Statement, 40 vol

COLOUR Full gold.

NOSE Sea breezes. Slight salt. Barley-malt sweetness.

BODY Lean but smooth. Textured.

PALATE Teasing, appetizing, balance of slight salt and shortbread-like fresh malt. Faint hint of raspberries.

FINISH Plum-skin dryness.

SCORE 76

BALBLAIR 10-year-old, 40 vol

COLOUR Shimmery, pale gold.

NOSE Fresh. Salty. Vanilla. A hint of chocolate.

BODY Light on tongue.

PALATE Malty dryness. Shortbread sprinkled with sugar.
Custard. Summer pudding.

FINISH Concentrated fruity dryness. Summer pudding. Comforting.

COMMENT Approachable and well structured, with delicious flavours.

SCORE **77**

BALBLAIR 16-year-old, 40 vol

COLOUR Pale amber.

NOSE Nutty. Light, fresh spiciness. Fragrant.

BODY Firm, smooth, textured.

PALATE Smooth and surprisingly satisfying. Again, the saltiness and
shortbread. This time, it is chocolate shortbread. A light whisky but
packed with flavours. Very lively.

FINISH Toffee apples. Cedary dryness.

SCORE **78**

BALBLAIR 27-year-old, 46 vol

COLOUR Dark chestnut.

NOSE Cocoa powder. Winey.

BODY Firm, dusty.

PALATE More chocolate, but more bitter. Good quality cooking chocolate.

FINISH Slightly gritty and astringent. Much improved with
a splash of water.

SCORE **77**

BALBLAIR 31-year-old, Bottled 2002,
Highland Selection Limited Edition, 55 vol

COLOUR Very bright pale gold.

NOSE Grassy. Sun-dried grass. Dusty. Restrained cedar.

BODY Cedary, but rather woody for most tastes

PALATE Dry. Some spiciness.

FINISH Stern. Unyielding. Dry, but not astringent.

SCORE **76**

A 31-year-old for the French market begins with a more open, malty, fresh brioche character, but quickly retreats into its own thoughts. SCORE 77

BALBLAIR 33-year-old, 54.4 vol

COLOUR Bright gold.

NOSE Peaty, earthy, almost pungent.

BODY Firm, smooth.

PALATE Oily. Seed cake. Banana cake. Spicy.

FINISH Big. Spicy. Lemon grass. Fragrant peat. Long.

COMMENT A whisky that starts life with some restraint has
certainly developed over the years.

SCORE **79**

CASK No 893

ADELPHI DISTILLERY LIMITED

3 GLOUCESTER LANE, EDINBURGH EH3 6ED, SCOTLAND

FROM BALBLAIR, 37 YEARS OLD

**54.3%
vol**

DISTILLED AT BALBLAIR DISTILLERY 1965
BOTTLED IN SCOTLAND 2002
SELECTED BY ADELPHI DISTILLERY LIMITED

70cl

INDEPENDENT BOTTLING
BALBLAIR 37-year-old, Adelphi, 54.3 vol

COLOUR Apricot.

NOSE Again, cedary.

BODY Drying.

PALATE Cedary, but also spicy and liquorice-like.
The rich spiciness rounds out the flavours.

FINISH Robust.

SCORE **78**

BALMENACH

PRODUCER Inver House Distillers Ltd
REGION Highlands DISTRICT Speyside
ADDRESS Cromdale, Grantown-on-Spey, Morayshire, PH26 3PF
EMAIL enquiries@inverhouse.com WEBSITE www.inverhouse.com

Two new bottlings in the Highland Selection were a robust reminder of Balmenach just as its owners, Inver House, became part of Khun Charoen's interests. There had been loose talk of Balmenach being regarded by Inver House as a "flagship". Its distillate has the most powerful aromas and flavours among those produced in the group, but Balmenach today seems geographically very remote. In the upper reaches of Speyside, beyond the Livet and Avon, the bowl known as Cromdale ("crooked plain") was once alive with illicit distillers. When Balmenach emerged there as a legal distillery in 1824, it was in the heart of whisky country.

The family that founded Balmenach, in 1824, also produced two appropriately distinguished authors: Sir Compton Mackenzie (*Whisky Galore*) and Sir Robert Bruce Lockhart (*Scotch, in fact and story*, and other books on soldiering, espionage, and travel). Balmenach later had its own spur on the Strathspey railway. The distillery contributed malt whisky to many blends, especially Crabbie's and Johnnie Walker.

In 1991 a bottled single malt was issued at 43 vol in the flora and fauna series. A review appeared in subsequent editions of this book, praising the whisky for its depth of heather-honey flavours, herbal dryness, and sherry (SCORE 77). Two years later, United Distillers announced that Balmenach was to be mothballed. Four years on, it passed to Inver House. In the interim, very flowery expressions of Balmenach were bottled under the name Deerstalker, by Aberfoyle & Knight, of Glasgow (SCORE 79).

HOUSE STYLE Big. Herbal, savoury. Hints of peat.
Distinctive. Teasing. Surprisingly food-friendly.

BALMENACH 27-year-old, Bottled 2001, Highland Selection, 46 vol

NOSE Sweet tropical fruits. Bananas. Plantains being cooked on a barbecue.

PALATE Becoming drier. Vegetal. Yeasty. Perhaps the meal is
in Thailand or China?

FINISH A touch of smokiness. Roasted bell-peppers. Some chilli-like heat.

SCORE **79**

BALMENACH 1972, 28-year-old, Highland Selection, 46 vol

NOSE Sweet at first. Honeydew melons. Then leafy: a suggestion of sorrel.
A hint of grass and peat-smoke.

PALATE Lightly honeyish, becoming creamy. Quite rich, leathery. Some peat.

FINISH Dry, big. Gingery. Black treacle. Smoky, sulphury, heady.

COMMENT A robust malt, but with many subtleties of character.

SCORE **80**

SOME INDEPENDENT BOTTLINGS

BALMENACH 30-year-old, 1972 Port Wood, Released 2002, Hart Brothers, 50.1 vol

NOSE Honey, with a suggestion of chocolate, but also herbal notes.

PALATE Peppery and dry, but also creamy.

FINISH Orangey, zesty. Appetizingly spicy. Cilantro?

COMMENT Very distinctive. Bring on the chicken molé.

SCORE **77**

BALMENACH 1974, Connoisseurs Choice, 40 vol

COLOUR Deep bronze.

NOSE Glazed pastry. Savoury. Gingery.

BODY Softy. Oily.

PALATE Expressive. Spicy. Phenol.

FINISH Smoky, herbal.

SCORE **77**

A 1978 12-year-old Coopers Choice, at 43 vol, from the Vintage Malt
Whisky Company, had some curiously aromatic wood notes. SCORE 74

A 13-year-old, at 60.1 vol, from Adelphi, had an herbal,
aromatic, mint character. SCORE 77

A 1971 30-year-old from Cadenhead had a sweeter,
maltier richness. SCORE 77

THE BALVENIE

PRODUCER William Grant & Sons Ltd
REGION Highlands   DISTRICT Speyside (Dufftown)
ADDRESS Dufftown, Banffshire, AB55 4BB
TEL 01340 820373   WEBSITE www.thebalvenie.com

As SEDUCTIVELY HONEYED AS A SPEYSIDER can be; ever more aristocratic, in recent years introducing vintages as though they were eligible offspring, The Balvenie is increasingly recognized far from her domain. Her tendency toward voluptuousness, and her ready charm, win friends easily. A dalliance by the sea resulted in the birth, in 2001, of The Balvenie Islay Cask. Fellow Speysiders resented the notion of a whisky from their elevated territory even contemplating the addition of "Islay" to its name. Meanwhile, Islanders complained that The Balvenie was merely courting popularity. There have been no more Islay Casks. It was a holiday romance.

She may be a notably rich spirit, but Bad Penny offers the easiest mnemonic for Balvenie's vowel sounds. The Balvenie distillery was built in 1892 by the Grant family, who had already established Glenfiddich in 1886. It is highly unusual for a distillery to remain in the same ownership throughout its history, but both Glenfiddich and Balvenie have done so, on their original sites, which adjoin one another. One became the world's biggest selling malt and the other the epitome of luxury, but both were established, thriftily, with second-hand stills. Balvenie's are more bulbous, and that feature no doubt contributes to the distinct character of the whisky. The distillery also has its own small floor maltings, using barley from the family farm.

In 1990, Grant's added to the site a third distillery, Kininvie. This also produces a creamy spirit, but Kininvie has not thus far been bottled as a single malt. Adjoining the site is the silent Convalmore distillery, acquired by Grant's in 1992 to augment warehousing capacity.

Grant's site is at Dufftown, where the rivers Fiddich and Dullan meet on their way to the Spey. The Balvenie distillery is near the castle of the same name, which dates at least from the 1200s. The castle was at one stage known as Mortlach and was at another stage occupied by the Duff family, and is now owned by the nation of Scotland.

HOUSE STYLE The most honeyish of malts, with a distinctively orangey note. Luxurious. After dinner. Ages well.

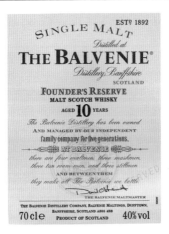

THE BALVENIE Founder's Reserve, 10-year-old, 40 vol

Matured in 90% American oak and 10% sherry.

COLOUR Bright gold.

NOSE Orange-honey perfume. Musky. Faint hint of peat.

BODY Medium.

PALATE Honeyed sweetness drying to lightly spicy notes. Very lively.
Just a touch of sherry.

FINISH A tingly surge of flavours, with lingering, syrupy honey.

SCORE **85**

THE BALVENIE Double Wood, 12-year-old, 40 vol

First- and second-fill bourbon casks, then six to twelve months in sweet oloroso casks.

COLOUR Amber.

NOSE Sherry and orange skins.

BODY Medium, rich.

PALATE Beautifully combined mellow flavours: nutty, sweet, sherry,
very orangey fruitiness, heather, cinnamon spiciness.

FINISH Long, tingling. Very warming.

SCORE **87**

THE BALVENIE Single Barrel, 15-year-old, 50.4 vol

All first-fill bourbon casks.

COLOUR Pale gold.

NOSE Assertive. Dry, fresh oak. Heather. Rooty. Coconut. Lemon pith.

BODY Firm.

PALATE Lively. Cedar. Orange skins, pineapple-like sweetness and acidity.

FINISH Very dry. Peppery alcohol.

SCORE **85**

THE BALVENIE Islay Cask, 43 vol

Seven years in bourbon barrels, then finished for six months at Balvenie in casks that had held Islay whisky for six months.

COLOUR Bronze with pinkish tinge.

NOSE Restrained, but distinct, seaweed and salt.

BODY A touch of syrupiness in the middle.

PALATE Honeyed, then some peaty smokiness. The smokiness is enwrapping, rather than attacking, as it might be in an Islay malt.

FINISH Fragrantly smoky. Orangey flavours emerge. Lively, emphatic finish. Bonus points for a bold idea.

SCORE **89**

BALVENIE Port Wood, 21-year-old, 40 vol

Primarily matured in bourbon casks, then a short period in first-fill port pipes.

COLOUR Reddish amber.

NOSE Perfumy, fruity. Passion fruit. Raisiny. Nutty dryness. Marzipan.

BODY Rich.

PALATE Very complex. Toffee, creamy, winey, aniseed.

FINISH Long, cedary, dry.

SCORE **88**

BALVENIE Single Barrel, 25-year-old, 46.9 vol

COLOUR Pale, bright, gold.

NOSE Honeyed.

BODY Lightly syrupy.

PALATE Surprisingly peaty, though the characteristic honey is always there.

FINISH Firm. Peaty.

SCORE **86**

BALVENIE 50-year-old, 45.1 vol

For the collector, rather than the taster, whiskies this old once won points simply for being. As more are released, they have to justify themselves.

COLOUR Mahogany.

NOSE The best feature. Heavy, dark red fruits. Plum strudel, dusted with cinnamon. Evokes images of cafés in Vienna. Incongruous? Perhaps. When this was being distilled, the Red Army was leaving.

BODY Light, drying. A curiously inky texture.

PALATE More plums. Passion fruit. Woody tannins. Iron-like flavours weigh down the palate. Spicy notes try to lift it, but eventually lose the struggle.

FINISH Quite bitter and astringent.

SCORE **85**

SOME VINTAGE BOTTLINGS OF THE BALVENIE
THE BALVENIE 1989, Port Wood, 40 vol

Finished for a year in second-fill port pipes with a view to a more subtle wine character.

COLOUR Warm gold.

NOSE Hint of cream toffee.

BODY Creamy, clinging.

PALATE A suggestion of passion fruit. Orange muscat, "peach stone" nuttiness, then spicy dryness. Port character very restrained.

FINISH Silky.

SCORE **87**

THE BALVENIE Vintage Cask, 1972, 49.4 vol

COLOUR Rich, warm, gold to amber.

NOSE Buttery richness. Butterscotch pudding. Bread and butter pudding. Honey.

BODY Rich, soft, delicious. Astonishingly syrupy smooth.

PALATE Still evoking thoughts of desserts, but the honeyed pastries of the Balkans. Then a suggestion of chocolate powder hints at tiramisu.

FINISH Bitter chocolate. Terry's chocolate oranges. The ultimate dessert whisky. Beautifully composed.

SCORE **92**

THE BALVENIE Vintage Cask, 1970, 44.6 vol

COLOUR Gold.

NOSE Fudge. Honey. A hint of heather. Very soft, floral.

BODY Lightly creamy.

PALATE Intensely sweet and Sauternes-like. Or perhaps orange Muscat? With water yet sweeter and fruitier.

FINISH The sweet components become more like dark, clear, liquid honey. The fruity element becomes more intense and perfumy. All the elements of a classic Balvenie, beautifully presented and combined.

SCORE **91**

THE BALVENIE 1968, Vintage Cask, 50.8 vol

COLOUR Full gold to bronze.

NOSE Clear liquid honey. Heathery.

More perfumy and orangey when water is added.

BODY Fudgey, soft.

PALATE Honeyed. Very pronounced orange zest. Lots of flavour development.

With water. Hazelnut or almond. Some smoke. Slight menthol. Mint.

FINISH Lemony. Dry. Warming. Very long.

SCORE **90**

THE BALVENIE Vintage Cask 1967, 49.7 vol

COLOUR Full gold.

NOSE Very aromatic. Butterscotch, honey. Acacia. Faint peat.

BODY Light syrupy. Slightly drying. Nutty. Chewy.

PALATE Buttery maltiness. Honey. Orange. Linctus-like.

Hint of vanilla. Juicy oak.

FINISH Orange skins. Lemon grass. Lightly peaty balancing dryness.

SCORE **88**

THE BALVENIE Vintage Cask 1966, 42.1 vol

COLOUR Full gold to bronze.

NOSE Very aromatic. Butter, honey, lemon. Grass. Faint peat.

BODY Medium, firm, rounded.

PALATE Buttery maltiness. Honey. Orange. Lemon grass. Juicy oak.

A beautifully balanced classic Speyside whisky.

FINISH Lemon. Grass. Lightly peaty balancing dryness.

SCORE **88**

EARLIER VERSIONS OF THE BALVENIE

A 1964 Vintage, long gone, was similar but nuttier and drier. SCORE 88
A 1951 had a dark brown colour and was full of peat and oak smoke, but
still with some malty smoothness underneath it all. Slightly astringent, but
bonus points for traditional values and distinctiveness. SCORE 88

OTHER VERSIONS OF THE BALVENIE

A rare independent bottling by Signatory in 1990, of a 1974 distillate:
bright full gold; dry, malty shortbread aroma; firm, lightly syrupy
body; honey, cinnamon, and lemon in palate; smooth,
long, rounded, satisfying, warming finish. SCORE 87

BANFF

PRODUCER DCL
REGION Highlands DISTRICT Speyside (Deveron)
SITE OF FORMER DISTILLERY Inverboyndie, on B9139, 1 mile west of Banff

THE HOUSE OF COMMONS was once supplied with whisky from this distillery, near the adjoining towns of Banff and MacDuff. The two face each other across the Deveron, where the river flows into the Moray firth. The county of Banffshire once stretched from the Deveron to the Spey. This eastern flank of Speyside embraced half the region's distilleries. It has fewer today, but it is still barley country, its coastal strip linking the Laich of Moray with Aberdeenshire. The county became Banff and Buchan and is now subsumed into Aberdeenshire.

The distillery, dating from at least 1824, closed in 1983, leaving a substantial amount of stock. Its buildings have gradually been dismantled, though remains loom through the sea mist. They are in a field next to a graveyard. The spirits of Banff are restless judging from the profusion of independent bottlings.

HOUSE STYLE Fragrant. Lemon grass. Sweet. Restorative or after dinner.

BANFF 1980, 21-year-old, Cask No 2914, Signatory Vintage, 43 vol

COLOUR	Vinho verde.
NOSE	Light. Fresh. Grassy.
BODY	Light, creamy, appetizingly dryish.
PALATE	Grassy. Oaty. A suggestion of golden syrup.
FINISH	Kendal mint cake.
COMMENT	A pleasant, easily drinkable malt. Showing few signs of age, good or bad.

SCORE 70

Earlier from Signatory, in its Silent Stills series, a 1978 bottling, at 18 years old and 58.8 vol, was drier and smokier. SCORE 67

BANFF 1978, 22-year-old, Bottled 2002, The Coopers Choice (The Vintage Malt Whisky Company), 56 vol

COLOUR	Greeny gold. Lime-tinged.
NOSE	Grassy. Aromatic.
BODY	Smooth. Creamy.
PALATE	Condensed milk. A hint of chocolate. Late flavour development. Becomes very lively.
FINISH	Big surge. Lemon zest.

SCORE 69

BANFF 1976, 25-year-old, James MacArthur's Old Master's, 57.1 vol

COLOUR	Full greeny gold.
NOSE	Soft. Warm. Burnt grass.
BODY	Slippery smooth.
PALATE	Peaty, earthy. Chocolate powder. Sweetish. A touch of vanilla. Some syrupiness.
FINISH	Long. Warming. Spicy. Minty. Extra strong peppermints.

SCORE 69

BANFF 24-year-old, Cadenhead, 58.3 vol

COLOUR	Bright gold.
NOSE	Clean, dry, peat-smoke fragrance. A hint of the sea?
BODY	Syrupy.
PALATE	Vanilla. Syrupy-sweet flavours. Grassy. Sun-dried grass.
FINISH	Lemon grass. Complex spiciness. Gingery, dry. Very long. Real depth and staying power.

SCORE 72

An earlier 1976, at 21 years and 58.2 vol, from Cadenhead, was peatier and earthier, with more vanilla. Less bright and clean. SCORE 67.

BANFF 1976, Connoisseurs Choice, 40 vol

COLOUR	Vinho verde.
NOSE	Fresh. Grassy. Lemon grass.
BODY	Smooth. Creamy.
PALATE	Fresh cream. Coconut. Tropical fruits.
FINISH	Fruity, aromatic dryness. Perhaps even a hint of phenol.

SCORE 73

BEN NEVIS

PRODUCER Ben Nevis Distillery Ltd
REGION Highlands DISTRICT West Highlands
ADDRESS Lochy Bridge, Fort William, PH33 6TJ
TEL 01397 702476 VC

MUCH-IMPROVED BOTTLINGS are beginning to emerge as Ben Nevis marks a dozen years under the ownership of the respected Japanese distillers Nikka. The distillery, at Fort William, lies at the foot of Scotland's highest mountain, Ben Nevis (1344m/4409ft). The peak does not have quite the significance of Fuji, but it is a powerful symbol of Scotland.

The distillery was established in 1825 by "Long John" McDonald. The well-known blended Scotch, Long John, was named after him. The distillery, with its curiously anthologous architecture, is in a very visible spot on a road with a heavy tourist traffic, but relatively distant from any other distilleries. Its regional appropriation to the western Highlands is supported by its being close to a sea loch. "We are a coastal distillery" insists manager Colin Ross, standing in front of the mighty mountain.

HOUSE STYLE Fragrant. Robust. Waxy fruitiness. Tropical fruit.
Oily, a touch of smoke. Restorative or book-at-bedtime.

BEN NEVIS 10-year-old, 46 vol

Found at 40 vol or 43 vol in some markets.

COLOUR Warm bronze to amber.

NOSE Perfumy, spicy, soft. Waxed fruit. Kumquats. Hard black chocolate.

BODY Emphatically big, firm, smooth.

PALATE Orange-cream pralines in black chocolate. Belgian toffee wafers.

FINISH Orange zest. Pithy dryness. Touch of cigar smoke.

SCORE **77**

Also at 10 years old, tasted as a work in progress, a single cask, aged entirely in sherry, emerged with orange marmalade colour; flavours of pickled peaches and rum butter; texture as dense as a mince pie; and a long, warming finish.

BEN NEVIS 21-year-old, Limited Edition in Decanter, 60.5 vol

Now hard to find.

COLOUR Bronze to amber.

NOSE Box of black chocolates.

BODY Big, smooth.

PALATE Oilier, juicier, chewier, drier.

FINISH Robust. Oaky spiciness.

SCORE **77**

BEN NEVIS 26-year-old, Distilled 1975, Cask No 945, Bottled 2001, 53.9 vol

COLOUR Bright greeny gold.

NOSE Leafy. Fruity.

BODY Firm. Smooth.

PALATE Fruity, A touch of honey. Dry maltiness. Chocolatey.

FINISH Spiciness. Chillis. Peppery. Rather aggressive.

SCORE **77**

DISTILLED AND BOTTLED IN SCOTLAND

BEN NEVIS

SINGLE HIGHLAND MALT SCOTCH WHISKY
BEN NEVIS DISTILLERY (FORT WILLIAM) LIMITED
Cask Nos. 946
DISTILLED IN 1975
BOTTLED IN 2001
70 cl.   52.3% vol.

Distilled and bottled in the same years as the previous whisky, cask no 946 emerged at 52.3 vol, slightly richer and sweeter. SCORE 78

An earlier 26-year-old (distilled 1972, bottled 1998), 57.4 vol, had a fuller colour, more sherry character, some smokiness, and a beautiful balance. SCORE 78

BEN NEVIS 1966, Bottled 1998, 51 vol

COLOUR Bright golden yellow.

NOSE Oily.

BODY Very oily.

PALATE Oily, flowery, surprisingly neutral. Disappointing, like some other Ben Nevis distillates from the 1960s.

FINISH Mustardy.

SCORE **62**

SOME INDEPENDENT BOTTLINGS

BEN NEVIS 35-year-old, Distilled April 1957, First Sherry Wood, Hart Brothers, 50.1 vol

COLOUR Very attractive reddish amber.

NOSE Tightly combined and balanced, fragrant smoke, oak and hard-toffee maltiness.

PALATE Chewy. Malty honeycomb in dark chocolate. As though the Belgians had upgraded the British Crunchie bar. Tropical fruits.

FINISH Clinging. Bittersweet. Firm. Intense black chocolate, but avoids astringency. An outstanding bottling.

SCORE **82**

A Cadenhead bottling of 1986 at 17 years old and 46 vol was oily, feinty, and hot. Rather harsh all round. SCORE 60

A Blackadder bottling of 1984 at 60.8, from cask no. 257, balanced its woodiness with a luscious, sweet, treacle-toffee character. SCORE 76

Cask no 258, at 61.2 vol, had winey, Syrah-like flavours, and hints of raspberry vinegar. Lots of sweetness suggested a dessert whisky, but the idyll was shattered by the intensity of woodiness. SCORE 78

BEN WYVIS

PRODUCER Whyte and Mackay Ltd
REGION Highlands   DISTRICT Northern Highlands
ADDRESS Invergordon Distillers, Cottage Brae,
Invergordon, Ross-shire, IV18 0HP

A NEW ENTRY IN THIS BOOK, yet it finally appears a quarter of a century after the distillery closed. The wait for whisky has been twice as long as the distillery's lifespan. Several distilleries had short lives and subsequently appeared in spirit, but Ben Wyvis is surely the ultimate ghost of the glens. Its name is pronounced with a short "y", as in myth: wyv-iss. It derives from the mountain peak Ben Wyvis (1046 metres or 3432 feet), variously translated into English as "big green slope" or "terrible hill", northwest of Inverness and the Black Isle; the peak is part of the northern Highland range.

The regional designation Ferintosh was used to identify whiskies from the Black Isle and Dingwall, on the Cromarty firth, in the late 1600s and 1700s. The name Ferintosh was later applied for a time to a distillery built as Ben Wyvis in Dingwall in 1879. This first Ben Wyvis closed in 1926. The buildings were later used as whisky warehouses, and some still stand, masquerading as a business park.

The economic recovery after the Second World War led to a boom in the whisky industry in the late 1950s and the 1960s. In 1965, a new Ben Wyvis distillery was built further north on the Cromarty firth, at Invergordon. It shared a site with the Invergordon grain distillery. The intention was that Ben Wyvis would provide malt whisky for the Invergordon blends. The Invergordon company had its own ups and downs, and Ben Wyvis ceased production in 1976.

It is said that one cask of Ben Wyvis was exported to the United States in 1974. There was still some stock of Ben Wyvis when the current century dawned and Invergordon was restructured as Kyndal, two very limited releases have been made. There have also been two bottlings from Signatory. It turns out to have been a highly distinctive malt.

Around the same time, in the opposite corner of Scotland, another half-forgotten distillery was suddenly back in view. Hedley Wright, proprietor of Springbank, announced that he was to reopen Glengyle after 70 years' silence. The stills had long gone, but they have been replaced with those from Ben Wyvis.

HOUSE STYLE Light, dry, herbal, savoury, appetizing.

BEN WYVIS 27-year-old, Distilled 1972, Cask No 745, Bottle No 11 of 187, Cask Strength, 45.9 vol

COLOUR Bright pale gold. Green tinge.

NOSE Very distinctive. Drily flowery. Herbal. Fresh mint. Pesto-like.

BODY Light but textured.

PALATE Herbal. Savoury.

FINISH Soft, buttery. Some mustard.

SCORE **81**

BEN WYVIS 37-year-old, Distilled 17 June 1965, 45.5 vol

COLOUR Full gold. Green tinge.

NOSE More perfumed. Mint. Leafy.

BODY Firmer. Drier.

PALATE Toasted pine nuts. Smoky. Roasted vegetables.

FINISH Very crisp dryness.

SCORE **80**

SIGNATORY BOTTLING

BEN WYVIS 31-year-old, Distilled 5 June 1968, Bottled 25 February 2000, Signatory, Cask No 687, 56.5 vol

COLOUR Full gold. Green tinge.

NOSE Slightly more vegetal. Cucumber.

BODY Firm. Smooth.

PALATE Dry, cleansing, appetizing.

FINISH Coriander seeds. Pepper.

SCORE **79**

BENRIACH

PRODUCER Chivas Brothers
REGION Highlands DISTRICT Speyside (Lossie)
ADDRESS Longmorn, Elgin, Morayshire, IV30 3SJ

Twin of the much loved Longmorn (but not identical). The two occupy adjoining sites. Both distilleries were built in the 1890s, but Benriach was silent from 1900 until it was restored in 1965. Benriach has its own floor maltings. This has not been used since the 1990s, but is beautifully maintained. Benriach is the more agricultural-looking distillery, Longmorn the more elaborate. Benriach has a traditional mash tun. Both distilleries have onion-shaped stills, but Benriach's are steeper. Benriach's whiskies are in general sweeter, those from Longmorn more complex. At older ages, Benriach begins to narrow the gap.

HOUSE STYLE Cookie-like, with touches of butterscotch. Restorative. A mid-afternoon malt?

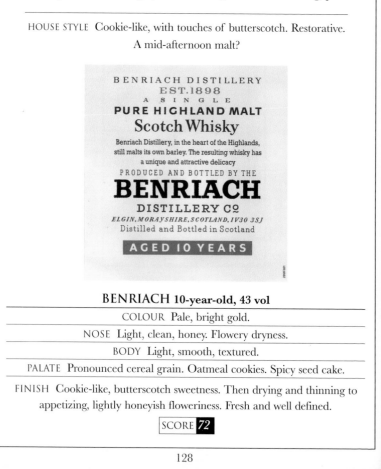

BENRIACH 10-year-old, 43 vol

COLOUR Pale, bright gold.

NOSE Light, clean, honey. Flowery dryness.

BODY Light, smooth, textured.

PALATE Pronounced cereal grain. Oatmeal cookies. Spicy seed cake.

FINISH Cookie-like, butterscotch sweetness. Then drying and thinning to appetizing, lightly honeyish floweriness. Fresh and well defined.

SCORE 72

BENRINNES

PRODUCER Diageo
REGION Highlands DISTRICT Speyside
ADDRESS Aberlour, Banffshire, AB38 9WN
TEL Contact via Dailuaine 01340 872500

As a mountain, Ben Rinnes spreads itself to two words and is hard to miss; as a distillery and a whisky, Benrinnes compounds itself so neatly that it is too easily overlooked. It is no novice. Benrinnes may have been founded as early as the 1820s, and was largely rebuilt in the 1950s. The distillery had a long association with the Crawford blends. Its malt whisky did not have official bottling until 1991, in a Flora and Fauna edition. Benrinnes' system of partial triple distillation places it among the handful of quirky, individualistic distilleries in the Diageo group.

HOUSE STYLE Big, creamy, smoky, flavoursome, long.
Restorative or after dinner.

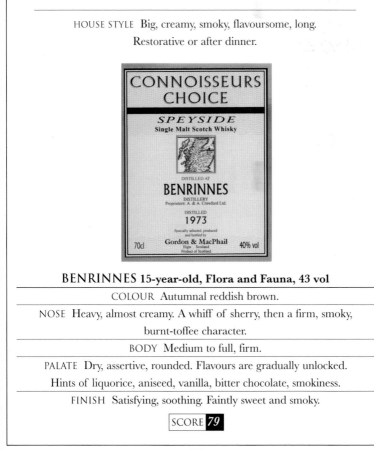

BENRINNES 15-year-old, Flora and Fauna, 43 vol

COLOUR	Autumnal reddish brown.
NOSE	Heavy, almost creamy. A whiff of sherry, then a firm, smoky, burnt-toffee character.
BODY	Medium to full, firm.
PALATE	Dry, assertive, rounded. Flavours are gradually unlocked. Hints of liquorice, aniseed, vanilla, bitter chocolate, smokiness.
FINISH	Satisfying, soothing. Faintly sweet and smoky.

SCORE **79**

BENRINNES 21-year-old, Distilled 1974, Rare Malts, 60.4 vol

COLOUR Bright gold.

NOSE Earthy. Hint of peatiness.

BODY Medium, firm.

PALATE Oily, nutty, toffeeish, creamy. Developing vanilla, orange, lime.

FINISH Delayed, surging finish. Sweetish spicy. Long, lingering, expressive.

SCORE **79**

A 1974, at 22 years old, from Adelphi, was grassy, flowery and fruity. SCORE 78

SOME INDEPENDENT BOTTLINGS
BENRINNES 1989, Signatory, 43 vol

COLOUR Greeny gold. Vinho verde.

NOSE Earthy, dry, and dusty. The aroma in a country store that stocks
everything from bacon and cheese to hardware.

BODY Medium, creamy.

PALATE Lightly nutty. Salty. Savoury. Tasty. Distinctive.

FINISH Lemony. Appetizing.

 SCORE **78**

An earlier Signatory bottling, a 1982 at 43 vol, had hints of peat and sherry,
but beautifully balanced. SCORE 79

BENRINNES 19-year-old, Douglas Laing, 50 vol

COLOUR Pale oak.

NOSE Cedary. Winey. Sherry. Reminiscent of amontillado.

BODY Very creamy. Unusually dense.

PALATE Creamy, earthy, slightly woody. Damson fruitiness.

FINISH Jammy fruitiness eventually blocked by woodiness.

SCORE **76**

BENRINNES 1973, Connoisseurs Choice, 40 vol

COLOUR Deep gold.

NOSE Creamy, toffeeish.

BODY Firm, toasty.

PALATE Gingerbread. Vanilla. Marshmallow. Rose-water.

FINISH Restrained, soothing warmth and balancing dryness.
Controlled oakiness. Beautifully composed.

 SCORE **78**

BENROMACH

PRODUCER Gordon & MacPhail
REGION Highlands DISTRICT District Speyside (Findhorn)
ADDRESS Invererne Road, Forres, Moray, IV36 3EB
TEL 01309 675968 WEBSITE www.gordonandmacphail.com
EMAIL info@gordonandmacphail.com VC

PRINCE CHARLES IS NO DOUBT among the malt lovers keen to taste this 100-year-old distillery's born-again whisky. Benromach appeared to have died while in the care of United Distillers in the mid-1980s. The distillery, the most immediately visible to travellers approaching Speyside from Inverness, was closed. Sadder still, its valuable copper stills were removed. United did subsequently issue one Rare Malts edition, at 20 years old. Apart from that isolated instance, Benromach was for many years available only in independent bottlings.

A flowery 12-year-old and a more fruity 15-year-old, both popular ages, and each scoring 77, have dried up since the fourth edition of this book. However much inventory a distillery has, its stocks are finite. Devotees mourn, and independent bottlers lose a source. On this occasion, Gordon & MacPhail decided to try and buy the distillery. Having succeeded, they re-equipped it with smaller stills. The idea was to adapt it to present demand, but also to produce a richer spirit. With its new still-house, Benromach was reopened in 1998 – by Prince Charles. The early batches have long passed the three-year transition from spirit to whisky, but will be given a few more summers before they are considered sufficiently mature to release. At that point, there will be a further ascent of the legend. "Bottled by Gordon & MacPhail" is no longer enough. This has already become "by the Proprietors". Eventually, the legend will say: "Distilled and bottled by Gordon & MacPhail."

HOUSE STYLE Assertive, flowery, sometimes creamy. With dessert or after dinner.

BENROMACH Centenary Bottling, 17-year-old, 43 vol

COLOUR Deep, full gold.

NOSE Very flowery, herbal, smoky, complex, long.

BODY Firm, smooth, oily.

PALATE Malty background. Richly sherryish. Peachy.
Flowery. Lively. Complex.

FINISH Nutty, juicy oak, soothing, very long.

SCORE 79

BENROMACH 18-year-old, 40 vol

COLOUR Full gold.

NOSE Very restrained at first, but gradually becomes very fragrant.
Flowery. Lime blossom. Ground almonds. Sugared almonds.
Mint imperials. Very faint smoke.

BODY Lightly soft, syrupy, flirtatious.

PALATE Perfumy, fragrant. Faint smoke again.

FINISH Very dry but well judged.

SCORE 80

BENROMACH Cask Strength, 1982, Cask Nos 112 and 114, 59.7 vol

COLOUR Deep, shining gold.

NOSE Fresh air. Ozone. So fresh as to be almost astringent.

BODY Firm, smooth, dryish.

PALATE Oily, liquorice. Treacle toffee. Toasted nuts. Toffee apples.

FINISH Peppermint.

SCORE 77

An earlier cask strength, at 61 vol, was more rounded, and had a more
obvious contribution from sherry. SCORE 78

BENROMACH 25-year-old, 43 vol

COLOUR Bright gold. Faint green tinge.

NOSE Hint of garden bonfires.

BODY Very light. Spring water. As though the whisky had
attenuated in the bottle.

PALATE Slightly vegetal. Rooty. Chlorophyll. Gin-like.

FINISH Lightly dry. Eccentric, but appetizing.

SCORE 77

BENROMACH Vintage 1973, 40 vol

COLOUR Full, refractive gold.

NOSE Distinctly sweeter, but also with acidity. Pear syrup. Fresh apples. Some crème fraîche acidity.

BODY Firm. Dry.

PALATE Apple pie with butterscotch and cream.

FINISH Burnt pie crust. Slight phenol.

SCORE **77**

BENROMACH Port Wood Finish, 19-year-old, 45 vol

COLOUR Attractive orange pink.

NOSE Lightly fruity. Dark, soft fruits as it opens. Nut toffee. A hint of coffee.

BODY Surprisingly light, soft, smooth.

PALATE Sweet. Some fruitiness, but lacks complexity.

FINISH Proposes a seduction, then vanishes. A tease.

SCORE **77**

OTHER VERSIONS OF BENROMACH

The Rare Malts 20-year-old, bottled in 1998 at cask strength, is creamy, fruity, almondy, and cedary. SCORE 77

A Scott's Selection from the same year, at 52.1 vol, is very flowery, fruity, and dry. SCORE 77

A Cadenhead 1965, bottled at 28 years old and 47.6 vol, is heavily sherried and smoky, attenuated with age, but still with a delicate nuttiness and floweriness. SCORE 77

BLADNOCH

PRODUCER Raymond Armstrong
REGION Lowlands DISTRICT Borders
ADDRESS Bladnoch, Wigtownshire, DG8 9AB
TEL 01988 402605 WEBSITE www.bladnoch.co.uk VC

FINALLY DISTILLING AGAIN, since 2001, and producing a very flowery "new make". Some time before the end of the decade, this spirit should be ready for release as mature whisky. It promises to restore a corner of pride to the Lowlands as malt whisky region. Meanwhile, new proprietor Raymond Armstrong has been buying casks and bottles of Bladnoch whisky from previous owners UDV and from the trade in general, to ensure that he has something to sell in the distillery shop.

Bladnoch is the southernmost working distillery in Scotland. It takes its water from the river Bladnoch, which flows into the Solway Firth, which forms the border with England.

The pretty little distillery, established between 1817 and 1825, was originally attached to a farm, and used local barley. For a time, it triple distilled. It was mothballed in 1993 by its then owner, United Distillers.

The distillery gave rise to the hamlet of Bladnoch. Nearby is Wigtown, noted for its bookshops. A little farther away is Dumfries, where Robbie Burns's house can be visited.

Raymond Armstrong, from Northern Ireland, bought the distillery buildings with a view to converting them into a holiday home, but came to feel they should be returned to their original purpose. He spent two years restoring the distillery to working order. Armstrong, a surveyor and builder, had no connections with the whisky industry, but had family links with Wigtownshire. The area is geographically very close to Northern Ireland.

HOUSE STYLE Grassy, lemony, soft, sometimes with a suggestion of bananas. A classic Lowlander. Perhaps a dessert malt.

BLADNOCH 10-year-old, Flora and Fauna, 43 vol

Launched in UDV period. Becoming hard to find.

COLOUR Amber.

NOSE Hint of sherry, fragrantly fruity, lemony.

BODY Fuller, firm.

PALATE Lots of development from a sherryish start through cereal-grain grassiness to flowery, fruity, lemony notes.

FINISH Again, surprisingly assertive.

SCORE *85*

BLADNOCH 23-year-old, Rare Malts, Distilled 1977, Bottled 2001, 53.6 vol

COLOUR Pale bright gold.

NOSE Aromatic. Straw, grass, lemon grass.

BODY Light, oily.

PALATE Dry. Bamboo-like woodiness. Some vanilla smoothness.

FINISH Exotic fruits. Chillis. Hot. Needs softening with a good splash of water.

SCORE *78*

CASKS OF BLADNOCH ACQUIRED BY THE DISTILLERY.

Tasted as works in progress.

1991, Refill Barrel, Cask No 3998, 54.3 vol

COLOUR Vinho verde.

NOSE Floral, vegetal.

BODY Light. Firm.

PALATE Starts very sweet. Then develops coriander-like dryness.

FINISH Hint of liquorice. Cough sweets. Hot. Fisherman's Friend.

1990, Cask Unspecified, 52.9 vol

COLOUR Shimmery. Very pale greeny gold.

NOSE Fresh, light, fruitiness. Passion fruit.

BODY Light, drying.

PALATE Oily. Lemon curd. Lemon zest.

FINISH Zesty. More liquorice.

1988, Refill Hogshead, Cask No 2631, 57.3 vol

COLOUR Gold.

NOSE Morning dew. Wet grass.

BODY Firm. Smooth.

PALATE Lively start. Fruity. Bananas. Grassy coriander, lemons. Cream.

FINISH Leafy. Vegetal.

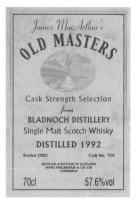

SOME INDEPENDENT BOTTLINGS

BLADNOCH 1992, James MacArthur, Cask No 720, 57.6 vol

COLOUR Very pale, green-tinged.

NOSE Light, dusty fruitiness.

BODY Oily.

PALATE Zest of lemon. Sweet lime cordial. Leafy dryness.

FINISH A suggestion of old books.

SCORE **78**

BLADNOCH 1990, Signatory, 43 vol

COLOUR Gold. Faint green tinge.

NOSE Warm. Banana-like.

BODY Textured.

PALATE Bananas. Cream, cereal grain. Falls away in middle.

FINISH Late recovery. Some lively acidity.

SCORE **79**

A 1974 from Signatory, at 50.6 vol, had a full gold colour and a generous spoonful of liquorice in the aroma and palate. This expression seemed to have reached its conclusion very quickly, but this proved to be a grandstand finish, exploding with fruitiness and spiciness. SCORE 84

BLADNOCH 1989, 13-year-old, Cadenhead, 54.9 vol

COLOUR Very pale greeny gold.

NOSE Lime peels.

BODY Delicate. Petal-like.

PALATE Slow to open up, but water helps. Chlorophyll. Herbal. Vanilla.

FINISH Drying.

SCORE **79**

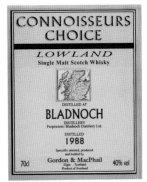

BLADNOCH 1988, Connoisseurs Choice, 40 vol

COLOUR Bright, greeny gold.

NOSE Fresh. Green. Grassy. Leafy.

BODY Soft.

PALATE Clean. Perfumy. Rounded. Superbly balanced. Beautifully combined flavours. Banana toffee? Nougat, perhaps.

FINISH Anis.

SCORE **86**

Gordon & MacPhail also released a cask strength
(cask nos 3151 and 3158, 58.8 vol) bottling from the same year.
This had a warm, bronze colour; discreetly suggesting sherry.
The hint was more strongly spelled out in the aroma and palate,
but Bladnoch's typical citrus and banana esters
smile through. SCORE 87

BLADNOCH 1987, Scott's Selection, 58.9 vol

COLOUR Pale vinho verde.

NOSE Heavy tropical flowers. Some fruity acidity.

BODY Firm, rounded.

PALATE Very sweet. Scottish tablet.

FINISH Bittersweet, geranial. Assertive.

SCORE **76**

BLADNOCH Distilled June 1980, Bottled January 1997, Royal Mile Whiskies, 56.6 vol

COLOUR Gold.

NOSE Lightly honeyed.

BODY Light, thin.

PALATE Honey again, developing orange-flower and acacia notes. Pleasant
enough, but neither as complex or as rounded as might have been hoped.

FINISH Seville orange marmalade.

SCORE **77**

BLAIR ATHOL

PRODUCER Diageo
REGION Highlands DISTRICT Eastern Highlands
ADDRESS Pitlochry, Perthshire, PH16 5LY
TEL 01796 482003
WEBSITE www.discovering-distilleries.com/www.malts.com VC

B LAIR IS A SCOTTISH NAME, referring to a tract of flat land, a clearance, a battlefield, or someone who originates from such a place. Blair Castle is the home of the Duke of Atholl. The village of Blair Atholl ends with a double "l", while the distillery prefers to keep it single. The distillery is nearby at the inland resort of Pitlochry, known for its summer theatre. The well-designed, beautifully maintained distillery, overgrown with ivy and Virginia creeper, traces its origins to 1798. It has been sympathetically expanded several times.

Its malt whisky is extensively used in the Bell's blends. The whisky matures quickly, and behaves like a gentleman. It is a sturdy, well-proportioned whisky rather than a big bruiser, but it can take a lot of sherry without becoming showy or belligerent.

HOUSE STYLE Redolent of shortbread and ginger cake. Spicy, nutty.
A mid-afternoon malt?

139

BLAIR ATHOL 12-year-old, 43 vol

Released in 2000 in the Single Distillery Malt series, a further development of the flora and fauna selections.

COLOUR Attractive dark orange. Satin sheen.

NOSE Rich. Moist, cake-like. Lemon grass. Assam tea. (A hint of peat?)

BODY Silky smooth.

PALATE Spiced cake. Candied lemon-peels. Lots of flavour development.

FINISH Lightly smoky. Rooty. Treacley. Impeccable balance between sweetness and dryness.

SCORE 78

BLAIR ATHOL 12-year-old, Commemorative Limited Edition, 43 vol

A much more sherryish version.

COLOUR Distinctively deep. Orange liqueur.

NOSE Very complex. Fragrant, candied orange peels, dried fruit, cinnamon.

BODY Medium, silky.

PALATE Walnuts. Sweetish. Cakey. Faint treacle or molasses.

FINISH Very smooth, round, soothing, lightly smoky.

Very sophisticated for its age. Blair Athol matures quickly, gaining perfuminess, sweetness, richness, spiciness, complexity, and length. The sherry helps to emulsify the elements.

SCORE 77

BLAIR ATHOL 18-year-old, Bicentenary Limited Edition, 56.7 vol

COLOUR Full peachy amber (but less dark than the 12-year-old).

NOSE Very delicate, finessed, orange and cinnamon.

BODY Bigger and firm.

PALATE Dates. Raisins. Dried figs. Moist cake. Butter.

FINISH Toasty. The slightly burnt crust on a cake.

SCORE 78

BLAIR ATHOL 1981, Bottled 1997,
Cask Strength Limited Bottling, 55.5 vol

Now becoming hard to find.

COLOUR Deep, bright orange red.

NOSE Oakier and smokier, but appetizingly so.

BODY Medium, firm, smooth.

PALATE Delicious, clean toffee. Firm, slightly chewy. Pronounced black treacle. Lively. Hints of banana, orange, lemon. Faint fragrant smokiness.

FINISH Ginger, toasty oak.

SCORE 78

SINGLE Cask BOTTLING

**DISTILLED AT
BLAIR ATHOL DISTILLERY**

∿SINGLE MALT SCOTCH WHISKY∿

DISTILLED 1975 MARCH

BOTTLED 2000 NOVEMBER

Aged **25** *Years*

NO CHILL FILTRATION. NO COLOURING
BOTTLED AT NATURAL CASK STRENGTH

THIS BOTTLE IS ONE
OF *192* BOTTLES
FILLED FROM CASK

700ml   DISTILLED, MATURED AND BOTTLED IN SCOTLAND 49.3% ALC/VOL
DOUGLAS LAING & CO LTD, GLASGOW G3 6EQ
PRODUCT OF SCOTLAND

BLAIR ATHOL 25-year-old, Douglas Laing & Co, 49.3 vol

COLOUR Bright pale, greeny gold.

NOSE Candied orange peel. Marzipan. Sponge cake with
fresh fruit.

BODY Clean, syrupy.

PALATE Creamy, perfumy. Fresh citrus. Pineapple.

FINISH Beautifully rounded dryness,

SCORE **78**

BLAIR ATHOL 1973, Signatory Cask Strength Series, 55 vol

COLOUR White wine.

NOSE Lightly smoky. Lightly fruity.

BODY Light to medium, textured.

PALATE Lemony, syrupy, lightly smoky.

FINISH After a palate that seems to lack complexity, a very long finish.
Starts flowery and fruity, with suggestions of an almost-ripe pear or
dessert apple. Develops to buttery shortbread. Then a late, surprising
hit of gingery warmth.

SCORE **74**

BOWMORE

PRODUCER Morrison Bowmore Distillers Ltd
REGION Islay DISTRICT Lochindaal
ADDRESS Bowmore, Islay, Argyll, PA34 7JS
TEL 01496 810441 WEBSITE www.bowmore.com VC

EVOCATIVE NAMES like Dawn, Dusk, Voyage, and Legend accentuate the dream-like nature of the place. The village of Bowmore is the "capital" of Islay, but barely more than a hamlet, where the river Laggan flows into Lochindaal. On the edge of the boggy moor, the round church looks down the hill to the harbour.

The distillery, founded in 1779, is kept in beautiful condition – but not to be confused with the local school, which has decorative pagodas. In both geography and palate, the whiskies of Bowmore are between the intense malts of the south shore and the gentlest extremes of the north. Their character is not a compromise but an enigma, and tasters have found it difficult to unfold its complexity. The water used rises from iron-tinged rock, and picks up some peat from the earth as it flows by way of the Laggan, through moss, ferns, and rushes, to the distillery. While the peat higher on the island is rooty, that at Bowmore is sandier.

The company has its own maltings, where the peat is crumbled before it is fired to give more smoke than heat. The malt is peated for a shorter time than that used for the more intense Islay whiskies. Up to 30 per cent of the whisky is aged in sherry. The distillery is more exposed to the westerly winds than others, so there may be more ozone in the complex of aromas and flavours.

HOUSE STYLE Smoky, with leafy notes (ferns?) and sea air.
Younger ages before dinner, older after.

EXPRESSIONS WIITH NO AGE STATEMENT
BOWMORE Legend, 40 vol

A light, young version, identified in some markets as an eight-year-old.

COLOUR Full gold.

NOSE Firm, peaty, smoky, very appetizing.

BODY Slightly sharp.

PALATE Very singular flavours, deftly balanced: a touch of iron,
leafy, ferny, peaty. Underlying earthy sweetness.
A fresh, young whisky, but no obvious spiritiness.

FINISH Sweet, then salty.

SCORE **80**

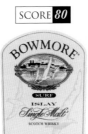

BOWMORE Surf, 43 vol

COLOUR Bright gold.

NOSE Fresh peat smoke.

BODY Light but smooth.

PALATE Light, dry, some nutty malt. A light, smooth, entry-level Bowmore.
Seems very tame at first, with a cookie-like maltiness, but the characteristic
ferny lavender, fragrant smoke and sea air gradually emerges.
One of the sweeter Bowmores.

FINISH Sweet smokiness. With water, later saltiness, honey-roast peanuts.

SCORE **78**

BOWMORE Dusk, Bordeaux (Claret) Wine Casked, 50 vol
This is a wine finish.

COLOUR Seems fractionally paler than claret finish. Orangey.

NOSE Seems slightly smokier than the version labelled Bowmore Claret.
Peaty. Leathery. Deliciously evocative and appetizing.

BODY Chewy.

PALATE Rich, fruity, smoky. Lots of flavour development: fruit,
nuts (almonds?), vanilla.

FINISH Toffeeish, oaky, smoky. Long.

SCORE **86**

BOWMORE Dawn, Ruby Port Cask Finished, 51.5 vol

COLOUR Very interesting pinkish amber.

NOSE Sooty smoke.

BODY Soft, textured, lightly toffeeish.

PALATE Smoky and fruity, lively.

FINISH Leafy, peaty. Slightly chewy.

SCORE 83

BOWMORE Voyage, Port Casked, 56 vol

COLOUR Bright orange.

NOSE Less obviously smoky. More perfumy. Drier.

BODY Less toffeeish than most port finishes.

PALATE Smooth, light on the tongue. Develops some fruitiness.

FINISH More lively. Seems crisp at first, but lingers
very warmly, with late saltiness.

SCORE 84

BOWMORE Claret, Bordeaux Wine Casked, 56 vol

COLOUR Rich, dark, honey.

NOSE Very big in both departments. Lots of recognizably claret-like
fruit-and-cedar notes – and a powerful response from Bowmore smokiness.

PALATE Bowmore beats Bordeaux.

FINISH Toffeeish (more port-like) fruit fights back convincingly. Oak keeps
the contestants apart. Finally a salty battle is won by the distillery character.

COMMENT The fighter beat the boxer, but it was wonderfully enjoyable.

SCORE 90

BOWMORE Cask Strength, 56 vol

Vatting of whiskies in mid-teens.

COLOUR Sunny, yellowy gold.

NOSE Sea air. Cereal-grain oiliness. Nutty. Malty sweetness. Syrupy. Scenty.

BODY Medium, substantial, smooth.

PALATE Earthy dryness. Some tasters have found "wet wool". Others find it
carbolic. Lively. Flavours not very well integrated.

FINISH Orange peel. Leafy. Ferns. Peaty.

SCORE 81

BRACKLA

PRODUCER John Dewar & Sons Ltd
REGION Highlands ISLAND Arran DISTRICT Speyside (Findhorn Valley)
ADDRESS Royal Brackla Distillery Cawdor, Nairn,
Inverness-shire, IV12 5QY TEL 01667 402002 VC

THE FIRST BOTTLING OF BRACKLA under Dewar's ownership was scheduled for 2003–04, but has been subject to delay. The bottling, at 10 years old, will replace a Flora and Fauna at the same age. The latter, and a Rare Malts bottling, were introduced in the 1990s, when Royal Brackla was owned by Diageo/United Distillers. The distillery was extended in the 1970s, and was twice rebuilt in earlier years. In 1835, Brackla became the first distillery to receive the royal warrant. This is granted to companies that supply goods to the royal household. The distillery was founded in 1812, on the estate of Cawdor, not far from Nairn, on the western fringes of Speyside.

HOUSE STYLE Fruity, cleansing, sometimes with a dry, hot finish.
A refresher or a pousse-café.

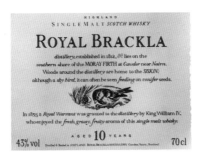

ROYAL BRACKLA 10-year-old,
Flora and Fauna, 43 vol

COLOUR Pale gold.

NOSE Smoky, slightly sulphurous, burnt, molasses.

BODY Medium, drying on the tongue.

PALATE Starts malty and sweet, becoming robustly fruity,
then spicy notes.

FINISH Cedary, smoky.

SCORE 74

ROYAL BRACKLA 20-year-old, Bottled 1998, Rare Malts, 59.8 vol

COLOUR Bright gold.

NOSE Flowery, melony, gingery.

BODY Rich, syrupy.

PALATE Very sweet. Honey. Anis.

FINISH Warming. Late angelica, pepper, cedary dryness. Slightly astringent.

SCORE **75**

ROYAL BRACKLA 1991, Distilled 1991, Bottled 2002, Butt No 6367, Signatory, 43 vol

COLOUR Greeny gold.

NOSE Sweet, oaty.

BODY Oaty. Oily. Slightly drying.

PALATE Marshmallow. Cookies. Oatcakes.

FINISH Curiously short. That typical dry, hot, finish.

SCORE **71**

An earlier bottling of a 1979 Brackla from Signatory, at 43 vol, was fruity and dryish, with a weak finish. SCORE 69

From the same bottler, a 1975 at 58.6 vol was a great deal more impressive, with an appetizing balance of restrained fruit and big spiciness. SCORE 75

"Green" BRACKLA 1975, 27-year-old, The Whisky Exchange, 59.7 vol

COLOUR Very dark. Somewhere between onyx and ironstone.

NOSE Saddlesoap.

BODY Lightly chewy.

PALATE Butter. Rum butter. Toffee. Rich and enjoyable.

FINISH Warming. Rummy. Gently oaky.

SCORE **77**

BRACKLA 1975, Murray McDavid "Mission" Series, 46 vol

COLOUR Deep gold.

NOSE Candyfloss, peach ice cream.

BODY Very rich and chewy.

PALATE Buttery. Mint humbugs. Liquorice.

FINISH Rooty. Some astringency.

SCORE **78**

An earlier bottling from Murray McDavid, a 1979 at 17 years old
from refill sherry, was drier and fruitier. SCORE 72

ROYAL BRACKLA 1975, 25-year-old,
The Coopers Choice, 43 vol

COLOUR Full gold to bronze.

NOSE Tea-like, perfumey.

BODY Slightly thin. Perfumey. Drying on the tongue.

PALATE Oily. Darjeeling tea. Malty.

FINISH Madeira-like. Tired.

SCORE **69**

An earlier Coopers Choice, a 1984, bottled in 1998 at 13 years old, was the
peatiest among the examples reviewed here. SCORE 76

ROYAL BRACKLA 15-year-old, Cadenhead, 58.2 vol

COLOUR Bright pale gold.

NOSE Lemon grass. Honeydew melon.

BODY Much richer.

PALATE Syrup, vanilla, ginger, then spicy smokiness.

FINISH Deliciously smoky, lively and warming. Quite aggressive.
A muscular malt of a style that is sadly vanishing
from the Highlands. Very enjoyable.

SCORE **77**

ROYAL BRACKLA 1975, Cask No 5467, Adelphi, 59.5 vol

COLOUR Burnished bronze to copper.

NOSE Rich heavy sherry. Butter. Rum. Moist fruitcake.

BODY Firm, smooth.

PALATE Chewy. Mint toffee. Treacle toffee.

FINISH A small explosion of spiciness. Ginger, allspice.
Hot, dry. Very long.

SCORE **78**

BRAEVAL

PRODUCER Chivas Brothers
REGION Highlands DISTRICT Speyside (Livet)
ADDRESS Chapeltown, Ballindalloch, Banffshire, AB37 9JS

BRAES OF GLENLIVET was the distillery's name when the whiskies reviewed here were distilled. This name had the merit of linking this distillery with its famous neighbour and parent – but made it difficult for the owners to dissuade other companies from treating Glenlivet as a region or style. The current name, Braeval, is an even older form. Brae is Scottish Gaelic for a "hillside" or "steep bank". Against a mountain ridge, this distillery is perched on a stream that feeds the River Livet. Despite its romantic name, and handsomely monastic appearance, it is a modern distillery, built between 1973 and 1978. It can be operated by one man, or even from its parent distillery. Braeval's whisky is a component of Chivas Regal, among others.

HOUSE STYLE Light, sweet, honeyish, with a zesty finish. Aperitif.

BRAES OF GLENLIVET 1975, Connoisseurs Choice, 40 vol

COLOUR Very pale greeny gold.

NOSE Fragrant. Vanilla.

BODY Dancing on the tongue.

PALATE Flowery. Herbal. Very appetizing.

FINISH Lightly dry. Zesty.

SCORE **77**

BRUICHLADDICH

PRODUCER The Bruichladdich Distillery Co. Ltd
REGION Islay DISTRICT Loch Indaal
ADDRESS Bruichladdich, Islay, Argyll, PA49 7UN
TEL 01496 850221 WEBSITE www.bruichladdich.com
EMAIL laddie@bruichladdich.com VC

ISLANDERS CARRIED CHILDREN on their shoulders to witness the historic moment. They lined the Islay shore to watch the reopening in 2001 of Bruichladdich, Scotland's most westerly distillery. The single morning plane, bringing more guests, was running late. The people on the shore scanned the skies. They had waited ten years; what was another hour? Lovers of Bruichladdich had come from London, Seattle, and Tokyo. There were tears of joy, a ceilidh, and fireworks at midnight.

The new owners, headed by Mark Reynier, of the London wine merchants La Reserve, bought the distillery with plenty of maturing stock. Like many distilleries, Bruichladdich has a miscellany of former bourbon barrels and sherry butts, some containing their first fill of Scotch whisky, others their second or third. In any distillery, the selection of casks to make a bottling is critical. On the new team at Bruichladdich, this task is in the hands of one of the principals, veteran Islay whisky maker Jim McEwan. In his early vattings, McEwan has juggled casks to shake off the notion that Bruichladdich is almost too mild to be an Islay whisky.

The whisky has long combined light, firm maltiness with suggestions of passion fruit, seaweed, and salt. McEwan has coaxed out more fruitiness and some sweetness, and has given everything more life and definition. The latter qualities are heightened by the use of the distillery's own water in reduction and by the lack of chill filtration. These changes in procedure were made possible by the installation in 2003 of a bottling line. Bruichladdich thus becomes the third distillery to have its own bottling line on site. (The others are Springbank and Glenfiddich/Balvenie.)

The new range began with whiskies at 10, 15, 17, and 20 years old. As these are vatted from stock, their ages will increase over the next decade, until spirit distilled by the new team is ready. An annual vintage is also being released, and a bottling of yet older whiskies under the rubric Legacy. Yet further ranges are planned – under the rubrics Links and Full Strength. At the distillery, visitors who wish to buy a bottle are invited to sample from three current casks. The visitors bottle their own whiskies, under the rubric Valinch. This refers to the oversized pipette that is used in distilleries to remove samples from casks. This device is sometimes known as a "thief".

When Bruichladdich reopened, McEwan immediately reset the stills to produce a spirit to his requirements. This will remain light to medium in its peating. Two new spirits were added, with a heavier peating.

Bruichladdich (pronounced "brook laddie") is on the north shore of Lochindaal. The new owners have promoted the nickname "The Laddie", and introduced labels in a pale seaside blue to match the paintwork at the distillery. The distillery's water rises from iron-tinged stone, and flows lightly over peat. Unlike the other Islay distilleries, Bruichladdich is separated from the sea loch, albeit only by a quiet, coastal road.

The distillery was founded in 1881, rebuilt in 1886 and, despite an extension in 1975, remains little changed. All maturing spirit in its ownership is warehoused on the island, either at Bruichladdich or in the vestiges of the Lochindaal distillery, at Port Charlotte, the nearest village. Some independent bottlers of Bruichladdich have labelled the whisky Lochindaal.

The name Port Charlotte will be used on one of the new heavily peated spirits from Bruichladdich. An even peatier whisky will be called Octomore, after another former distillery at Port Charlotte. Parts of that distillery survive as Octomore Farm, home of Port Charlotte's lighthouse keeper, fire fighter and lifeboatman – who was also one of the pipers on the opening day at Bruichladdich.

HOUSE STYLE Light to medium, very firm, hint of passion fruit, salty, spicy (mace?). Very drinkable. Aperitif.

BRUICHLADDICH 10-year-old, 46 vol

COLOUR Bright greeny gold.

NOSE Fresh, clean. Very soft "sea air". Wild flowers among
the dunes. A picnic at the beach.

BODY Satin.

PALATE Summer fruits. Passion fruit. Zesty, almost
effervescent, Bruichladdich at its fruitiest.

FINISH The flavours meld, with a late frisson of sharpness.

SCORE *82*

BRUICHLADDICH 15-year-old, 46 vol

COLOUR Bright yellow.

NOSE Sea air. Perfumy. Slightly sharp.

BODY Firm, cracker-like, malt background.

PALATE Starts with a clean, grassy sweetness, then manifests an
astonishingly long, lively series of small explosions. Peppery.

FINISH Underlying iron. Savoury. Appetizing.

SCORE *80*

BRUICHLADDICH 17-year-old, 46 vol

COLOUR Deep gold, with green tinge.

NOSE Firm, confident, fruity. Passion fruit and sea air.

BODY Firm. Very dry.

PALATE Powerful. Long, sustained development of fruity,
estery flavours.

FINISH Iron. Salt. Muscular. Stimulating.

SCORE *83*

BRUICHLADDICH 20-year-old, 46 vol

COLOUR Bright solid gold.

NOSE Seafront aromas. Like standing on the jetty at Bruichladdich.

BODY Smooth. Malty. Oily.

PALATE More cereal grain. More fruit. More salt.

FINISH Ironish, but also very flowery; more so than the others in this flight. A well-rounded whisky. Deceptively powerful, with a great depth of character.

SCORE 84

SOME VINTAGE-DATED BOTTLINGS
BRUICHLADDICH 1984, Vintage, 46 vol

COLOUR Pale gold.

NOSE Very flowery, leafy. Dry earth, sand. Sea air.

BODY Lightly creamy. Drying.

PALATE Salt and pepper.

FINISH Sandy. Cayenne pepper. Very peppery indeed. Try it with a Baltimore crab-feast or New Orleans crawdads.

SCORE 78

BRUICHLADDICH 1970, Vintage, 44.2 vol

COLOUR Medium to full gold.

NOSE Heavy, blossomy aroma. Fruit trees. Fresh limes.

BODY Oily.

PALATE Gentle, slow start. Leafy, malty. Brooding.

FINISH Surge of spicy, sandy flavours. Very spicy.

SCORE 80

SOME VALINCH BOTTLINGS
BRUICHLADDICH 1990, Cask No 998, 60.2 vol

COLOUR Gold, green tinge.

NOSE Dry. Slightly peaty.

BODY Marshmallow.

PALATE Bay leaves, peppercorns, ground white pepper.

FINISH Grainy, savoury, dry, hot.

SCORE **78**

BRUICHLADDICH 1966, Legacy, 40.6 vol

COLOUR Full gold. Orange tinge.

NOSE Estery. Apple crumble.

BODY Lean.

PALATE Estery. Calvados. Cider. Some refreshingly fruity acidity.

FINISH Passion fruit.

SCORE **82**

BRUICHLADDICH 1986, Cask No 700, 53.3 vol

COLOUR Full greeny gold.

NOSE Grassy. Dunes. Salty.

BODY Beeswax. Oily.

PALATE More maltiness and especially fruitiness.

FINISH Still hot and dry, but softened by the oiliness of the spirit.

SCORE **78**

BRUICHLADDICH 1983, Fresh Sherry Butt, 58.8 vol

COLOUR Mandarin orange.

NOSE Pralines. Bitter chocolate. Filled with orange cream.

BODY Rich and creamy.

PALATE Sweet. Gingery.

FINISH Very spicy More ginger. Lively.

SCORE **79**

BRUICHLADDICH 1972, Cask No 9, 48.8 vol

COLOUR Very full gold.

NOSE Clean, sweet. Sea breezes.

BODY Smooth, oily.

PALATE Temptingly approachable. Very expressive and full of flavour.
Orange and passion fruit meld with spicy, salty notes.

FINISH Gently dry. Very appetizing.

SCORE **79**

BRUICHLADDICH 1970, Cask No 5079, 48.2 vol

COLOUR Apricot.

NOSE Malty. Dusty. Short pastry.

BODY Syrupy. Juicy.

PALATE Fruity. Delicious. The maltiness and fruitiness of Bruichladdich
at its best. Bring on the clootie dumplings.

FINISH Late perfuminess. Fragrant. Resiny.

SCORE **80**

SOME INDEPENDENT BOTTLINGS OF BRUICHLADDICH
BRUICHLADDICH 12-year-old, Royal Mile Whiskies,
Distilled July 1985, Bottled April 1998, 336 Numbered Bottles, 46 vol

COLOUR Very pale, clear, greenish.

NOSE Fruity, vegetal, wild garlic.

BODY Rounded, dry.

PALATE Malty, marshmallow-like. Fruity.

FINISH Dusty. Herbal. Light, balancing bitterness.

SCORE **76**

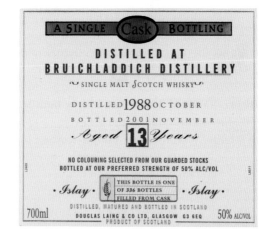

BRUICHLADDICH 13-year-old, Distilled October 1988,
Bottled November 2001, The Old Malt Cask, 50 vol

COLOUR Vinho verde.

NOSE Freshly cut grass.

BODY Syrupy but light.

PALATE Vegetal. Faint peatiness. Ash. Earthy.

FINISH Fruity. Dry.

SCORE **76**

BRUICHLADDICH 13-year-old, Adelphi, 57.9 vol

NOSE Heather. Flowery. Mint. Menthol. Faintly medicinal. Salt.

PALATE Very light but oily. Passion fruit. Grassy.

FINISH Peppermint, drying.

COMMENT Interesting, but not typical.

SCORE **72**

Also from Adelphi, a 1970 vintage at 30 years old and 49.4 vol, released in 2001, had a bright, golden colour; a palate that was fruity, but also full of almondy nuttiness; and a late crescendo of mace-like spiciness. SCORE 80

BRUICHLADDICH 1988, Gordon & MacPhail, Cask Nos 1955 and 1956, Distilled 25 October 1988, Bottled 3 January 2003, Cask Strength, 54.2 vol

COLOUR Bright gold, with a greenish tinge.

NOSE Perfumy. Talc-like.

BODY Slippery-smooth.

PALATE Good malty background. Dry and, by the standards of Bruichladdich, quite a peat accent.

FINISH Sting of peat, then lingering dryness.

SCORE **80**

Also from Gordon & MacPhail, in their Cask Strength series, a 1969 Bruichladdich, bottled in 2003 at 52.5 vol. This is sherry-led expression, but with a beautiful interplay of creamy maltiness and salty flavours. For a picnic by Lochindaal? SCORE 80

An earlier Gordon & MacPhail bottling of a 1969 Bruichladdich, at 54.3, emerged with a classically seaweedy aroma; a malty, cakey palate; and a salty finish; while still having enjoyed a close encounter with sherry. SCORE 81

BRUICHLADDICH 16-year-old, Distilled 1986, Bottled March 2003, Bourbon Hogshead, Cadenhead, 55.9 vol

COLOUR Primrose.

NOSE Salty, sandy.

BODY Slippery-smooth. Seems to slip away.

PALATE Creamy, then fruity, then sandy. Three big hits.
Bruichladdich in assertively unfancy mood.

FINISH Slightly blood-like. One of the hits connected.
It's not real blood, just passion fruit.

SCORE 78

BRUICHLADDICH 1986, Scott's Selection, 57.2 vol

COLOUR Very pale, bright, vinho verde.

NOSE Leafy, grassy, peaty.

BODY Syrupy, but very light.

PALATE Oaty, dusty, developing some sweetness.

FINISH A touch of lactic acidity. Appetizing and refreshing.

SCORE 77

BRUICHLADDICH 1970, Raw Cask, 53.8 vol

COLOUR Deep gold. Almost orange marmalade.

NOSE Warm, sweet, fruity.

BODY Densely creamy.

PALATE Sweet. Oily. Slightly perfumey. Smoky. Peaty.

FINISH Some maritime notes.

SCORE 77

BRUICHLADDICH 26-year-old, Stillman's Dram, 45 vol

COLOUR Full gold to amber.

NOSE Spicy (some tasters have found mace),
fruity, sherry, lightly toasty oak, sea air.

BODY Medium, very smooth.

PALATE Light oak, malt, salt, passion fruit, sherry sweetness.
Flavours tightly locked together.

FINISH Lightly toasty oak, seaweed, salt and pepper.

SCORE 77

BRUICHLADDICH 33-year-old, Distilled May 1969, Bottled December 2002, Cask No 2329, Duncan Taylor, 48.7 vol

COLOUR Full gold.

NOSE Very perfumey.

BODY Light, lapping on tongue.

PALATE Butter, syrupy but dryish. Fennel. Italian spices.

FINISH Restrained but tasty. Appetizing.

SCORE **79**

OTHER VERSIONS OF BRUICHLADDICH

A 25-year-old (1968), at 53.8 vol, from Cadenhead,
is flowery and complex. SCORE 78

A 1968, at 52.9 vol, in Signatory's 10th anniversary series, is sherryish,
malty, and salty, with a distinct smoky fragrance in the finish. SCORE 79

A 1965, at 53.5, from Gordon & MacPhail, is even
more sherryish, with lots of oak and smoke. SCORE 78

BUNNAHABHAIN

PRODUCER Burn Stewart Distillers plc
REGION Islay DISTRICT North Shore
ADDRESS Port Askaig, Islay, Argyll, PA46 7RP
TEL 01496 840646 WEBSITE www.blackbottle.com
EMAIL enquiries@burnstewartdistillers.com VC

A NEW LIFE for the elusive Bunnahabhain set the seal on the Islay revival in the new millennium. Elusive? Bunnahabhain has the most hidden location of the Islay distilleries, the most superficially difficult name (pronounced "boona'hhavn"), and the most delicate whisky. Even its new owners, since 2003, are the smallest group in the industry. Bunnahabhain joins the Tobermory and Deanston distilleries in the Burn Stewart group, well known in the Far East for its Scottish Leader blends. With the acquisition of Bunnahabhain, Burn Stewart also gain the cult blend Black Bottle, which contains malts from all the Islay distilleries. At the time of the takeover, Burn Stewart had recently joined the worldwide group that includes the "super-premium" vodka Belvedere and has as its unlikely flagship Angostura Bitters.

The Bunnahabhain distillery had been well maintained by its previous owners, Edrington, but both production and marketing of its products had been sporadic. Stocks were sinking – not a happy state of affairs for the whisky whose packaging bears the words of the Islay anthem, "Westering Home". Despite its delicacy, Bunnahabhain does have a touch of Islay maritime character.

The distillery, expanded in 1963, was built in 1881. It is set around a courtyard in a remote cove. A kerb has been built to stops visitors' cars from rolling into the sea. A ships' bell, salvaged from a nearby wreck, hangs from the wall. It was at one time used to summon the manager from his home if he were urgently needed. The distillery's water rises through limestone, and because it is piped to the distillery, it does not pick up peat on the way. The stills are large, in the style that the industry refers to as onion-shaped.

HOUSE STYLE Fresh, sweetish, nutty, herbal, salty. Aperitif.

BUNNAHABHAIN 12-year-old, 43 vol

COLOUR	Gold.

NOSE Remarkably fresh, sweet, sea-air aroma.

BODY Light to medium, firm.

PALATE Gentle, clean, nutty-malty sweetness.

FINISH Very full flavour development. Refreshing.

 SCORE **77**

BUNNAHABHAIN Auld Acquaintance Hogmanay Edition, 1968, Bottle 1 of 2000, 43.8 vol

COLOUR Orange satin, with pinkish tinge.

NOSE A rich, moist Dundee cake. Toasted nuts. Salty. Sea breezes.

BODY Creamy.

PALATE Malted milk. Chocolate. Nonetheless avoids
being cloying. Deftly balanced.

FINISH Dark cocoa powder.

COMMENT A brilliantly sunny winter's day; a long walk by the sea in the
late afternoon; oatcakes and cheese; Dundee cake; a dram at dusk. Still
recognizably Bunnahabhain, but so different. More such essays, please.

SCORE **86**

BUNNAHABHAIN 1968, The Family Silver, 40 vol

Now hard to find.

COLOUR Attractive pale walnut.

NOSE Fragrant sea air and polished wood.

BODY Firm, creamy.

PALATE Depth of flowery nuttiness and creamy flavours.

FINISH Delightful teasing subtlety of nuttiness and gently salty sea air.

SCORE 79

BUNNAHABHAIN 1966, Cask No 4379, 46.1 vol

COLOUR Blood orange

NOSE Smoky. Fresh sea breezes. Could that be the puffer
leaving for Glasgow?

BODY Rich, creamy.

PALATE Fresh, concentrated flavours. Unusually estery. Ginger-toffee.
Becoming nutty. Very concentrated flavours.

FINISH Dusty. Spice-shop. Long. Warming

SCORE 80

BUNNAHABHAIN 1963, 750 bottles, 42.9 vol

COLOUR Gold, with a touch of olive.

NOSE Cashew nuts.

BODY Light and satin smooth.

PALATE Gunpowder tea. Ginseng.

FINISH Just enough bitterness to be appetizing. Salty.

SCORE 83

SOME INDEPENDENT BOTTLINGS
BUNNAHABHAIN 20-year-old, James MacArthur, 57 vol

COLOUR Deep orange satin.

NOSE Mango chutney. Pickled walnuts.

BODY Oily, buttery.

PALATE Toffee. Japanese plum wine.

FINISH Sweetness and bitter coffee. Nice drink. Where's the whisky?

SCORE 71

BUNNAHABHAIN 1980, Cask No 9064, Bottled 2002,
Unchillfiltered, Berry Brothers and Rudd, 55.6 vol

COLOUR Iridescent greeny gold.

NOSE A walk by the seafront.

BODY Extraordinarily oily.

PALATE Sweet, caramel, shortbread.

FINISH Sudden surge of salt. Slight astringency.

SCORE **79**

BUNNAHABHAIN 22-year-old, Distilled 1980, Bottled 2003
Cask No 5899, Dun Bheagan, 58 vol

COLOUR Full, refractive, gold.

NOSE Expressive, full, honeyish.

BODY Light, firm, smooth.

PALATE Rounded. Some vanilla. Honey. Nutty. Salty.

FINISH Spicy. Salty. Long. Appetizing.

SCORE **81**

BUNNAHABHAIN 35-year-old, Distilled March 1967,
Bottled September 2002, Hart Brothers, Cask Strength, 40.5 vol

COLOUR Deep, iridescent, gold.

NOSE Dried fruits. Caramel. Smoke from an open fire.
Some cellar character.

BODY Surprisingly light.

PALATE Sweetness, saltiness and some oakiness.

FINISH Some musty woodiness.

SCORE **79**

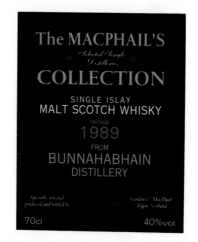

BUNNAHABHAIN 1989, The MacPhail's Selection, 40 vol

COLOUR Full gold.

NOSE Fragrant. New leather upholstery in a luxury car.

BODY Surprisingly light.

PALATE Cream toffee. Shortbread. Afternoon tea.

FINISH Ginger cookies. Spicy.

SCORE 79

An earlier bottling of a 1989 Bunnahabhain by Gordon & MacPhail was richer all round: sherryish, gingery, toasty, salty. A breakfast whisky for the truly decadent. SCORE 80

BUNNAHABHAIN 1982, Distilled 1982, Bottled 2001, Scotts Selection, 52.5 vol

COLOUR White wine.

NOSE Light. Fragrant. Some vanilla. Hint of lemon grass.

BODY Slightly oily but very light.

PALATE Light, sweet, toast.

FINISH Late surge of salt. Quite stinging – and sustained.

SCORE 78

From the same bottler, a 1981 Bunnahabhain, at 51 vol, is more flowery and complex. SCORE 80
A 1969, at 40.1 vol, is drier and cedary, but seems to have lost some dimension with age. SCORE 79

BUNNAHABHAIN 1979, Murray McDavid, Bourbon Barrel, 46 vol

COLOUR Old gold.

NOSE Salt, fresh limes. Citrus peel.

BODY Creamy. Oily.

PALATE Lightly nutty. Clean, grassy, peat.

FINISH Fragrant.

COMMENT Surprising peatiness, but without smokiness.

SCORE **80**

From the same bottler, a 1979 Bunnahabhain from sherry wood
has vibrant flavours of toffee, ginger, and malt, but they are
eventually overpowered by the wood. SCORE 76

BUNNAHABHAIN 36-year-old, Distilled June 1966,
Bottled November 2002, Cask No 4872, Duncan Taylor, 40.1 vol

COLOUR Dark gold.

NOSE Fresh. Salty. Harbourfront.

BODY Surprisingly light. Drying.

PALATE Cookie-like. Chocolate digestives? Very subtle flavours,
mellowed by age. Some Maderisation?

FINISH Very late salt, a reminder of the whisky's maritime youth.

SCORE **79**

CAOL ILA

PRODUCER Diageo
REGION Islay DISTRICT North shore
ADDRESS Port Askaig, Islay, Argyll, PA46 7RL
TEL 01496 302760 Distillery has shop
WEBSITE www.discovering-distilleries.com/www.malts.com

AT THE ISLAY FESTIVAL OF 2002, three stylishly boxed expressions of Caol Ila were released by owners Diageo, as part of a new range with the rubric "Hidden Malts". Public attending the festival were invited to join whisky writers at the tasting. The tools of modern marketing were much in evidence, but so was the patrimony of Islay malt. Manager Billy Stichell, an Ileach, with four generations of family in the industry, provided an accomplished commentary. It was the first time he had spoken in public.

It was further announced at Caol Ila that Hidden Malts would also emanate from another three Diageo distilleries: Clynelish, Glen Elgin, and Glen Ord. For the moment each of them would release only one age.

The launch of Caol Ila in an official bottling, in such a public way, and implicitly as the flagship in the new range, finally confirmed that it was far from hidden. Its malts had become more readily available, and appreciated, in recent years.

The name, pronounced "cull-eela", means "Sound of Islay". The Gaelic word "caol" is more familiar as "kyle". The distillery is in a cove near Port Askaig. The large windows of the still-house overlook the Sound of Islay, across which the ferry chugs to the nearby island of Jura. The best view of the distillery is from the ferry.

Its 1970s façade is beginning to be accepted as a classic of the period, after years of being deemed brutal. Inside, the distillery is both functional and attractive: a copper hood on the lauter tun; brass trim; wash stills like flat onions, spirit stills more pear-shaped; Oregon pine washbacks. Some of the structure dates from 1879, and the distillery was founded in 1846.

Behind the distillery, a hillside covered in fuchsias, foxgloves, and wild roses rises toward the peaty loch where the water gathers. It is quite salty and minerally, having risen from limestone. As a modern, well-engineered distillery, making whisky for several blends, it has over the years used different levels of peating. This is apparent in the independent bottlings.

HOUSE STYLE Oily, olive-like. Junipery, fruity, estery. A wonderful aperitif.

THE HIDDEN MALTS

CAOL ILA 12-year-old, 43 vol

COLOUR Vinho verde.

NOSE Soft. Juniper. Garden mint. Grass. Burnt grass.

BODY Lightly oily. Simultaneously soothing and appetizing.

PALATE Lots of flavour development. Becoming spicy. Vanilla, nutmeg, white mustard. Complex. Flavours combine with great delicacy.

FINISH Very long.

 SCORE **83**

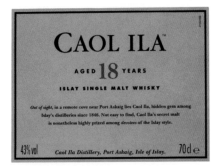

CAOL ILA 18-year-old, 43 vol

COLOUR Fullest of the three. Fino sherry on a sunny day.

NOSE Fragrant. Menthol. Markedly vegetal. Nutty vanilla pod.

BODY Firmer. Much bigger.

PALATE More assertively expressive. Sweeter. Leafy sweetness. Spring greens. Crushed almonds. Rooty, cedary.

FINISH Powerful reverberations of a remarkable whisky.

SCORE **86**

CAOL ILA Cask Strength, 55 vol

COLOUR Palest of the three, remarkably pale. White wine.

NOSE Intense. Sweetish, smokiness. Coconut. Grapefruit.

PALATE A very lively interplay of flavours, with malty sweetness fruity esteriness and peppery dryness. Perfumy, with suggestions of thyme.

FINISH The flavours come together in a rousing finale, with the alcohol providing a back beat.

SCORE 85

SOME EARLIER OFFICIAL BOTTLINGS, NOW HARD TO FIND

CAOL ILA 15-year-old, Flora and Fauna, 43 vol

COLOUR Fino sherry, bright.

NOSE Aromatic, complex.

BODY Light, very firm, smooth.

PALATE Rounder, with the flavours more combined.

FINISH Oily and warming enough to keep out the sea.

SCORE 80

CAOL ILA 1981, Bottled 1997,
Cask Strength Limited Bottling, 63.8 vol

COLOUR Bright limey yellow.

NOSE Fragrant peat smoke, juniper, seaweed. Very appetizing.

BODY Firm, oily.

PALATE Assertively oily, junipery. Late surge of peaty dryness. Very dry.

FINISH Wonderfully long and warming.

SCORE 82

CAOL ILA 20-year-old, Bottled 1996, 57.86 vol
150th Anniversary Edition

COLOUR Orange.

NOSE Sweet seaweed. Juniper. Pine nuts.

BODY Medium, smooth, rounded.

PALATE Enormously complex and distinctive. Nutty, appetizingly seaweedy, peppery, salty. Tightly combined flavours. Beautifully balanced.

FINISH Sherry, toasty oak, seaweed, lemon skin, pepper.

SCORE 85

SOME RARE MALTS
CAOL ILA 20-year-old, Rare Malts, 61.3 vol
Becoming hard to find.

COLOUR Full greeny gold.

NOSE Powerfully aromatic. Roasted peppers. Olives. Salt.

BODY Medium but gentle, oily, soothing.

PALATE Oily. Roasted peppers, olives, lemon juice.

FINISH Dry, junipery, vine leaves, stemmy. Intense, expressive.

SCORE 83

CAOL ILA 21-year-old, Rare Malts, 61.3 vol

Becoming hard to find.

COLOUR Attractive, subtle pale gold.

NOSE Very fresh. Sea air.

BODY Medium, oily, smooth.

PALATE Astonishingly fresh. More sea air. Almost a sandy taste.
Fresh seaweed. Sweet and dry, olivey. Sustained development of flavours.

FINISH Big, long. Expressive. Smoky fragrance. Appetizing. Oaky dryness.

SCORE **82**

CAOL ILA 23-year-old, Rare Malts, 61.7 vol

Released 2002.

COLOUR Warm gold to pale amber.

NOSE Distinctly peaty. A robust, straight-ahead,
Caol Ila in traditional Islay style.

BODY Firm, dry.

PALATE Peaty, gritty, salty.

FINISH Sweet, smoky. Some underlying estery fruitiness.

SCORE **84**

SOME GORDON & MACPHAIL BOTTLINGS
CAOL ILA 1988, Gordon & MacPhail,
Cask Strength Series, 57.6 vol

COLOUR White wine.

NOSE Hugely peppery.

BODY Lightly syrupy.

PALATE Flowery. Oily, buttery. Then a surge of pepper.

FINISH A smoky explosion.

SCORE **84**

CAOL ILA 1988, Connoisseurs Choice, 40 vol

COLOUR White wine. Very pale.

NOSE White pepper. Juniper.

BODY Light. Soft.

PALATE Vegetal, smoky.

FINISH Delicate leafy, dry.

SCORE **79**

GORDON & MACPHAIL WOOD FINISHES, ALL AT 40 VOL

CAOL ILA 1988, Calvados finish. Pale, shimmery, greeny gold. Fruity, tannic notes in aroma and palate? SCORE 79

CAOL ILA 1988, Claret finish. Warm gold. Starts enticingly, with sweet, creamy flavours, but becomes very astringent. SCORE 77

CAOL ILA 1988, Cognac finish. Quite big-bodied. A heavyweight struggle between the world's two great spirits. The whisky wins, but the Cognac goes the distance and even rallies in the final round. Extraordinarily long.
SCORE 81

CAOL ILA 1990, Vintage Cognac finish. Much smoother proceedings. Restrained, concluding in a gentlemanly draw. A charming after-dinner companion. SCORE 80

CAOL ILA 1990, Port finish. Tell-tale pinkish-bronze colour. Nutty. Port establishes a harmony with the maritime notes of the whisky. SCORE 80

CAOL ILA 1988, Sherry finish. The warm amber colour delivers all it promises. Dried apricots, spices, and lightly salty Islay character. A dryish but deftly balanced whisky. SCORE 79

SOME INDEPENDENT BOTTLINGS OF CAOL ILA

CAOL ILA 1983, 19-year-old, Unchillfiltered, Berry Brothers & Rudd, 46 vol. Pale gold. Textured. Very fruity and spicy. Sweetish and warming.
SCORE 77

CAOL ILA, Distilled 1992, Bottled 2000, Black Adder Raw Cask, 58.6 vol. White wine colour. Starts creamy and sweet; becomes appetizingly dry, with suggestions of sea-salt. Well-rounded. SCORE 78.
From the same bottler, a 1990, at 58.5, is oilier, drier, and longer. SCORE 79

CAOL ILA 1993, 10-year-old, Cadenhead, 60.8 vol. Bright gold. Fresh sea air on the nose. Lemony fruitiness in the palate. Salty dryness in the finish.
SCORE 78

CAOL ILA 1990, 12-year-old, Rum Finish, Chieftain's Choice, 46 vol. Medicinal aroma; sudden rush of peat. Big, fresh flavours. Creamy sweetness in background presumably from rum. SCORE 79

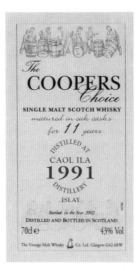

CAOL ILA 1991, 11-year-old, The Coopers Choice, 43 vol. Very pale, greenish. Clean, oily, light, dry. Grassy crispness in the finish. Reminiscent of bison-leaf vodka. SCORE 77

CAOL ILA 1992, 10-year-old Dun Bheagan, 43 vol. Very pale colour. Fresh aroma. Soft, lean malt character. Becoming fruity and junipery. Then crisp, grassy finish. SCORE 77

CAOL ILA 1990, 12-year-old, Duncan Taylor Whisky Galore, 46 vol. Greenish tinge. Quite big bodied. Oily. Mustardy. SCORE 77

CAOL ILA 23-year-old, Kingsbury, 60 vol. Primrose. Oily, waxy, junipery. Hints of blackcurrant. Where is the whiff of the sea? It blows in eventually. SCORE 77

CAOL ILA 1989, Bourbon Cask. Murray MacDavid, 46 vol. Aromatic, nutty. Palate warm, oily, butter. Vanilla. Late, laconic, mustardy finish. SCORE 77 An earlier counterpart, distilled in 1989, had more of the house character, notably a touch of iodine. SCORE 77

CAOL ILA 1991, Port Wood, Signatory, 48 vol. Very pale, white wine. Touch of estery, figgy sweetness. Nuttiness and sandy dryness in the middle. Late fruity (brambles) warmth. SCORE 78. A 1989, at 46 vol, in Signatory's unchillfiltered series, was briny, medicinal and a fine example of the more peated style of Caol Ila. SCORE 83. A 1981 Caol Ila at 58.2 vol had a fuller amber colour and big flavours, with sherry, spices, and oak Finished dry but not astringent. SCORE 82

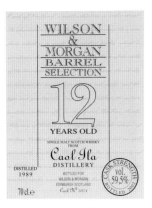

CAOL ILA 1989, 12-year-old, Wilson & Morgan, 59.5 vol. Very pale greenish. Oily, viscous. Cereal-grain notes. Touch of peat. A winter warmer. SCORE 77

CAPERDONICH

PRODUCER Chivas Brothers
REGION Highlands DISTRICT Speyside (Rothes)
ADDRESS Rothes, Morayshire, AB38 7BN

LESSER KNOWN PARTNER to the renowned Glen Grant. The two distilleries, under the same ownership, are across the street from one another in the whisky town of Rothes. This little Speyside town has five distilleries. Caperdonich, founded in 1898, was rebuilt in 1965 and extended in 1967. Its name is said to indicate a "secret source". From the start, it has been a back-up to Glen Grant. When young, the malts of both distilleries are light and fragrant in their bouquet, medium-bodied, and nutty-tasting.

Of the two, Caperdonich is perhaps a dash fruitier and slightly more smoky. It, too, is a component of the Chivas Regal blend. The Chivas group kept a tight control of its malts during the last years of its ownership by Seagram, of Canada. This policy seems to have been maintained since the takeover by Pernod Ricard, of France. There are official bottlings of Glen Grant, but not of Caperdonich. The independent bottlings tend to be very old. The fourth edition of *Malt Whisky Companion* commented "Some malt lovers would dismiss them for an overpowering oakiness; others would love them for their sherry and intensity." In the years since the last edition, the industry has used less peat and been stingier with sherry. Bottlings that have become available since the fourth edition are each two or three decades old, less intense, oaky, and sherryish, with more grainy notes.

HOUSE STYLE Dried fruits, grainy, toasty. Breakfast? After dinner?

CAPERDONICH 1980, Gordon & MacPhail, 40 vol

COLOUR Yellow-amber.

NOSE Chocolate-covered dates. Fruity. Cherry brandy.

BODY Firm. Very smooth. Silky.

PALATE Oily. Hazelnut liqueur. Very mild indeed.

FINISH Restrained ginger. Woody dryness, as though the tongue had encountered the stick in a lollipop.

SCORE 74

CAPERDONICH 1979, Signatory, 43 vol

COLOUR Extraordinarily pale. Almost "white", with a tinge of green.

NOSE Lollipop sticks. A suggestion of vanilla. A hint of raspberry.

BODY Very light but slightly syrupy.

PALATE Toasted marshmallow.

FINISH Very lightly spicy.

SCORE 69

CAPERDONICH 1970, Duncan Taylor & Co., 51.7 vol

COLOUR Full yellow gold.

NOSE A crusty loaf, fresh from the oven, dusted with flour and sitting on a wooden bread board.

BODY Medium. Chewy. Mozzarella on a pizza.

PALATE Malty. Grainy. Slightly vegetal.

FINISH Mustard cress. Hot.

SCORE 75

CAPERDONICH 1968, Lombard, 46 vol

COLOUR Gold, with faint green tinge.

NOSE Slightly smoky. Oily. Linseed.

PALATE Bath Oliver biscuits. Some perfumy notes. (Lavender. Potpourri?)

FINISH Dry. Drying. Woody.

SCORE 79

CARDHU/CARDOW

PRODUCER Diageo
REGION Highlands DISTRICT Speyside
ADDRESS Aberlour, Banffshire, AB38 7RY
TEL 01340 872555 WEBSITE www.discovering-distilleries.com VC

A CONTROVERSIAL CHANGE, seen by some whisky lovers as a threat to the future of single malts, lay behind the adjustment to this distillery's name in 2003.

Such a threat could not issue from a less congruous location. Cardow has several claims to renown. It provided the industry with a dynastic family, the Cummings, and contributed twice to the tradition of strong women running distilleries. Helen Cummings distilled illegally on the family farm. Her daughter-in-law, Elizabeth, developed the legal distillery, which produced malt whisky as a substantial component of the Johnnie Walker blends.

The distillery was founded as Cardow (Gaelic for "black rock", after a nearby point on the river Spey). An alternative spelling, "Cardhu", better reflecting the pronunciation, was adopted when the distillery began to promote a bottled single malt. This mild, easily drinkable whisky was launched to compete with the popular malts in the early days of consumer interest.

It was a modest success in the United Kingdom, but enjoyed far greater sales in new markets for malts, such as France and Spain. In the latter country, the distinction between malts and blends seems to engage the consumer less than the age statement. Cardhu found itself head to head with the blend Chivas Regal, both being 12 years old. The Spaniards' taste for Scotch whisky is so great that the success of Cardhu in that market rendered it the world's fastest growing malt, outstripping the capacity of the distillery. Rather than "rationing" Cardhu, or increasing its price, owners Diageo decided to drop the designation "single" malt and substitute the imprecise "pure". Thus Cardhu was consumed by its own success.

The distillery, having reverted to the name Cardow, continues to produce whisky for bottling as Cardhu, but this is augmented by other Speyside distilleries under the same ownership.

Had Cardhu never been the name of a distillery and a single malt, there would be no cause for concern. Given that Cardhu was a single malt for between 30 and 40 years, and is now merely "pure" (meaning, in this instance, a vatted malt), there is a risk of confusion. The singularity of the name has been compromised, however good the "pure" malt.

How good, in this instance, is the pure malt? It seems a very good match, perhaps fractionally bigger: darker, oilier, nuttier, and drier. Initially, the only other component whisky to have been identified is Glendullan, but there are at least two others.

Diageo concedes the danger of confusion, and has worked hard to steer clear, but does not rule out more such transformations. If a single malt can, without changing its name, become less singular, how long before devotees become sceptics?

Other drinks try to set apart something special: microbrewed beers, real ales, first-growth clarets, Napoleon brandies, … but none is as clearly defined as a single malt. It would be monumentally foolish to squander that advantage. The tasting notes below refer to Cardhu as a single malt.

HOUSE STYLE In the original form: light, smooth, delicate; an easy-drinking malt. Greater ages are richer, more toffeeish, and often work well with desserts.

CARDHU 12-year-old, 40 vol
Was widely distributed, and therefore still to be found, though it has been replaced by Cardhu Pure Malt.

COLOUR Pale.

NOSE Light, appetizing, hints of greengage, and the gentlest touch of smoke.

BODY Light and smooth.

PALATE Light to medium in flavour, with the emphasis on malty sweetness and vanilla.

FINISH A lingering, syrupy sweetness, but also a rounder dryness with late hints of peat, although again faint.

SCORE 72

CARDHU 1974, Signatory, 54.1 vol

COLOUR Distinctive reddish orange. Reminiscent of blood oranges.

NOSE Very rich and toffeeish.

BODY Syrupy. Soothing.

PALATE Treacle toffee. Underlying fruity complexity. Apricots. Nectarines. Plums.

FINISH Perfumy. Fragrant. Smoky. Slightly bitter.

SCORE 75

CARDHU 1973, 27-year-old, Cask Strength, Rare Malts, 60.02 vol

COLOUR Full, bright, greeny gold.

NOSE Much more peaty than today's Cardhu. Hint of hessian, peat fire. Oaky.

BODY Big. Very malty. Marshmallow-like.

PALATE Complex. Toasted marshmallows. Very assertive. Softens a little with
late flavour development. Slightly burnt grassiness and fruitiness.
Grated tangerine peel. Lemons. Just a hint of sherbet.

FINISH Firm, very dry, lingering.

SCORE 77

An earlier Rare Malts bottling of Cardhu (distilled 1973), at 60.5 vol,
has a richer, marshmallow maltiness, a suggestion of crystalized fruit,
and a hint of tangerine in the finish. SCORE 76

CLYNELISH

PRODUCER Diageo
REGION Highlands DISTRICT Northern Highlands
ADDRESS Brora, Sutherland, KW9 6LR
TEL 01408 623003
WEBSITE www.discovering-distilleries.com/www.malts.com VC

CULT STATUS SEEMS TO have been conferred in recent years on the Clynelish distillery and its adjoining predecessor, Brora, which command the middle stretch of the northern Highlands.

The appeal of their malts lies partly in their coastal aromas and flavours. Sceptics may question the brineyness of coastal malts, but some bottlings of Brora and Clynelish make that characteristic hard to deny. They are the most maritime of the East Coast malts, and on the Western mainland are challenged only by Springbank.

For a time, the big flavours of Clynelish and Brora were heightened by the use of well-peated malts. Clynelish cultists are always keen to identify distillates from this period. A similar preoccupation is to distinguish malts made at the Brora distillery from those that were distilled at Clynelish.

The two distilleries stand next door to each other on a landscaped hillside near the fishing and golfing resort of Brora. They overlook the coastal road as it heads toward the northernmost tip of the Scottish mainland.

The older of the two distilleries was built in 1819 by the Duke of Sutherland to use grain grown by his tenants. This distillery was originally known as Clynelish: the first syllable rhymes with "wine", the second with "leash". The name means "slope of the garden". After a century and half, a new Clynelish was built in 1967–68, but demand was sufficient for the two distilleries to operate in tandem for a time. They were initially known as Clynelish 1 and 2. Eventually, the older distillery was renamed Brora. It worked sporadically until 1983.

Brora is a traditional 19th-century distillery, in local stone (now overgrown), with a pagoda. Clynelish's stills greet the world through the floor-to-ceiling windows, in the classic design of the period, with a fountain to soften the façade.

Inside, the still-house has its own peculiarities, in which the deposits in the low wines and feints receivers play a part. The result is an oily, beeswax background flavour – another distinctive feature.

For years, this robustly distinctive malt was available only as a 12-year-old, bearing a charmingly amateurish label, from Ainslie and Heilbron, a DCL subsidiary, whose blends were given brand names of equal charm. The Real McTavish was a good example. Since the United Distillers and Diageo eras, Brora and Clynelish have been positively anthologous. Editions have been issues by Flora and Fauna, The Rare Malts, Cask Strength Limited Editions, Hidden Malts, as well as Special Releases.

HOUSE STYLE Seaweedy, spicy. Mustard-and-oil.
With a roast-beef sandwich.

CLYNELISH, 14-year-old, 46 vol, Hidden Malts

*Replaces more seaweedy Flora and Fauna edition reviewed in
the fourth edition of* Malt Whisky Companion.

COLOUR Bright pale orange.

NOSE Fragrant. A stroll in the sand dunes.

BODY Firm, oily and seductively smoky.

PALATE Firm hit of cleansing flavours. Coriander. Orange. Dry. Spicy.
Distinctively mustardy.

FINISH The spiciness becomes yet more perfumy and exotic.
Both satisfying (without being satiating).

SCORE **81**

BRORA 1977, 24-year-old, Cask Strength, The Rare Malts, 56.1 vol

COLOUR Very bright primrose. Lime tinge?

NOSE Very flowery. Camomile. Suggestion of sweet lime.

BODY Lightly oily.

PALATE Lively, fruity, refreshing. Distinctive gorse or whin; that coconut flavour. Then fresh lime, then peppery seaweed.

FINISH Sandy, grainy, mustardy. Wasabi?
Does the 18th hole at Brora serve sushi?

SCORE **84**

BRORA 30-year-old, Special Release, Limited Bottling of 3000, 52.4 vol

COLOUR Greeny gold.

NOSE Fruity. Fresh limes. Indian lime pickle.

BODY Light but firm.

PALATE Powerfully peaty, with "island" flavours of spinach-like seaweed, salt and pepper.

FINISH Stingingly mustardy. Joyously extrovert.

SCORE **86**

EARLIER "OFFICIAL" BOTTLINGS

A 1982 Clynelish at 57.7 vol, in the Cask Strength series of Limited Editions, was assertive, seaweedy and slightly metallic. SCORE 81

A 1975 Brora, at 20 years and 59.1 vol, also in the Rare Malts series, had an intensely flowery aroma; a flowery, seaweedy, medicinal palate; and iodine, seaweed and salt in its long, lingering finish. A classic. SCORE 84

A 1977 Brora, at 21 years and 56.9 vol, in the Rare Malts series, had a good maritime character and a distinctively tar-like note. SCORE 85

A 1972 Clynelish, at 22 years and 58.95 vol, in the Rare Malts series, had more spice. Earlier Rare Malts from Brora have included a more flowery 1975. SCORE 84

There was also a wonderfully seaweedy, medicinal 1972. SCORE 86

SOME ADELPHI BOTTLINGS OF CLYNELISH

One independent bottler with a particular enthusiasm for Clynelish is Adelphi. Here is a selection of recent bottlings, all scoring more than 80.

CLYNELISH 1989, 9-year-old, Cask No 6081, Adelphi, 61.6 vol

COLOUR Very pale gold.

NOSE Very flowery. Soft for a relatively young example.

BODY Light, smooth.

PALATE Flowery. Cress. Pepper. Salt. Delicate interplay of flavours. A lovely, flowery aperitif.

FINISH Lightly seaweedy. Late sweetness.

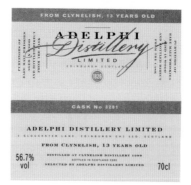

CLYNELISH 1989, 13-year-old, Cask No 3281, Adelphi, 56.7 vol

COLOUR Brassy gold.

NOSE Aromatic: fruity, flowery, vegetal (dock leaves?), appetizing

BODY Dry, biscuity, cracker-like

PALATE Reminiscent of edible seaweed. Interplay of sweetness, spicy mustard and vegetal dryness.

FINISH Peppery. Very salty Not the most peaty Clynelish, but a lovely distinctive whisky.

A 12-year-old Clynelish from Adelphi, cask no 3280 at 57.2 vol, was unusually sweet. Syrupy, creamy, peppery, dry (passion-fruit?). It had a long, peaty glow. Enjoyable, but very restrained for a Clynelish. SCORE 81

A 27-year-old Clynelish from Adelphi, cask no 2569 and at 56.3 vol, had wet grass, fresh earth, and peat in the aroma. Deliciously smooth. Syrupy without being cloying. Developing peat. Finish was typically mustardy. SCORE 84

MORE INDEPENDENT BOTTLINGS
OF BRORA AND CLYNELISH

CLYNELISH 1972, 29-year-old, Berry Brothers & Rudd, 43 vol

COLOUR Very clear pale gold or *eau-de-nil*.

NOSE Very fresh. Sliced limes. Lemon zest. Vanilla.

BODY Light and delicate but beautifully rounded.

PALATE Light cereal-grain character. Sliced dessert apple, but very rounded. Hint of lemony acidity.

FINISH Crisp, gingery, refreshing.

SCORE **79**

CLYNELISH 1976, Cask No 6501, Blackadder, Bottled 2002, 59 vol

COLOUR Dark oak.

NOSE Treacle toffee. Mint toffee.

BODY Cough syrup.

PALATE Fig-like. Fig Newtons. Ginger biscuits. Intense.

FINISH Maritime character emerges. Salty. Long. Woody.

SCORE **78**

CLYNELISH 1989, 13-year-old, Cask No 3287,
South African "Sherry" Wood, Chieftain's, 46 vol

COLOUR Full gold. Faint greenish tinge.

NOSE Lemony. Winey acidity.

BODY Rich, smooth.

PALATE Lemony. Oily. Anis. Lively flavours that seem to be trapped in malt like plums in a pancake.

FINISH Lemon curd. Zest of lemon.

SCORE **78**

CLYNELISH 1990, Connoisseurs Choice, 40 vol

COLOUR Attractive warm bronze.

NOSE Harbourfront. Seaweed. Slightly sour.

BODY Firm. Steely. Stern.

PALATE Iron-like flavours. Passion fruit. Gorse. Sea mist.
Flavours tightly combined.

FINISH Salty. Savoury. Appetizing.

SCORE 80

A Clynelish 1989, cask no 3248, at 57.9 vol, from the same merchant, has a considerably fuller colour, more like dark oak. With that hue comes a sherry creaminess, butteriness, and hint of cocoa. Then, through all those flavours, comes the salty tang of the sea. A deft balance of two extremes, and a luxurious nightcap. SCORE 84

BRORA 1982, Connoisseurs Choice, 40 vol

COLOUR Full, bright, yellowy gold.

NOSE Powerful. Gorse in a sea mist.

BODY Very firm.

PALATE Salsify, asparagus, edible cactus, juicy cucumber. Very unusual.
Both refreshing and appetizing, though rather weak in the middle.

FINISH Oily, olivey, peppery.

SCORE 79

THE COOPERS CHOICE
CLYNELISH 1990, 12-year-old, The Coopers Choice, 43 vol

COLOUR Old gold to bronze.

NOSE Dried orange skins.

BODY Dry, toffeeish.

PALATE Orange toffee. Banana toffee. Rather thin and one-dimensional.

FINISH Lemony. Just a suggestion of salt and seaweed.

SCORE **76**

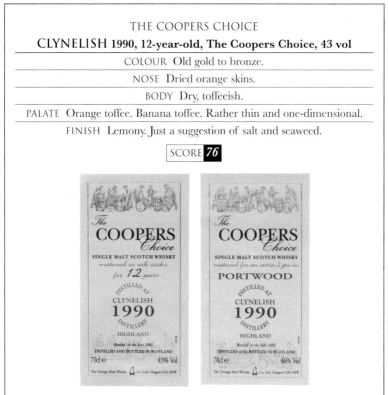

CLYNELISH 1990, 12-year-old, port finish, 46 vol, Coopers Choice.
Fresh sea smells. A walk in the dunes. Creamy. Reminiscent of a mustardy
hollandaise sauce (perhaps served with samphire). Fruity, mustardy,
dry finish is not quite enough of a foil. SCORE 79

CLYNELISH 1983, 16-year-old, 43 vol, Coopers Choice. Very fresh
and aromatic. Pears. Cress. Pepper. Suggestions of olive oil in the
palate. Falls away in the middle. Then develops sweet mustard
notes. The finish is grassy, sandy, peppery, seaweedy. SCORE 80

HART BROTHERS
CLYNELISH, 14-year-old, Cask Strength, Hart Brothers, 53.3 vol

COLOUR Bright, shimmery gold, with faint greenish tinge.

NOSE Vegetal. Seaweedy. A walk on the beach.

BODY Smooth, rounded, promising.

PALATE Clean, sweet. Suggestions of liquorice. Children's sweetshops.
Liquorice allsorts. Develops more adult flavours. Fennel? Celeriac?
Becomes more typically vegetal. Complex. Satisfying.

FINISH Sweet, peppery, lively.

SCORE **81**

KINGSBURY'S
CLYNELISH 1990, Amontillado Sherry Cask, Bottled 2000, Kingsbury's, 54.2 vol

The sherry complements rather than overpowers the classic Clynelish character.

COLOUR Very full gold.

NOSE Very oily. Orange zest. Citrus peels. Lemon

BODY Medium, firm.

PALATE Oily. Lemon. Mustard. Pine nuts. Cream.

FINISH Bitter salad leaves. Powerfully dry.

SCORE **82**

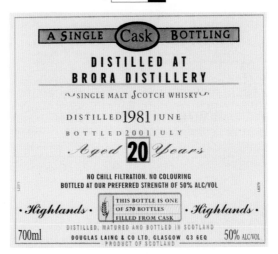

DOUGLAS LAING
BRORA 20-year-old, Single Cask Bottling, 50 vol

COLOUR Bright, greeny gold.

NOSE Curiously cloth-hall aroma, as though the whisky were being nosed among rolls of silk and satin. Or perhaps just among the occupants of sleek evening dresses.

BODY Oily. Slightly buttery.

PALATE Cereal grain. Restrained apple and lemon. Toast.

FINISH Touch of ginger marmalade.

SCORE **79**

Brora 18-year-old, 50 vol. This earlier bottling of Brora from the same house at the same strength, but two years younger, was much peatier, to the point of evoking Islay. It fell away somewhat in the middle, but came back for a stinging, fruity finish. Reminiscent of citron pressé. Very long saltiness. SCORE 82

LOMBARD
CLYNELISH 1982, Lombard, 50 vol

COLOUR Extraordinarily pale. *Eau-de-nil.*

NOSE Peaty.

BODY Oily but light and drying.

PALATE Peaty, grassy, peppery.

FINISH Dry, sharp, penetrating.

SCORE **76**

LOMBARD

JEWELS OF SCOTLAND
SINGLE MALT SCOTCH WHISKY

distilled at the
BRORA
Distillery

DISTILLED 1982   BOTTLED 2002

Rich and smooth with a nutty flavour.
Distillery now closed.

This whisky has been carefully selected and bottled under the sole
responsibility of Lombard Scotch Whisky, Glasgow PA4 8AN.
Distilled, Matured and Bottled in Scotland.

700ml/70cl   **HIGHLAND**   50%alc./vol.

BRORA 1982, Lombard (Jewels of Scotland), 50 vol

COLOUR Greeny gold.

NOSE More maritime, harbourfront character.

BODY Firm, slippery.

PALATE Slightly chewy. Both fruity and vegetal.
Lemons and spinach with Indian spices.

FINISH Spicy, perfumy, rounded.

SCORE **78**

JAMES MACARTHUR
CLYNELISH 10-year-old, James MacArthur, 59.8 vol

COLOUR Attractive greeny primrose.

NOSE Hint of the sea.

BODY Textured.

PALATE Sweet, mustardy, iron iodine salty, very lively.
Lots of flavour development. Light but warm smokiness.

FINISH Salty. Long. Stinging. Very appetizing indeed.

SCORE **83**

CLYNELISH 1989, Cask No 1122, James MacArthur, 58 vol

COLOUR Pale, greeny gold.

NOSE Hint of the sea.

BODY Medium to full, textured.

PALATE Like biting into crudités. Celery, palm hearts, artichokes, spinach.

FINISH Robust. Salty. Peppery.

SCORE 82

Another 1989 Clynelish, at a mere 1.1% stronger in alcohol, is milder in flavours, but crisp, clean, and decisive. Sweet, becoming grassy and mustardy, long, and appetizing. SCORE 80

MURRAY McDAVID
CLYNELISH 1972, Mission Range Series, 46 vol

COLOUR Pale gold. Almost iridescent.

NOSE Very aromatic. Strawberry jam. Marzipan. Almonds.
Spice-shop aromas.

BODY Silky.

PALATE Oily. Very lively. Extraordinarily spicy. Mustard, cumin seeds, coriander seed, cilantro.

FINISH Slightly sour, acid tang. Very appetizing. Perfect with salmon.

SCORE 85

SIGNATORY
CLYNELISH 1983, Signatory, 43 vol

COLOUR Very pale white wine.

NOSE Light seaweed and sea air.

BODY Lightly silky.

PALATE Light, refreshing, weak in the middle, developing some peppery notes.

FINISH Peppery, light, fruity seaweed, sea salt, pepper.
Very late, mustardy dryness, and heat.

SCORE 78

BRORA 1982, Cask No 278, Signatory, 58.6 vol

COLOUR Vinho verde.

NOSE Sweet. Vanilla.

BODY Lightly creamy.

PALATE A gentle approach to the sea. Across the grassy dunes
to the sandy, salty shore.

FINISH Intensely vegetal. Juicy. Tasty. Nettle soup with the sting intact.

SCORE **79**

BRORA 1981, 21 year-old, Butt No 1422,
Signatory Unchillfiltered Collection, 46 vol

COLOUR Fractionally greener.

NOSE Slight cellar character.

BODY Creamier.

PALATE Creamy. Grassy sweetness. Earthy.

FINISH Late, restrained, maritime notes. Vegetal, seaweed.

SCORE **79**

Also from Signatory, a 1989 Clynelish at 56.7 vol, finished in South
African "sherry" casks. Buttery sweetness in the aroma. Palate
suggests banana liqueur. Then smoky, like a pancake that has burned
slightly. Caramel-ish, spicy finish. A very unusual expression of Clynelish.
SCORE 75

THE WHISKY SHOP

BRORA 1972, 30-year-old, Cask Strength, The Whisky Shop, 47.4 vol

COLOUR Dark mahogany.

NOSE A hint of sweetish smoke.

BODY Firm. Smooth.

PALATE Chewy. Dry. Treacle toffee. Prunes encased in chocolate.
Some fruity-vegetal Brora character squeaks through.

FINISH Cigar boxes. Woody. For those who like woody whiskies.
Or for collectors.

SCORE **79**

AN CNOC

PRODUCER Inver House Distillers Ltd
REGION Highlands DISTRICT Speyside (Isla/Deveron)
ADDRESS Knock by Huntly, Aberdeenshire, AB5 5LJ
WEBSITE www.inverhouse.com EMAIL enquiries@inverhouse.com

AN CNOC IS SCOTTISH GAELIC for "the hill", and the most distinctively simple among a confusing variety of styles used on labels. The full name of the distillery, in Gaelic, is Cnoc Dubh ("black hill"). In English, this is rendered as "Knockdhu", not to be confused with another wholly unrelated distillery, Knockando ("little black hill"). There was probably no thought of confusion when these two distilleries were established, both in the 1890s, as their original purpose was to produce whisky for blending, rather than as single malt.

Knockdhu was built in 1894 to supply malt for the Haig blends, and closed in 1983. Only after its acquisition by its present owners, and its reopening, did official bottlings, albeit on a small scale, begin to be issued in the 1990s.

HOUSE STYLE Creamy and fruity. A dessert malt?

AN CNOC 12-year-old, 40 vol

COLOUR Pale gold.

NOSE Very aromatic, smooth, fruity. Pineapple?

BODY Light but very smooth.

PALATE Smooth, creamy vanilla notes. Very soft note of fruit.
Very drinkable and enjoyable.

FINISH Creamy, oaty. Sweet herbs.

SCORE **75**

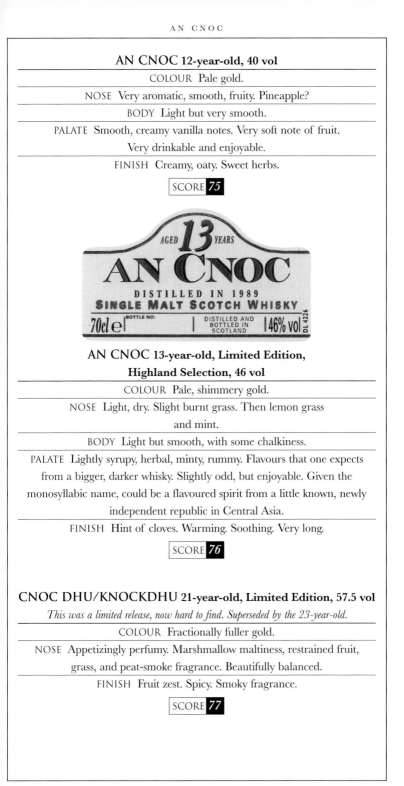

AN CNOC 13-year-old, Limited Edition,
Highland Selection, 46 vol

COLOUR Pale, shimmery gold.

NOSE Light, dry. Slight burnt grass. Then lemon grass
and mint.

BODY Light but smooth, with some chalkiness.

PALATE Lightly syrupy, herbal, minty, rummy. Flavours that one expects
from a bigger, darker whisky. Slightly odd, but enjoyable. Given the
monosyllabic name, could be a flavoured spirit from a little known, newly
independent republic in Central Asia.

FINISH Hint of cloves. Warming. Soothing. Very long.

SCORE **76**

CNOC DHU/KNOCKDHU 21-year-old, Limited Edition, 57.5 vol

This was a limited release, now hard to find. Superseded by the 23-year-old.

COLOUR Fractionally fuller gold.

NOSE Appetizingly perfumy. Marshmallow maltiness, restrained fruit,
grass, and peat-smoke fragrance. Beautifully balanced.

FINISH Fruit zest. Spicy. Smoky fragrance.

SCORE **77**

KNOCKDHU 23-year-old, Limited Edition, 57.4 vol

COLOUR Refractive, greeny gold.

NOSE Softly sweet lemon grass. Hint of fragrant smoke. Marshmallow.

BODY Smooth. Cinder toffee.

PALATE Toffeeish. Textured. Full of flavour. Clotted cream. Dessert apples.
Sweet without being cloying. Delicious.

FINISH Lemony. Rounded. The lightest touch of peat.

SCORE 78

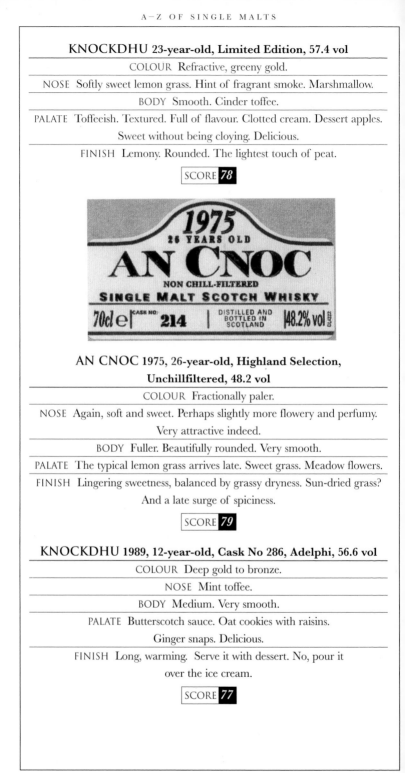

AN CNOC 1975, 26-year-old, Highland Selection, Unchillfiltered, 48.2 vol

COLOUR Fractionally paler.

NOSE Again, soft and sweet. Perhaps slightly more flowery and perfumy.
Very attractive indeed.

BODY Fuller. Beautifully rounded. Very smooth.

PALATE The typical lemon grass arrives late. Sweet grass. Meadow flowers.

FINISH Lingering sweetness, balanced by grassy dryness. Sun-dried grass?
And a late surge of spiciness.

SCORE 79

KNOCKDHU 1989, 12-year-old, Cask No 286, Adelphi, 56.6 vol

COLOUR Deep gold to bronze.

NOSE Mint toffee.

BODY Medium. Very smooth.

PALATE Butterscotch sauce. Oat cookies with raisins.
Ginger snaps. Delicious.

FINISH Long, warming. Serve it with dessert. No, pour it
over the ice cream.

SCORE 77

COLEBURN

PRODUCER Diageo
REGION Highlands   DISTRICT Speyside (Lossie)
ADDRESS Longmorn by Elgin, Moray, IV38 8GN

THE USHER'S WHISKIES, pioneer blends, once relied heavily upon malt from this distillery. Coleburn was built in the booming 1890s. It closed in the grim 1980s, the year before its owners DCL were subsumed into United Distillers, which in turn became part of Diageo. The Coleburn distillery still stands, but has not been licensed since 1992, and is unlikely to work again. There have been sporadic proposals to redevelop the site for other uses. Its whisky, always intended for blending, was never destined for solo stardom. A valedictory Rare Malts vintage was as enjoyable as any Coleburn to have been bottled in recent decades.

HOUSE STYLE Dry, fruity. Aperitif.

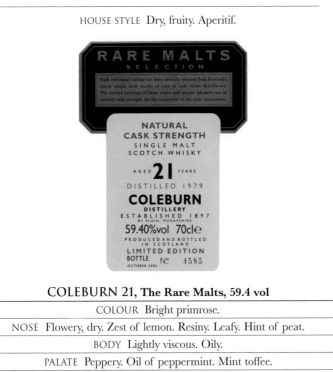

COLEBURN 21, The Rare Malts, 59.4 vol

COLOUR Bright primrose.

NOSE Flowery, dry. Zest of lemon. Resiny. Leafy. Hint of peat.

BODY Lightly viscous. Oily.

PALATE Peppery. Oil of peppermint. Mint toffee.

FINISH Ginger. Spicy. Medicinal. Warming. Soothing.

SCORE **73**

CONVALMORE

PRODUCER William Grant & Sons Ltd
REGION Highlands DISTRICT Speyside (Dufftown)
ADDRESS Dufftown, Banffshire, AB55 4BD

A RARE MALT OF Convalmore from Diageo in 2003 was something of a surprise – and a very pleasant one, given the quality of the whisky. The pagodas of Dufftown make an impressive congregation of landmarks, and Convalmore's is one of the most strikingly visible. Sadly, the distillery no longer operates.

For much of its life, Convalmore contributed malt whisky to the Buchanan/Black & White blends. The distillery was built in the 1870s; seriously damaged by fire, and rebuilt in 1910; modernized in 1964–65, but mothballed a couple of decades later by its owners at the time, DCL. Their successors, Diageo, still have the right to issue bottlings of Convalmore whisky from stock. In 1992, the premises were acquired by William Grant & Sons, owners of nearby Glenfiddich and Balvenie, but purely as warehousing.

HOUSE STYLE Malty, syrupy, fruity, biggish.
After dinner.

CONVALMORE 1981, Signatory, 43 vol

COLOUR *Eau-de-nil.*

NOSE Aromatic. Perfumy. Lavender. Wild mint.

BODY Very silky.

PALATE Fleshy. Musky. White rum. Cocoa butter. Pralines.
Mint chocolates.

FINISH Fresh, clean, stinging.

SCORE 71

CONVALMORE 1978, 24-year-old,
Rare Malt, 59.4 vol

COLOUR Shimmery pale gold.

NOSE Gently sweet. Oily cereal character. A fresh day on Speyside,
with a little smoke wafting quickly past.

BODY Medium. Creamy. Syrupy.

PALATE Chocolate cream in a cookie sandwich. Becoming less
chocolatey, more biscuity and drier.

FINISH Fruity. Lemon pith. Slightly woody. Alcoholic. Warming.
Long. Powerful.

SCORE 79

CONVALMORE 1977, 21-year-old,
Cadenhead, 64.4 vol

COLOUR Old gold. Dusty, full gold.

NOSE Oily. Passion fruit. Iron-ish, but sweet.

BODY Drying on the tongue. Clinging syrupiness.

PALATE Gritty. Dry. Sherbety. Peppery.

FINISH Big, long, rummy, warming syrupiness. After dinner.

SCORE 75

CONVALMORE 1960, Gordon & MacPhail, 40 vol

Released in 1999 as part of a new Rare Old series.

COLOUR Rich, lemony gold.

NOSE Aromatic. Oily. Very "clean" smoke.

BODY Medium. Oily. Clean.

PALATE Begins with a good malt background. Distinctly oily.
Again, lightly smoky.

FINISH Light malt. Hint of honey. Yet more oiliness. Hint of sulphur.
Clean peatiness. Warming. Long.

SCORE 70

CRAGGANMORE

PRODUCER Diageo
REGION Highlands DISTRICT Speyside
ADDRESS Ballindalloch, Banffshire, AB37 9AB TEL 01479 8747000
WEBSITE www.discovering-distilleries.com/www.malts.com

A WONDERFULLY COMPLEX SPECIAL RELEASE in 2003 demonstrated what a great malt this is. Cragganmore, one of Diageo's six "Classic Malts", is still less widely known than might be expected. The distillery, founded in 1869–70, is very pretty, hidden in a hollow high on the Spey. Its water, from nearby springs, is relatively hard, and its spirit stills have an unusual, flat-topped shape. These two elements may be factors in the complexity of the malt. The usual version, from refill sherry casks, some more sherried independent bottlings, and the port finish, are each in their own ways almost equal delights. Cragganmore is a component of Old Parr.

HOUSE STYLE Austere, stonily dry, aromatic. After dinner.

CRAGGANMORE 12-year-old, 40 vol

COLOUR Golden.

NOSE The most complex aroma of any malt. Its bouquet is astonishingly fragrant and delicate, with sweetish notes of cut grass and herbs (thyme perhaps?).

BODY Light to medium, but very firm and smooth.

PALATE Delicate, clean, restrained, with a huge range of herbal, flowery notes.

FINISH Long.

SCORE 90

CRAGGANMORE 1984, Double Matured, 40 vol
Finished in ruby port.

COLOUR Pale amber.

NOSE Heather honey. Scented. Beeswax. Hessian.

BODY Firm, smooth. Fuller.

PALATE Flowery. Orange blossom. Sweet oranges. Cherries. Port.

FINISH Flowery, balancing dryness. Warming. Soothing.
Connoisseurs might miss the austerity of the original – or enjoy
the added layer of fruity, winey sweetness.

SCORE **90**

CRAGGANMORE 1973, 29-year-old,
Special Release Issued 2003, 52.5 vol

COLOUR Gold, with a faint green tinge.

NOSE Fragrant, grassy, herbal, with both dryness and sweetness.

BODY Soft, slightly oily, dry.

PALATE Dry notes like bison grass, thyme and pepper, but also sweeter
flavours like liquorice and orange blossom.

FINISH Long, dry, flowery, cleansing.

SCORE **92**

SOME INDEPENDENT BOTTLINGS OF CRAGGANMORE:

Murray McDavid's bottling of a cask from 1990 at 46 vol is pale straw
in colour. A subtle refined nose hinting at berry fruits, mandarin, dried
apple, white pepper and a grassy note. Medium weight. The palate
is slightly flat. SCORE 80.

A 1989 bottling from Blackadder at 59.6 vol is light gold in colour; water
brings out slightly grubby wood. The palate and body shows a light
whisky which has had little interaction with the cask. SCORE 70

Signatory's 1989, 55.7 vol, is light gold with a nose of powdered almond,
sultana, and suggestions of weight; the palate is soft and sweet with good
character, but lacks the depth of the official bottlings. SCORE 83

CRAIGELLACHIE

PRODUCER John Dewar & Sons Ltd
REGION Highlands DISTRICT Speyside
ADDRESS Craigellachie, Banffshire, AB38 9ST
TEL 01340 881212

FOR ITS 2003/04 selection, the Craigellachie Hotel, with its renowned whisky bar, went for the first time to the local distillery. The whisky of Craigellachie had a very low profile under the ownership of Diageo; perhaps it will rediscover itself under Dewar's. The distillery was founded in 1891 and remodelled in 1965.

The village of Craigellachie – between Dufftown, Aberlour, and Rothes – is at the very heart of Speyside distillery country. It also has the Speyside Cooperage. Here, the Fiddich meets the Spey, and the latter is crossed by a bridge, designed by the great Scottish engineer Thomas Telford. Craigellachie is pronounced "Craig-ella-ki" – the "i" is short.

HOUSE STYLE Sweet, malty-nutty, fruity. After dinner.

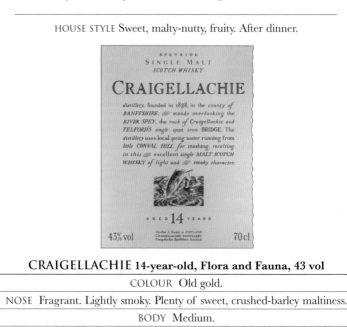

CRAIGELLACHIE 14-year-old, Flora and Fauna, 43 vol

COLOUR Old gold.

NOSE Fragrant. Lightly smoky. Plenty of sweet, crushed-barley maltiness.

BODY Medium.

PALATE Starts sweet, slightly syrupy, and malty, then becomes nutty, developing a very fruity, Seville-orange character.

FINISH Orangey, lightly smoky, aromatic, warming.

SCORE 75

CRAIGELLACHIE 1982, 2003 Single Cask Bottling for the
Craigellachie Hotel, 60 vol

COLOUR Pale, bright gold. Almost iridescent.

NOSE Very evocative. Warm. Fresh earthiness. The forest floor.
Wild mushrooms. Chanterelle vol-au-vents.
Pastry fresh out of the oven. Shortbread.

BODY Firm. Smooth. Lightly syrupy.

PALATE Creamy. Slight accent towards maltiness, but very well balanced.
Starts sweet, but develops some fruity acidity. Apricots. Fruit pies.
Apple, especially. Flavours tightly bound together.

FINISH Soothing warmth.

SCORE **78**

CRAIGELLACHIE 13-year-old, Adelphi,
Cask No 3783, 59.2 vol

COLOUR Bright gold.

NOSE Sweet, malty, nutty, buttery.

BODY Medium but rich.

PALATE Creamy, nutty. Lacks complexity, but delicious.

FINISH Light, clean fruitiness. Orange zest. Quick.

SCORE **75**

A 40 vol from the same year, bottled by Gordon & MacPhail, was
superbly balanced, with a more peaty smokiness and the faintest
suggestion of sherry. SCORE 78

CRAIGELLACHIE 1981, Signatory, 43 vol

COLOUR White wine.

NOSE Fragrant. Restrained dessert apples, grass, and fragrant smokiness.

BODY Oily.

PALATE Cereal-grain oiliness. Very oily. Perfumy. Soapy.

FINISH Flowery. Dessert apples again.

SCORE **75**

OTHER VERSIONS OF CRAIGELLACHIE

A 1973 22-year-old Rare Malts edition, at cask strength, begins with
crushed barley, moving to fudgey nuttiness and peanut brittle. SCORE 77

DAILUAINE

PRODUCER Diageo
REGION Highlands DISTRICT Speyside
ADDRESS Carron, Aberlour, Banffshire, AB38 7RE
TEL 01340 872500

BETWEEN THE MOUNTAIN BEN RINNES and the river Spey, at the hamlet of Carron, not far from Aberlour, the Dailuaine ("Dal-oo-ayn") distillery is hidden in a hollow. The name means "green vale", and that accurately describes the setting. It was founded in 1852, and has been rebuilt several times since.

It is one of several distilleries along the Spey valley that once had its own railway halt for workers and visitors – and as a means of shipping in barley or malt and despatching the whisky. A small part of the Speyside line still runs trains for hobbyists and visitors, at the Aviemore ski resort, and Dailuaine's own shunting locomotive has appeared there under steam, but is now preserved at Aberfeldy, a distillery formerly in the same group. Most of the route from the mountains to the sea is now preserved for walkers, as the Speyside Way. Dailuaine's whisky has long been a component of the Johnnie Walker blends. It was made available as a single malt in the Flora and Fauna series in 1991, and later in a Cask Strength Limited Edition.

HOUSE STYLE Firmly malty, fruity, fragrant.
After dinner.

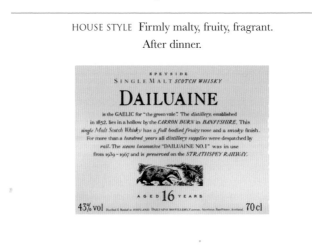

DAILUAINE 16-year-old, Flora and Fauna, 43 vol

COLOUR Emphatically reddish amber.

NOSE Sherryish but dry, perfumy.

BODY Medium to full, smooth.

PALATE Sherryish, with barley-sugar maltiness, but balanced by a dry cedar or oak background.

FINISH Sherryish, smooth, very warming, long.

SCORE **76**

DAILUAINE 1980, Bottled 1997, Cask Strength Limited Edition, 63 vol

COLOUR Bright deep orange. Very distinctive.

NOSE Lightly smoky. Orange marmalade. Sherry. Oak.

BODY Medium to full. Smooth.

PALATE Sherryish. Firm maltiness. Surge of peat smoke. Oak.

FINISH Oaky, dry, earthy, peppery.

SCORE **77**

DAILUAINE 1973, 22-year-old, Rare Malts, 60.92 vol

COLOUR Full gold.

NOSE Distinctly peaty.

BODY Light to medium. Very smooth.

PALATE Long-lasting flavours. Tightly combined barley-sugar sweetness and flowery dryness. Less sherried and big than the above, but with more distillery character.

FINISH Fruity, perfumy. Violets?

SCORE **77**

SOME INDEPENDENT BOTTLINGS OF DAILUAINE

A 22-year-old Adelphi bottling at 55.2 vol, cask no 4151, has a nose of Olde English marmalade, ripe fruit, vanilla oak cream, and menthol; sweet soft body and a palate that delivers soft vanilla fruits, blackberry, grilled nut fruit. A gentle giant. SCORE 80

The 21-year-old (1979 distillation, 43 vol) from Cooper's Choice has a perfumed nose akin to geranium and with water soft cooked fruits; the body is quite light and the palate has grassy notes mixed with soft creaminess. SCORE 75

A 1975 Connoisseurs Choice from Gordon and MacPhail at 40 vol is malty and rich with more European oak influence: leather, nut, stewed orange. A heavier-bodied dram with an oozy, soft depth. Plenty of chocolate in here. Deep. SCORE 77

DALLAS DHU

PRODUCER DCL
REGION Highlands DISTRICT Speyside (Findhorn)
ADDRESS Forres, Morayshire, IV36 2RR
TEL 01309 676548 VC

THE NAME MEANS "black water valley". This Dallas accommodates a hamlet rather smaller than its indirect descendant in Texas (named after US Vice-president George Mifflin Dallas, who seems to have been of Scottish origin). The Dallas Dhu distillery was established in 1899. Despite a fire in 1939, it does not appear to have changed greatly. Latterly, its whisky appeared in the Benmore blends and vattings, and as Dallas Mhor single malt.

The distillery closed in 1983 and reopened to the public in 1988, under the aegis of Scotland's Historic Buildings and Monument Directorate. There are no plans to restart production, but the later batches continue to appear in independent bottlings.

HOUSE STYLE Silky, honeyish, sometimes chocolatey. After dinner.

DALLAS DHU 1980, Gordon & MacPhail, 40 vol

COLOUR Gold.
NOSE Some oak. Cox s apple. Heavy perfumed greenhouse aromas: tomato, flowers. Spice.
BODY Round and soft.
PALATE Ripe fruits, lush and sweet.
FINISH Spices.

SCORE *83*

DALLAS DHU 1979, Murray McDavid Mission Range, 46 vol

COLOUR Rich gold.

NOSE Soft orchard fruit. Fruitcake, dried peach. Elegant and soft.

BODY Silky and chewy.

PALATE Sweet, complex, long, and elegant. Orange, date, juicy fruits. toffee.

FINISH Nutmeg.

SCORE **83**

DALLAS DHU 1978, Signatory, 43 vol

COLOUR Amber.

NOSE Dried sweet fruits. Caramelized fruits, toffee, date. Rich, voluptuous.

BODY Soft and rich.

PALATE Thick. Apricot, dried mango, singed notes. Great balance.

FINISH Light spice.

SCORE **80**

DALLAS DHU 21-year-old, Distilled 1975, Rare Malts, 61.9 vol

COLOUR Old gold.

NOSE Orange blossom. Honey. Musk. Heathery. Peat smoke.

BODY Smooth, light on the tongue, syrupy.

PALATE Orange zest, crème brûlée, burnt sugar.

FINISH Slightly chewy, treacle toffee. Late warmth. Long.

SCORE **81**

DALLAS DHU 1978, Signatory, 59.7 vol

COLOUR Bright greeny gold.

NOSE Quick hit of intense syrupy fruit.

Becoming more floral, perfumy and soapy.

BODY Syrupy.

PALATE Very appetizingly, pleasantly grassy and smoky. Creamy in the
middle, with a suggestion of white chocolate. Then smoky again.

FINISH Quite hot. Ginger cookies.

SCORE **75**

DALLAS DHU 1970, 32-year-old, Coopers Choice, 46 vol

COLOUR Old Gold to dull bronze. Quite full.

NOSE Soft. Malty. Buttery. Cinnamon.

BODY Light. Firm. Textured. Chewy.

PALATE Sticky toffee pudding.

FINISH Powerful. Fruity. Warming.

SCORE **80**

THE DALMORE

PRODUCER Whyte and MacKay Ltd
REGION Highlands DISTRICT Northern Highlands
ADDRESS Alness, Morayshire, IV17 0UT
TEL 01349 882362 WEBSITE www.dalmoredistillery.co.uk

A RECORD PRICE FOR A BOTTLE OF WHISKY was established in 2002, when a Dalmore 62-year-old single malt was sold at auction to an anonymous bidder for just over £25,000/$38,000. Records are made to be broken, but this was a timely boost to the distillery, not long returned to Scottish ownership. The record-breaking sale took place at McTear's, the Glasgow auction house. The whisky was vatted from vintages of 1868, 1878, 1926, and 1939. Over the years, it had been racked several times, latterly in an oloroso sherry butt from Gonzalez Byass.

The man who makes the vattings and blendings for Whyte and Mackay, Richard Patterson, is one of the industry's extroverts. He may well have celebrated with a cigar. One of his creations is Dalmore The Cigar Malt, a rich whisky intended to accompany a fine Havana. It is easy to imagine the finest cigars being smoked in the oak-panelled offices at Dalmore. The panels previously graced a shooting lodge.

Dalmore, said to have been founded in 1839, was once owned by a distinguished local family, the Mackenzies, friends of James Whyte and Charles Mackay, who created a famous name in blended Scotch. Latterly, the proprietor was Jim Beam, of Kentucky. The management buy-out of Jim Beam's Scottish distilleries led to the restoration of the Whyte and Mackay name.

Dalmore has an unusual still-house. The wash stills have a conical upper chamber and the spirit stills are cooled with a water jacket – another distinctive feature. There are two pairs of stills, identical in shape but different sizes. The warehouses are by the waters of the Cromarty Firth. About 85 per cent of the whisky is matured in bourbon casks, mainly first-fill, the rest in sweet oloroso and amontillado, but it is all married in sherry butts.

HOUSE STYLE Rich, flavourful, orange marmalade. After dinner.

THE DALMORE 12-year-old, 40 vol

COLOUR An attractive amber hue.

NOSE Arousing, with rum butter, malt loaf, and soda bread.

BODY Medium. Silky smooth.

PALATE Gradual flavour development. Malty sweetness,
orange jelly beans, spiciness (anise?), perfuminess, heather,
light peat Even a faint, salty tang of the sea.

FINISH Toasty. Grainy, Long

SCORE **79**

THE DALMORE "Black Isle", 12-year old, 43 vol

COLOUR Slightly darker and redder. Copper.

NOSE More obvious sherry. Apricot jam. Morello cherries. Pipe tobacco.

BODY Velvety.

PALATE Seville oranges. Candied orange peels in mincemeat. Mince pies.

FINISH Rooty. Liquorice. Lingering.

SCORE **80**

THE DALMORE Cigar Malt, 40 vol

A marriage of Dalmore whiskies between ten and 20 years old,
mainly in the-mid teens.

COLOUR Dark orange.

NOSE A soft smokiness. Suggestions of black chocolate and orange creams.

BODY Firm.

PALATE Rich, rounded. A hint of rum butter, then dryish and firm.
Hard caramel toffee. Hint of burnt sugar. Faint smoke. Never cloying.
With the cigar, a complement rather than a contrast.

FINISH Light, smoky, wood bark, ground almonds, dryness. Scores points
for originality and for balance.

SCORE **81**

THE DALMORE 1978, 21-year-old, 43 vol

COLOUR Pale orange.

NOSE Soft, perfumy, fruity.

Body Silky.

PALATE A distinctly finessed and elegant interpretation. Very well combined, complex flavours. Orange, chocolate, flowers, late spices, hint of smoke.

FINISH Light touch of citrus. Whiff of smoke.

SCORE **81**

THREE BOTTLINGS FOR JAPAN

A 1980, at 22 years old and 60.8 vol (cask no 158), has
suggestions of pastry, apple pie (a little too long in the oven)
and a dousing with calvados. SCORE 79

A 1979, at 23 years and 54.8 vol (cask no 595) has more fruit –
albeit rather tannic apples. SCORE 80

A 1974, at 28 years old, and 57.9 vol (cask no 5883) has a smoother start
and a much more mature middle palate, with typically rich, spicy,
Dalmore flavours, but ends abruptly and rather woodily. SCORE 81

THE DALMORE 30-year-old Stillman's Dram, 45 vol

Releases under this rubric vary in age and style.

COLOUR Tangerine

NOSE Musky. Curaçao orange peels. Tomatoes in a hothouse. Geraniums.

BODY Lightly creamy.

PALATE Very sustained flavour development. Very spicy.
Christmas spices. Nutmeg, cinnamon.

FINISH Dusted pastry. Salt.

SCORE **81**

THE DALMORE 30-year-old Special Cask Finish
(Gonzalez Byass), 42 vol

COLOUR Full amber. Tawny.

NOSE Clotted cream stirred with honey, poured over nectarines.

BODY As sensuous as a massage.

PALATE Sweet, creamy, caramelized flavours. Crème brûlée.

FINISH Biscuity, with dark flavours. Like tiramisu with lots of
espresso and no vanilla sugar.

SCORE 82

THE DALMORE 50-year-old, 52.6 vol

*Occasional bottlings. Some have contained proportions of far older whiskies, dating to
1868. The enjoyment is in the pleasure of tasting history. A whisky of this age has more
memory than muscle. (Available at the Sheraton Hotel, Edinburgh.)*

COLOUR Chestnut.

NOSE Astonishingly, the fruit is still discernible. Perfumy, polished oak.
Quickly moving to surprisingly fresh smokiness and oakiness.

BODY Has lost some fullness with age, but still some substance.

PALATE Orange, lemon pith, flowering currant, sap, oak, smoke.

FINISH Caramelized charred oak.

SCORE 85

THE DALMORE 62-year-old, 40.5 vol

COLOUR Dark oak.

NOSE Hickory smoke. Mesquite. Or perhaps apple wood.
Very appetizing.

BODY Beeswax oiliness.

PALATE Orange. Mint. Menthol. Pipe tobacco. The big Dalmore
flavours have settled down in harmonious maturity.

FINISH Mild. Surprising lack of woody astringency.
There is even some sweetness.

SCORE 86

DALWHINNIE

PRODUCER Diageo
REGION Highlands DISTRICT Speyside
ADDRESS Dalwhinnie, Inverness-shire, PH19 1AB
TEL 01540 672219 VC
WEBSITE www.discovering-distilleries.com/www.malts.com

ONE OF THE HIGHEST DISTILLERIES in Scotland, at 326 metres (1073 feet), Dalwhinnie has the Monadhliath Mountains to one side, and the Forest of Atholl, the Cairngorms, and the Grampians to the other. Its name is Gaelic for "meeting place". The village of the same name stands at the junction of old cattle-droving routes from the west and north down to the central Lowlands. Much whisky smuggling went on along this route. The distillery was called Strathspey when it opened in 1897. It is near the upper reaches of the Spey, although Dalwhinnie represents the Highlands in Diageo's Classic Malts range.

HOUSE STYLE Lightly peaty. Cut grass and heather honey. Clear flavours against a very clean background. Aperitif.

DALWHINNIE 15-year-old, 43 vol

COLOUR Bright gold.
NOSE Very aromatic, dry, faintly phenolic, lightly peaty.
BODY Firm, slightly oily.
PALATE Remarkably smooth, long-lasting flavour development. Aromatic, heather-honey notes give way to cut-grass, malty sweetness, which intensifies to a sudden burst of peat.
FINISH A long crescendo.

SCORE **76**

DALWHINNIE 15-year-old,
Friends of the Classic Malts Bottling, 56.9 vol

COLOUR Light gold.

NOSE Hard to get much on nose: sulphur, guava, coconut cream. Alcohol.

BODY Light and delicate.

PALATE Delicate, but better weight than the nose suggests. Tropical fruit.
More about feel than aroma.

FINISH Crisp. Oaky.

SCORE **70**

DALWHINNIE 1980, Double Matured, 43 vol
Oloroso finish.

COLOUR Sunny gold to bronze.

NOSE Oloroso, liquorice, rooty, grassy.

BODY Firm, rounded.

PALATE Very sweet, toffeeish start. Honey. Lemons. Long flavour
development to peatiness, cut grass, vanilla, and fresh oak. Beautiful
interplay and balance. The sherry sweetness seems, by contrast, to
accentuate the usually light peatiness of Dalwhinnie.

FINISH Very long. Cut grass, peat, smoke, oak.

SCORE **79**

DALWHINNIE 1973, 29-year-old, Special Release of 2003, 57.8 vol

COLOUR Restrained, warm gold.

NOSE Appetizingly fruity. Lemon grass. Orange juice on breakfast pancakes.

BODY Smooth. Textured.

PALATE Bursts with fruitiness. Apples, bananas?
Against cereal-grain background.

FINISH Refreshing. Lively. Scenty.

SCORE **78**

DALWHINNIE 1966, 36-year-old, Limited Bottling of 1500,
Bottled 2002, 47.2 vol

COLOUR Full gold. Hint of bronze.

NOSE Aromatic. Oily. Restrained peat. Some grassy, moorland aromas.

BODY Very light. As fresh as spring water.

PALATE Clean, very firm maltiness. Honey-glazed biscuits.
Pronounced vanilla. Slowly developing lively, appetizing moorland grass
and faint smokiness.

FINISH Very long and warming.

SCORE **79**

DEANSTON

PRODUCER Burn Stewart Distillers plc
REGION Highlands DISTRICT Eastern Highlands
ADDRESS Deanston, near Doune, Perthshire, FK16 6AG
TEL 01786 841422 WEBSITE www.burnstewartdistillers.com
enquiries@burnstewartdistillers.com

THE TOWN OF DOUNE was known in the 17th century for the manufacture of pistols, some of which may have seen service on the Spanish main. Now the old empire strikes back. The Trinidadian drinks company, Angostura, has acquired Burn Stewart, owners of the town's Deanston distillery. That enterprise itself has an interesting history. It is housed in a cotton mill, designed in 1785 by Richard Arkwright and extended in 1836. The mill was driven by the waters of the river Teith. The supply of good water apparently contributed to the decision to turn the building into a distillery at a time when the whisky industry was doing very well.

It opened as the Deanston distillery in 1965–66, with the vaulted weaving shed serving as a warehouse. The distillery prospered during the 1970s, but closed during the difficult mid-1980s. At the time it was owned by Invergordon. With the growth of interest in single malts in the late 1980s and early 1990s, Deanston was bought by the blenders, Burn Stewart, and more versions of this pleasant whisky became available.

HOUSE STYLE Light, slightly oily, nutty, accented toward a notably clean, malty sweetness. Restorative.

DEANSTON 6-year-old, 40 vol

Mainly for the French market.

COLOUR Light gold.

NOSE Lightly perfumed, grass, cream, muesli, slightly nutty.

BODY Soft and light.

PALATE Cereal-like with a soft mid-palate and a malty note. Slightly hard.

FINISH Green grape. Immaturity still there.

SCORE **70**

DEANSTON 12-year-old, 40 vol

COLOUR Very pale, greeny gold. Fino sherry.

NOSE Linseed oil.

BODY Light, smooth, soothing.

PALATE Malty, drying in finish. Reminiscent of a lightly nutty, dry sherry.

FINISH Again, very light, but a touch of nuttiness. In character, less of a
Highland malt than a very good Lowlander.

SCORE **70**

DEANSTON 17-year-old, 40 vol

COLOUR Markedly fuller. Bright bronze.

NOSE Linseed oil, grass, cereal grain, barley sugar.

BODY Light to medium.

PALATE Cereal grain, more emphatically nutty. Slightly creamy.

FINISH Nutty, appetizing.

SCORE **71**

DEANSTON 21-year-old, Limited Edition Decanter, 43 vol

COLOUR Copper.

NOSE Shows good maturity. Cashew, fruitcake, basil, coconut, box tree.

BODY Soft and gentle.

PALATE Oaky, light orange notes, clean juicy malt. Slight bitter note.

FINISH Dry, spicy, short.

SCORE **75**

DEANSTON 1992, Signatory, 46 vol

COLOUR Rich gold.

NOSE Sweet, clotted cream, estery. Privet, dry oak.

BODY Fir and dry.

PALATE Cashew nut, strawberry, becoming very dry. Dry oak and dry malt.

FINISH Nutty.

SCORE **67**

DRUMGUISH

PRODUCER Speyside Distillers Co. Ltd
REGION Highlands   DISTRICT Speyside
ADDRESS Tromie Mills, Glentromie, Kingussie, PH21 1HS
TEL 01540 661060
WEBSITE www.speysidedistillers.co.uk   VC By appointment

ONE OF THE NEWEST DISTILLERIES in Scotland, having made its first spirit in 1991, and now beginning to develop a portfolio of more mature whiskies. The handsome, gabled stone building intentionally looks a hundred years old. Its opening was the realization of a dream for its owner, George Christie, who had planned it for three or four decades, his progress on the project ebbing and flowing with the fortunes of the industry. One of his earlier essays was a vatted malt, popular in the United States, under the name Glentromie.

Christie's distillery is at Drumguish, where the tiny river Tromie flows into the highest reaches of the Spey. His company, Speyside, takes its name not only from its location, but also from a distillery by that name that operated in nearby Kingussie between 1895 and 1910.

HOUSE STYLE Oily, nutty, lightly peaty. Aperitif.

DRUMGUISH No Age Statement, 40 vol

COLOUR Full gold.

NOSE Flowery. Jasmine. Passion fruit.

BODY Medium, soft.

PALATE Cashew nuts and a sweetish dried-grass note that recalls great Scotch whiskies of the past. Cookies. Toasted marshmallows.

FINISH Faintly kirsch-like, dry fruitiness. A bit abrupt.

SCORE **73**

SPEYSIDE 10-year-old, 43 vol

COLOUR Golden satin.

NOSE Pronounced oily nuttiness.

BODY Very light and soft.

PALATE Sweet, buttery, rich. Some cream toffee, cookies, and caramel.

FINISH Lightly dry. Leafy. Grain mustard. long

SCORE **75**

DUFFTOWN

PRODUCER Diageo
REGION Highlands   DISTRICT Speyside (Dufftown)
ADDRESS Dufftown, Keith, Banffshire, AB55 4BR
TEL 01340 822100   WEBSITE www.malts.com

THE EARL OF FIFE, James Duff, laid out this handsome, hilly little town of stone buildings in 1817. The town's name is pronounced "duff-ton". Dufftown lies at the confluence of the rivers Fiddich and Dullan on their way to the Spey. There are six active malt distilleries in the town; a further two survive as buildings but are highly unlikely ever to operate again. A ninth, Pittyvaich, has recently been bulldozed.

Only one of the distilleries appropriates Dufftown as its name. This distillery and Pittyvaich, its erstwhile next-door neighbour, were both owned by Bell's until that company was acquired by United Distillers, now Diageo. Dufftown's stone-built premises were a meal mill until 1896, but they have since sprouted a pagoda, and were twice expanded in the 1970s. They now comprise one of Diageo's larger distilleries, but most of its output goes into Bell's, the biggest selling blend in the UK.

HOUSE STYLE Aromatic, dry, malty. Aperitif.

DUFFTOWN 15-year-old, Flora and Fauna, 43 vol

COLOUR Pale golden.

NOSE Assertively aromatic.

BODY Lightly syrupy.

PALATE Malty, on the dry side, becoming flowery.

FINISH Lingers, but very light.

SCORE **71**

DUFFTOWN 1979, Bottled 1997, Refill Sherry, Murray McDavid, 46 vol

COLOUR	Full amber.
NOSE	Toast. Marmaladey sherry.
BODY	Medium, firm, oily.
PALATE	Butter, honey, oranges. Toasty and grainy. Sesame-seed bagels.
FINISH	Smoky. Slightly burnt and astringent.

SCORE **74**

A version distilled and bottled in those years, but with more sherry, at 57.1 vol, from Cadenhead, had an attractive, dark orange colour; a big aroma of oak, toast, orange, and cinnamon; a syrupy body; and a very fruity palate; finishing with dry malt and lots of sappy oak. SCORE 72

DUFFTOWN 1976, 20-year-old, Cask Strength, Rare Malts

Tasted as a work in progress.

COLOUR	White wine.
NOSE	Heather honey. Very honeyish.
BODY	Medium, firm.
PALATE	Lively, fruity, perfumy. Flapjacks. Shortbread. Fudge.
FINISH	Ginger cookies. Sweetish smokiness.

DUFFTOWN 1975, 21-year-old, Cask Strength, Rare Malts, 54.8 vol

COLOUR	Vinho verde.
NOSE	Honey. Honeydew melon. Glace cherries. Waxy. Lipstick.
BODY	Creamy, firm.
PALATE	Remarkably fudgey. Treacle toffee.
FINISH	Very gingery. Sweet, "leafy bonfires" smokiness.

SCORE **72**

EDRADOUR

PRODUCER Signatory Vintage Scotch Whisky Co. Ltd
REGION Highlands   DISTRICT Eastern Highlands
ADDRESS Pitlochry, Perthshire, PH16 5JP   TEL 01796 472095
WEBSITE www.edradour.co.uk   EMAIL info@edradour.fsbusiness.co.uk   VC

THE COUNTRY'S SMALLEST DISTILLERY was returned to Scottish – and independent – ownership in 2002. Edradour is a working commercial distillery on a farmhouse scale, using very old, open equipment, the function of which is easy to understand – a bonus for the visitor. It is near the inland resort of Pitlochry, and within easy reach of Edinburgh and Glasgow. The change in the ownership of Edradour was greeted with widespread goodwill.

With the much bigger Speyside distillery, Aberlour, it had for some years been a Scottish outpost of Pernod Ricard. With the acquisition of Chivas Brothers' ten distilleries, the French found their hands full. They had looked after Edradour well, but such a small distillery might benefit from ownership by an individual. It was sold to Andrew Symington, the enterprising founder of the independent bottler Signatory. The creation of a new range is still in its early stages, with the assistance of Iain Henderson, renowned manager of Laphroaig until his reluctant retirement.

Edradour likes to trace its history back to the beginning of legal whisky production in the Highlands in 1825, although the present distillery is believed to have been founded in 1837. The distillery, at the hamlet of Balnauld, above Pitlochry, is secreted by the hills.

HOUSE STYLE Spicy. Minty. Creamy. After dinner.

EDRADOUR 10-year-old, 40 vol

COLOUR Dark gold to pale amber.

NOSE Minty. Leafy.

BODY On the thin side. Firm.

PALATE Syrupy. Smoky.

FINISH Barbecue. Charcoal.

SCORE *79*

EDRADOUR 1991, 11-year-old, "Straight from the Cask", 60.2 vol

COLOUR Mahogany, with pink highlights.

NOSE Applewood. The embers of a fire.

BODY Syrupy.

PALATE Lots of sherry. Raisins. Nutty. Almonds.

FINISH Cloves. Peppermint. Medicinal. Hot.

SCORE *80*

EDRADOUR Cask Strength, 58 vol

COLOUR Dark amber.

NOSE Perfumy. Cherry blossom. Toffee.

BODY Fudgey creaminess.

PALATE Lovely balance of creaminess and toasty dryness.

FINISH Very spicy ginger marmalade and burnt toast.

SCORE *81*

EDRADOUR 1992, Unchillfiltered, 48 vol

COLOUR Bright gold. Paradoxically, the brightest of the flight.

NOSE Leafy. Vegetal.

Body Soft, smooth.

PALATE Creamy. Vanilla. Pepper.

FINISH Gentle. Soothing.

SCORE *81*

EDRADOUR 1976, Signatory Cask Strength Series, 54 vol

COLOUR Full gold to bronze.

NOSE Garden mint, grass, and peat.

BODY Decidedly creamy.

PALATE Very creamy-tasting. Slightly buttery.

FINISH Late, lively, spiciness.

SCORE *81*

FETTERCAIRN

PRODUCER Whyte and Mackay Ltd
REGION Highlands   DISTRICT Eastern Highlands
ADDRESS Distillery Road, Fettercairn, near Laurencekirk,
Kincardineshire, AB30 1YE   TEL 01561 340244   VC

T HE ESTATE OF THE GLADSTONE FAMILY, who provided Queen
Victoria with a famous Prime Minister, accommodates Old
Fettercairn. This pretty, cream-painted distillery is amid farmers' fields
on the edge of the village of attractive Georgian cottages from which
it takes its name. The distillery was founded in 1824, and that date is
now incorporated in the names of the whiskies. A malt called
Fettercairn 1824, at 12 years old, is being introduced to replace the 10-
year-old below. This new version will probably emerge with a similar
score. Tasted as a work in progress, it seemed slightly paler in colour,
with a Riesling aroma and a syrupy, spicy, palate.

HOUSE STYLE Lightly earthy, nutty. Easy drinking or aperitif.

OLD FETTERCAIRN 10-year-old, 40 vol

COLOUR Full gold.

NOSE Fresh, wet earth. Recent bottlings seem to have more (positive) wood
extract. Freshly cut wood. Resiny. Distant sherry note. Scottish tablet. Honey.

BODY Smooth and light.

PALATE Clean and crisp. Toffee notes. Soft spiciness.

FINISH Dry, nutty, slight bitterness.

SCORE **77**

OLD FETTERCAIRN 30-year-old, Stillman's Dram, 45 vol

This replaces the 26-year-old Stillman's Dram.

COLOUR Bright, shimmering gold.

NOSE Creamy sherry. Toffee, raisins. Elegant sweetness.

BODY Medium, silky.

PALATE Sherry sweetness, then an outburst of spices.
Cinnamon, ginger. Dry hazelnut.

FINISH Dry, warm, and lingering.

SCORE **78**

OLD FETTERCAIRN 1972, 30-year-old, Cask No 2895, 53.6 vol

Mainly for Japan.

COLOUR Bright gold.

NOSE Malty and fruity. Stewed apples, vanilla. Hint of peat.

BODY Light to medium.

PALATE Smooth and surprisingly fresh. Cedary.
Delicate fudgey touch. Toasted almonds.

FINISH Dry, lingering, gently spicy.

SCORE **79**

OLD FETTERCAIRN 1973, 29-year-old, Cask No 1966, 54.3 vol

Mainly for Japan.

COLOUR Deep gold.

NOSE Sherry. Sultanas, dried apricots. Spices. Touch of burnt wood.

BODY Medium.

PALATE Assertively spicy (fresh ginger), almost tangy ,
with an oaky background.

FINISH Dry, warm and tingling.

SCORE **77**

OLD FETTERCAIRN 1966, 49.6 vol

COLOUR Autumn gold (or blazing gold ?).

NOSE Superb. Opulent sherry. Rich fruit. Flowery.
Toffeeish. Cedary, peppery. Beeswax.

BODY Light, silky.

PALATE At first, the promise of the aroma is not fulfilled. The palate
seems sweetly mellow and soft, but to the point of seeming tired.
Then the fruit and oak elegantly combine.

FINISH Warm, then quickly fading away. Soft spices in aftertaste.

SCORE **79**

GLEN ALBYN

PRODUCER DCL
REGION Highlands DISTRICT Speyside (Inverness)
SITE OF FORMER DISTILLERY Telford Street, Inverness,
Inverness-shire, IV3 5LD

A COMPUTER SUPERSTORE AND a home-improvement store now stand on the site in Inverness once occupied by Glen Albyn, a distillery for 140 years, founded by a Provost (Mayor) of the city (generally regarded as the capital of the Highlands). Before the distillery, there was a brewery on the site. There is still a small pub, The Caley. The site is alongside one of Scotland's great feats of engineering, the Caledonian Canal, the dream of James Watt and Thomas Telford. The canal links the North Sea with the Atlantic by joining Loch Ness with a series of further lochs in the Great Glen (also known in parts as Glen Albyn or Glen Mor, More, or Mhor). There is an unconnected Glen Albyn pub in the centre of Inverness. Albyn is a variation on Albion or Alba, old names applied to Scotland, especially the Highlands.

The shopping strip from nowhere (or everywhere?) has not yet buried the individuality, the sensuous pleasure, and the Scottish pride afforded by a local distillery. There is still whisky, but for how long?

HOUSE STYLE Light. Fruity, nutty, dry. Aperitif.

GLEN ALBYN 26-year-old, Distilled 1975, Rare Malts, 54.8 vol

COLOUR Full primrose.

NOSE Very aromatic. Soapy. Linen. Suede

BODY Light but firm. Slippery.

PALATE Lightly buttery. Briefly syrupy. Malty. Smooth. Dry. Slightly musty.

FINISH Bitter. Brimstone. Quite explosive.

 SCORE **70**

GLEN ALBYN 1974, 28 year-old, Coopers Choice, 46 vol

COLOUR Deep amber.

NOSE Sherry. Burnt wood. Dry hay. Fresh hazelnuts. Cloves.

BODY Light.

PALATE Cedary. A touch of harshness. Hint of cold smoke.

Seems to want a cigar.

FINISH Dry, nutty, quite lingering.

 SCORE **70**

GLEN ALBYN 1974, Gordon & MacPhail, 40 vol

COLOUR Lemony gold.

NOSE Citrusy, herbal. Beeswax.

BODY Light, silky.

PALATE A warm roundness. Beautifully balanced. Creamy maltiness.

FINISH Soft, elegant, and almondy.

 SCORE **74**

GLEN ALBYN 1974, Signatory, 58 vol

COLOUR Lemony gold.

NOSE Fragrant. Tangy. Earthy (wet soil after rain). Almond milk.

BODY Light.

PALATE Warm and fizzy. Open spiciness. Restrained nuttiness.

FINISH Dry, oaky, slightly astringent.

 SCORE **70**

GLEN ALBYN 34 year-old, Douglas Laing, The Old Malt Cask, 47 vol

COLOUR Amber.

NOSE Sherry. Candied chestnut. Creamy fudge. Hint of cherry.

BODY Light to medium.

PALATE Smooth and soft. Dried fruit. Biting spices.

FINISH Soft and gentle but elusive.

 SCORE **71**

GLEN DEVERON

PRODUCER John Dewar & Sons Ltd
REGION Highlands   DISTRICT Speyside (Deveron)
ADDRESS Macduff Distillery, Banff, Banffshire, AB45 3JT
TEL 01261 812612

A WELL-KEPT, smart premises that at first sight clearly accommodates some kind of agricultural industry, though not obviously a malt distillery. Glen Deveron was built during the optimistic 1960s, when distillers could not keep up with demand. This distillery has a more workaday appearance than some of the architectural landmarks built by the whisky industry around that time. Its clean, uncluttered interior has in general been mirrored in the character of its whiskies. They, too, have been clean and uncluttered – whiskies that tasted of malt. They still do, but a newish 10-year-old, now the principal product, has a strong wood influence too.

The distillery is at the point where the glen of the Deveron reaches the sea, at the old fishing town and former spa of Macduff. (Both the distillery and its whiskies are sometimes known by the name Macduff.) On the other side of the river is the town of Banff. At a stretch, this is the western edge of Speyside. Not only is it a fringe location geographically – Glen Deveron was for years somewhat lonely as the sole distillery of the William Lawson company. The distillery's output has largely gone into the Lawson blends. Now Lawson, through the international Martini & Rossi group, is part of Bacardi, which also owns Dewars. Perhaps when Bacardi eventually settles into the whisky business, Glen Deveron will be accorded a higher profile.

HOUSE STYLE Malty. Sweet limes in older versions. Restorative or after dinner.

GLEN DEVERON 10-year-old, 1992, 40 vol

COLOUR Deep gold.

NOSE Freshly cut wood. Cedar-like. Surprisingly assertive.

BODY Light to medium. Notably smooth.

PALATE Malted milk. Condensed milk. Fig toffee. Butterscotch. Thick yogurt. Slightly sour. Lemony

FINISH Crisp. Cinder toffee.

SCORE **72**

GLEN DEVERON 12-year-old, 40 vol

This version is now very hard to find.

COLOUR Gold.

NOSE Faint hints of sherry. Rich, sweet, fresh maltiness.

BODY Light to medium, but notably smooth.

PALATE Full, very clean, delicious maltiness.

FINISH Malty dryness. Quick but pleasantly warming.

SCORE **75**

A very malty 15-year-old, with a good balance of oak, is also hard to find. SCORE 76

INDEPENDENT BOTTLINGS (AS MACDUFF)
MACDUFF 1988, Gordon & MacPhail, 40 vol

COLOUR Greeny gold.

NOSE Fragrant and lively. Fresh lime juice.

BODY Smoothly flowing.

PALATE Sweet barley sugar. Citrusy, lime-like freshness. Hint of honey.

FINISH Mellow, pleasantly warm.

SCORE **73**

MACDUFF 1969, Duncan Taylor, 40.3 vol

COLOUR Bright, greeny gold.

NOSE Complex. Malty and citrusy. Toffee. Restrained sherry notes.

BODY Dense, velvety.

PALATE Mellow, soothing. Fulfilling maltiness. A nutty touch.

FINISH Lingering but in a whispering tone.

SCORE **74**

GLEN ELGIN

PRODUCER Diageo
REGION Highlands   DISTRICT Speyside (Lossie)
ADDRESS Longmorn, Elgin, Morayshire, IV30 3SL
TEL 01343 862000

A "HIDDEN MALTS" BOTTLING, at 12 years old, is a welcome response to those who have urged that this classic Speyside whisky be more readily available as a single. There had previously been a version at around the same level of maturity, but without an age statement. This had been marketed mainly in Japan. The newer expression seems more flowery and complex, while the previous version was more winey.

The distillery itself has never been hidden, but it was for some years heavily branded with the name White Horse, in recognition of its contribution to that blend. The Glen Elgin distillery is very visible on one of the main roads into the town whose name it bears. Although it is just over a hundred years old, its façade dates from 1964, and reflects the classic DCL still-house design of the period.

Where the River Lossie approaches the town of Elgin, there are no fewer than eight distilleries within a few miles. Elgin is also worth a visit for Gordon & MacPhail's whisky shop as well as 13th-century cathedral ruins.

HOUSE STYLE Honey and tangerines. Restorative or after dinner.

EST   1900

GLEN ELGIN™

**SPEYSIDE SINGLE
POT STILL MALT WHISKY**

HAND CRAFTED   B28

AGED **12** YEARS

43% vol.   GLEN ELGIN DISTILLERY,
ELGIN, MORAYSHIRE   750ml

North of *Scotland's mountainous Cairngorm region* the arable land is rich, the climate cool and dry. Here, where the River Lossie meanders toward the ancient Royal Burgh of Elgin, is the fine old distillery that bears its name. House martins, which have returned each April for as long as can be remembered, swoop among the now rare *worm tubs*. The distillery maintains *traditional* practices like these, in order to maintain its whisky's elusive fruity character. To this day, Glen Elgin stands out from the crowd for its HAND-CRAFTED approach to whisky making.

DISTILLERY MANAGER   Andrew C. Cant

DISTILLED AND BOTTLED IN SCOTLAND

GLEN ELGIN 12 year-old, Hidden Malts, 43 vol

COLOUR Deep gold.

NOSE Fruity and flowery. Heather honey. Pears poached in spices.
Hint of coffee beans.

BODY Light but firm.

PALATE Fresh and crisp, flowery, and gingery. A touch of mandarin.

FINISH Dry and spicy.

SCORE **77**

GLEN ELGIN Centenary, 19-year-old, 60 vol

Bottle 297 of 750 to commemorate the first distillation on 1 May 1900.

COLOUR Pale amber, pinkish tinge.

NOSE Flowery heather honey, with spicy, cedary, oaky notes.

BODY Textured.

PALATE Warm honey. Seville orange. Toasted nuts.
Beautifully rounded. Elegant.

FINISH Fragrant. Long and creamy. Delicate smokiness.

SCORE **82**

GLEN ELGIN 32-year-old, Distilled 1971,
Special Release 2003, 42.3 vol

COLOUR Full gold.

NOSE Fragrant. Cedary. Honeyed. Seductive.

BODY Soft, rich, tongue-coating.

PALATE Clean, sweet. A hint of Seville orange. Intense heather honey.
Cereal grain. Crunchy. A lovely whisky.

FINISH Gently drying. Shortbread.

SCORE **81**

GLEN ELGIN 1968, Gordon & MacPhail, 40 vol

COLOUR Deep old gold.

NOSE Distinctively sherry. Exotic wood. Rich sweetness.
Candied orange. Crème brûlée.

BODY Medium, velvety.

PALATE Lusciously smooth. Oak and fruit elegantly mingled.
A touch of cinnamon.

FINISH Dry but rich and long. Hint of bitter chocolate.

SCORE **77**

GLEN FLAGLER

PRODUCER Inver House Distillers Ltd
REGION Lowlands   DISTRICT Central Lowlands
ADDRESS Towers Road, Moffat, Airdrie, Lanarkshire, ML6 8PL
WEBSITE www.inverhouse.com   EMAIL enquiries@inverhouse.com

A SECOND MANIFESTATION of these ghostly spirits has occurred in the new millennium. This is officially their last appearance, but do ghosts respect such sanctions?

Two malt whiskies were produced, under the names Glen Flagler and Killyloch, in different sets of stills – and a grain whisky called Garnheath in a third – at a complex at Moffat, near Airdrie, from 1965. These were some of the shortest lived distilleries in the history of Scotch whisky. The modern complex, in former paper mills, was intended to support the Inver House blends, then owned by Publicker, of Philadelphia, but was hit by one of the industry's cyclical downturns. Killyloch ceased production in the early 1970s, Glen Flagler and Garnheath in the mid-1980s, and the distilleries were dismantled. The warehouses were retained, and a management buy-out created Inver House (*see p. 76*), now Thai-owned.

Glen Flagler was briefly marketed as a single malt. Both it and Killyloch later manifested themselves as vatted malts. In the 1990s, when they seemed to have been lost for ever, the independent bottler Signatory located very small stocks of both malts, and issued them as singles. They were reviewed in the fourth edition of this book.

In 2003, there were official bottlings of both. These were from the last five casks of Glen Flagler (yielding 931 bottles) held by Inver House and the last six casks of Killyloch (371 bottles). The collectibility of these bottles is indicated by the asking price, retail: £425/$680 and £899/$1500 respectively.

HOUSE STYLE Glen Flagler is a spicy, perfumy restorative or aperitif – or, the 1973 edition, with cheese? Killyloch is grainier and sweeter, with dessert. Both have Lowland characters, though these are more obvious in Killyloch.

GLEN FLAGLER 1973, Bottled 2003, 46 vol

COLOUR Old gold.

NOSE Pronounced aroma of new leather. Floral.

BODY Light, slippery.

PALATE Oily, creamy. Smoked cheese.
Drier and more intense than the earlier bottling.

FINISH Dry. Strong, muscular.

SCORE **70**

GLEN FLAGLER 24-year-old, Distilled 1972, Bottled 1997, 52 vol

COLOUR Bright yellow.

NOSE Grassy. Linseed. Young leather.

BODY Medium, firm. Soapy dryness.

PALATE Lemony, oily, peaty.

FINISH Dry. Late, warming, pepperiness.

SCORE **70**

KILLYLOCH 1967, Bottled 2003, 40 vol

COLOUR Lemony yellow.

NOSE Very aromatic. Sourness remarkably like fresh lemon juice.

BODY Light but smooth.

PALATE Lemon sweets. Sherbet. Sweet vanilla. Sharper and
less creamy than the earlier bottling.

FINISH Spicy dryness. Crisp. Refreshing. A lamented Lowlander.

SCORE **68**

GLEN GARIOCH

PRODUCER Morrison Bowmore Distillers Ltd
REGION Highlands DISTRICT Eastern Highlands
ADDRESS Old Meldrum, Inverurie, Aberdeenshire, AB51 0ES
TEL 01651 873450 WEBSITE www.glengarioch.com

HOPES THAT GLENGARIOCH would reopen its maltings were kindled when the distillery was refurbished five or six years ago. They have thus far not materialized, but should not be abandoned. The proprietors have highlighted traditional aspects of both their other distilleries, and have a good story to tell at Glen Garioch.

First, there is the distillery's antiquity. An announcement in *The Aberdeen Journal* in 1785 refers to a licensed distillery on the same site. This makes it Scotland's oldest licence holder. Then there is location. The glen grows some of Scotland's finest barley – and here is one of the few distilleries with its own malting floors. Finally, there is the question of peat. When the distillery was acquired by its present owners, in 1970, their maltster, trained on Islay, was relatively heavy-handed with the peat. The result was a whisky with the "old-fashioned", smoky flavour that the Highland/Speyside region had largely forgotten. The revival of smoky Highlander could be popular at a time when the island whiskies seem to have seized the initiative.

Production stopped in 1995, but distillation restarted in 1997. The building's stonework, decorated with a clock that might grace a municipal building, faces on to the small town of Old Meldrum, on the road from Aberdeen to Banff.

HOUSE STYLE Lightly peaty, flowery, fragrant, spicy.
Aperitif in younger ages. Digestif when older.

GLEN GARIOCH Highland Tradition, 40 vol

COLOUR Gold.

NOSE Attractive, malty. Fresh, mandarin zest. Simple but charming.

BODY Light

PALATE Fresh and direct. Lively summer fruits. Malty.

FINISH Short but refreshing.

SCORE **75**

GLEN GARIOCH 8-year-old, 40 vol

COLOUR Full gold.

NOSE Autumn leaves, grass, hint of peat.

BODY Medium, smooth.

PALATE Malty start, buttery, but very clean. Then flapjack, nutty, lively flavours.

FINISH Late surge of ginger, honey, and heather.

SCORE **76**

GLEN GARIOCH 10-year-old, 40 vol

COLOUR Gold.

NOSE Aromatic and citric. Lemon icing, tinned peach, bran.
New carpets. Drier with water.

BODY Rounded but crisp.

PALATE Cereal with a creamy note playing off the firm maltiness.

FINISH Nutty. Short.

SCORE **75**

GLEN GARIOCH 12 year-old, 40 vol *(Mainly for Asian markets.)*

COLOUR Bronze.

NOSE Fragrant, leafy peatiness. Touch of dry oloroso?

BODY Medium, firm.

PALATE Interlocked heather-honey sweetness and peat-smoky dryness.

FINISH Echoes of both elements. Quick and warming.

SCORE **77**

GLEN GARIOCH 15-year-old, 43 vol

COLOUR Full gold.

NOSE Good whiff of earthy peat, oily smoke. Very aromatic.

BODY Medium, rich.

PALATE Very gradual development from malty, liquorice-like, rooty notes through heathery, flowery, perfumy smokiness. Full of character.

FINISH Very long, spicy, warming.

SCORE **79**

GLEN GARIOCH 12-year-old, 40 vol

Special bottling for National Trust of Scotland.

COLOUR Rich gold

NOSE Tea bread, raisins, maltings, some sweetness. Chocolate.

BODY Medium.

PALATE Bran provides a crisp frame.
Dried fruits with some richness. Lunchtime.

FINISH Hay loft.

SCORE **75**

GLEN GARIOCH 21-year-old, 43 vol

The most recent bottlings have more peat, oak, and sherry than earlier versions at this age. A superb Highland malt.

COLOUR Burnished amber.

NOSE Leathery, leafy, peaty, smoky, phenolic.

BODY Medium to full.

PALATE Sweet, juicy oak. Butter. Nutty, treacly, gingery cake.

FINISH Big and very smoky, but smooth. Lots of lingering toffee and fruit. Currants. Flowering currant.

SCORE **81**

GLEN GARIOCH 18-year-old, Selected Cask Vatting, 59.4 vol

COLOUR Deep, warm gold.

NOSE Fresh, floral, fragrant, gentle. Peat-tinged.

BODY Surprisingly rich.

PALATE Rich, sweet, clean, syrupy maltiness.

FINISH Very long. Treacle toffee. Gingery spiciness. Rooty dryness.
Very warming. Extremely late echo of phenolic peat.

SCORE **80**

GLEN GARIOCH 27-year-old, Selected Cask Vatting, 49.6 vol

This bottling is now hard to find.

COLOUR Bright amber.

NOSE Softly peaty, still with a hint of phenol.

BODY Medium.

PALATE Interplay of malty sweetness and dryness.

FINISH Spicy. Pepper and earthy saltiness.

SCORE **80**

GLEN GARIOCH 1986, Individual Cask Bottling,
Cask No 3065, 250 Bottles Only, 54.4 vol

COLOUR Reddish.

NOSE Fig roll, black banana. Clove, boot polish, oloroso.
With water an artificial lavender note.

BODY Rich and rounded.

PALATE Rich, sweet perfumed and resinous.
The lavender perfume unbalances things.

FINISH Lightly smoky.

SCORE **70**

GLEN GARIOCH 29-year-old, Individual Cask Bottling,
Distilled April 1968, Cask No 626, Hogshead, 56.6 vol

Strictly for the lover of long-matured, oaky whiskies.

COLOUR Very dark orange to chestnut.

NOSE Charred oak. Phenol. Earthy saltiness again.

BODY Big, firm.

PALATE Black-treacle toffee, developing late mint notes. Extra-strong peppermints. Very drying on the tongue.

FINISH Extraordinarily long. Cough sweets.

SCORE **81**

GLEN GARIOCH 200th Anniversary Limited Edition, 43 vol

Distilled in 1961, when Glen Garioch was scarcely peated, and when the stills were heated by coal rather than steam. Matured in first-fill American oak.

COLOUR Bright, deep gold.

NOSE Astonishingly fresh for a whisky of such age. Remarkably minty.

BODY Medium, firm, rounded.

PALATE Freshly soft and clean. Almost menthol-like, developing to a leafier, garden-mint note. Some tasters have found flavours reminiscent of star-fruit. Dryish, against a lightly syrupy malt background.

FINISH Long, minty, warming. Dryish hints of vanilla pod. Remarkably gentle.

SCORE **81**

INDEPENDENT BOTTLINGS

Cadenhead bottles an 11-year-old, distilled 1990, at 56.6 vol. Straw coloured with a nose as soft as American cream soda, it develops an attractive floral quality with water. The palate is summery, light and soft with clover honey sweetening the maltiness. SCORE 76. A 16-year-old single cask no 1585, at 51.9 vol, exclusive to The Whisky Exchange, has an aroma reminiscent of Darjeeling tea; treacle toffee in the palate and liquorice in the finish. SCORE 80

GLEN GRANT

PRODUCER Chivas Brothers
REGION Highlands   DISTRICT Speyside (Rothes)
ADDRESS Rothes, Morayshire, AB38 7BS   TEL 01340 832118   VC

A CHIC SUCCESS IN ITALY, and a Victorian classic in Scotland. Glen Grant was the lone single malt in many a bar from Glasgow to Genoa in the days when this form of whisky was scarcely known outside the Highlands. The distillery, founded in 1840 by John and James Grant, quickly gained a reputation for the quality of its whisky. James Grant, who was a prominent local politician, played a big part in bringing railways to the area, and they in turn distributed his product. The turreted and gabled offices in the "Scottish baronial" style, and the distillery, are set around a small courtyard. James Grant's son, a military major, brought plants from his travels in India and Africa, and created a garden in the glen behind the distillery. In 1995, the garden was restored and is open to visitors.

For the greater part of its history, and until the last couple of decades, Glen Grant has won its renown as a single malt in versions bottled by merchants. Older vintages can still be found bearing in small type the name of bottlers Gordon & MacPhail. Much the same classic label is now used under the name Glen Grant Distillery. Since 1977, the enterprise has been owned by Chivas. The whisky has long been a contributor to Chivas Regal, and is highly regarded by most blenders.

Glen Grant itself remains among the world's big-selling whiskies, but much of its volume is in the younger ages, especially in the important Italian market, where it has been marketed at five years. The version with no age statement, which is the principal Glen Grant in Britain, contains malt less than 10 years old.

HOUSE STYLE Herbal, with notes of hazelnut. In younger ages,
an aperitif; with sherry age, after dinner.

GLEN GRANT 5-year-old, 40 vol

COLOUR Very pale, white wine.

NOSE Light, dry fruitiness, spirity.

BODY Light, slightly sticky, almost resiny.

PALATE Spirity. Pear brandy.

FINISH Fruity, quick.

SCORE **65**

GLEN GRANT No Age Statement, 40 vol

COLOUR Gold.

NOSE Fruity, flowery, nutty, faintly spirity.

BODY Light but firm.

PALATE Dry, slightly astringent at first, becoming soft and nutty.

FINISH Herbal.

SCORE **74**

GLEN GRANT 10-year-old, 43 vol

COLOUR Full gold.

NOSE Still dry, but much softer, with some sweetness.

BODY Light to medium, with no obvious intervention of sherry.

PALATE Lightly sweet start, quickly becoming nutty and very dry.

FINISH Very dry, with herbal notes.

SCORE **76**

GLEN GRANT 15-year-old, Gordon & MacPhail, 40 vol

COLOUR Medium amber.

NOSE Some sherry.

BODY Light to medium.

PALATE Sherryish, soft and nutty, dry.

FINISH Mellow, warming.

SCORE **80**

GLEN GRANT 21-year-old, Gordon & MacPhail, 40 vol

Take it slowly, and appreciate the subtlety and development.

COLOUR Full amber red.

NOSE Lots of sherry.

BODY Medium, soft.

PALATE Sherryish sweetness at first, then malt and grassy-peaty notes, finally the nutty Glen Grant dryness.

FINISH Lingering, flowery.

SCORE **81**

GLEN GRANT 25-year-old, Gordon & MacPhail, 40 vol

Not so much chess as wrist wrestling, with the sherry coming out on top. A robust version.

COLOUR Dark.

NOSE Lots of sherry.

BODY Medium, firm.

PALATE Dry oloroso character at first, then nutty dryness. A lot of depth.

FINISH Deep, flowery, peaty.

SCORE **81**

GOOD TO GO, AT 50-PLUS

The Grants of Rothes and the Urquharts of Elgin were both Victorian entrepreneurs in the durable Scottish mould. Some equally durable Glen Grants slumber among the 7000 casks in the warehouse of the Urquhart's little shop, Gordon & MacPhail. On the facing page is a trio that got away ... went on the bottle. Each is more than 50 years old.

GLEN GRANT 1950, Gordon & MacPhail, 40 vol

COLOUR Gold with copper glints.

NOSE Very perfumed. Violet, rhubarb, nutty, stewed fruit.
Complex slightly faded.

BODY Delicate, a lacy texture.

PALATE Ethereal. Oak, resin, sandalwood. Nutmeg, lanolin.
Soft smoke in background.

FINISH Lightly smoky.

SCORE **83**

GLEN GRANT 1952, Gordon & MacPhail, 40 vol

COLOUR Gold.

NOSE Gentle, sweet, and fragrant. Herbal, green fern,
light smoke, beechnut, smoky.

BODY Soft, rounded, and gentle.

PALATE Autumn bonfires, nuts, a rich complex body. Heather. Rooty. Old.

FINISH Smoke. Still sweet.

SCORE **86**

GLEN GRANT 1953, Gordon & MacPhail, 45 vol

COLOUR Mahogany with dull yellow/green rim.

NOSE Chicory coffee, acorn, walnut, chestnut paste.

BODY Tight and firm.

PALATE Dry, tannic, black tobacco, bitter chocolate. Very dry.

FINISH Espresso. Bitter.

SCORE **73**

GLEN KEITH

PRODUCER Chivas Brothers
REGION Highlands   DISTRICT Speyside (Strathisla)
ADDRESS Station Road, Keith, Banffshire, AB55 3BS

CHIVAS OWNS TWO DISTILLERIES next door to one another in the town of Keith, on the River Isla. One simply takes the name of the district, Strathisla; the other is Glen Keith, which was built on the site of a corn mill in 1957–60. It was one of the first of a new generation of malt distilleries at that time, and was intended as a showpiece for a blend called Passport. The branding on the building has the feel of a late 1950s time warp.

Glen Keith had the first gas-fired still in Scotland, and pioneered the use of computers in the industry. Some 1960s' distillates were bottled by Gordon & MacPhail in the 1980s. A less chewy official bottling, initially with a 1983 vintage date, made its debut in 1993–94. The whisky is now simply identified as being 10 years old.

HOUSE STYLE Gingery, rooty, tart. Before dinner.

GLEN KEITH 10-year-old, 43 vol

COLOUR Solid gold.

NOSE Flower petals. Lemon grass. Rooty. Ginger. Cedar. Oak.

BODY Medium.

PALATE Sweet, chewy, ginger cake.

FINISH Very late, fruity tartness.

SCORE **73**

GLEN MHOR

PRODUCER DCL
REGION Highlands   DISTRICT Speyside (Inverness)
SITE OF FORMER DISTILLERY Telford Street, Inverness, Inverness-shire, IV3 5LU

PURISTS PRONOUNCE IT the Gaelic way, "Glen Vawr", to rhyme with "law". The distillery, built in 1892 in Inverness and demolished in 1986, was one of several at which the poet, novelist, and pioneering whisky writer, Neil Gunn, worked as an exciseman. In his book, *Scotch Missed*, Brian Townsend writes that Gunn was inspired by Glen Mhor to let slip his observation that "until a man has had the luck to chance upon a perfectly matured malt, he does not really know what whisky is". Even in Gunn's day, Glen Mhor could be found as a single malt, and casks still find their way into independent bottlings.

HOUSE STYLE Aromatic, treacly. Quite sweet. With dessert or after dinner.

GLEN MHOR, 22-year-old, Distilled 1979, Bottled 2001, Rare Malts, 61 vol

COLOUR Shimmery old gold.

NOSE Surprisingly fresh, minty, and herbal.

BODY Lightly syrupy. Texture reminiscent of whipped cream. Rose-water, sherbet. Meringue on a shortbread base.

FINISH Distinctly leafy and grassy.

SCORE **78**

SOME INDEPENDENT BOTTLINGS

GLEN MHOR 1979, Gordon & MacPhail, "Cask" Series, 66.7 vol

COLOUR Deep gold to peach.

NOSE Liquorice. Rooty. Grassy.

BODY Rich.

PALATE Liquorice, treacle toffee, madeira.

FINISH Winey acidity. Hessian. Light oak. Toast. Spicy warmth.

SCORE **77**

GLEN MHOR Vintage 1977, Signatory, Cask No 1546, 43 vol

COLOUR Greeny gold.

NOSE Soft liquorice. Waxy.

BODY Light but smooth, and oily.

PALATE Liquorice. Fruit gums. Lemon jelly. Quite sweet.

FINISH Limes. Chilli.

SCORE **72**

GLEN MHOR 20-year-old, Distilled 1976, Cadenhead, 57.9 vol

COLOUR Primrose.

NOSE Light lipstick.

BODY Light to medium. Syrupy.

PALATE Sugary. Lemony. Flowery, perfumy, lemon character.

FINISH Sherbety. Spicy, becoming drier. Warming.

Wins points for balance, especially in that late dryness.

SCORE **74**

GLEN MHOR 21-year-old, Distilled 1976, Hart Brothers, 43 vol

COLOUR Pale greeny gold.

NOSE Fruit gums. Lemon. Lime. Developing to lemon grass.

BODY Syrupy but gritty (like a golden, sweet molasses).

PALATE Sugary. Lemony. Then a lemon-pith dryness.

FINISH Sugar. Strong peppermint sweets. Mint imperials.

Warming. Long. Digestif.

SCORE **73**

GLEN MORAY

PRODUCER Glenmorangie plc
REGION Highlands   DISTRICT Speyside (Lossie)
ADDRESS Bruceland Road, Elgin, Morayshire, IV30 1YE   TEL 01343 542577
WEBSITE www.glenmoray.com   EMAIL tdavidson@glenmorangieplc.co.uk

THE GRAPEY NOTE that some devotees find in Glen Moray is a house characteristic. It preceded the distillery's enthusiasm for wine finishes, most recently Vallée du Rhône. The earlier Chardonnay and Chenin Blanc finishes, launched in 1999, seemed to be aimed at ladies who lunch. The use of whites was an innovation in the industry. Glen Moray shares owners with the more northerly Glenmorangie distillery, which pioneered the notion of "wine" finishes but with reds, port, and madeira.

The two distilleries' similar names pre-date their common ownership. It is a second coincidence that both were formerly breweries. Glen Moray was converted into a distillery in 1897, acquired by its present owners in the 1920s, and extended in 1958. Its whiskies are admired, but have never enjoyed great glamour. Now they sport a change of orientation: skirts instead of kilts – the distillery previously favoured gift tins decorated with the liveries of Highland regiments. The smartly kept distillery is in boggy land near the river Lossie, just outside Elgin.

HOUSE STYLE Grassy, with barley notes. Aperitif.

GLEN MORAY 8-year-old, 43 vol

Mainly available in Italy.

COLOUR Very pale, satiny gold.

NOSE Fresh but soft. Sweet, with a late, oily hint of peat.

BODY Very light, but smooth and oily.

PALATE Very light indeed. Oily. Gin-like.

FINISH Light touch of cereal-grain firmness. Late, very light, smoky warmth.

GLEN MORAY Single Speyside Malt, No Age Statement, 40 vol

Six to ten years in bourbon casks, then "mellowed" in Chardonnay.

COLOUR Very pale gold.

NOSE Fresh, scented, fruity. Like an unpeeled dessert grape.
Perhaps a suggestion of banana. Very light hint of the sea.

BODY Very soft, textured.

PALATE Watermelon. Banana. White chocolate. Lightly creamy. Shortbread.

FINISH Grape skins. Apple cores. Hay. Cereal grains.
Lightly dry and very crisp.

GLEN MORAY 12-year-old, "Mellowed" in Chenin Blanc, 40 vol

COLOUR Softer, more yellowy.

NOSE Pears. Walnuts. Fresh oak.

BODY Smooth, oily. Beeswax. Honeyed.

PALATE Pears in cream. Late, lively, peachy fruitiness. Garden mint.

FINISH Raisiny. Also resiny. Fresh oak. Soothing warmth.

GLEN MORAY 16-year-old, "Mellowed" in Chenin Blanc, 40 vol

COLOUR Old gold.

NOSE Very aromatic. Hint of cloves. Apples. Tannin.

BODY Smooth and very firm.

PALATE More assertive. Toffee, apple, oak.

FINISH Long. Hints of peat. Grassy. Leafy. Resiny. Peppery.

SCORE **76**

GLEN MORAY 1981, Single Sherry Butt, Cask No 3661, 57.7 vol

COLOUR Chestnut.

NOSE Honeydew melon. A hint of garden mint. Milk pudding. Caramel. Cedar.

PALATE Creamy. Spicy. Sultanas. Plum cake. Nougat. Some toffeeish chewiness. Rich but mature.

FINISH Slightly burnt. Slightly rooty and woody.

SCORE **82**

GLEN MORAY 1976, Vallée du Rhône, 46 vol

COLOUR Pinky sunset.

NOSE Soft and ripe. Bruised plum, caramelized fruit, dried orange peel, vanilla.

PALATE Slick and soft, plum cake and crackerbread. Orange peel.

FINISH Winey, soft.

SCORE **75**

GLEN MORAY DISTILLERY Manager's Choice 1974, 53.2 vol

COLOUR Old gold.

NOSE Perfumed candles. Wax. Smoke. Joss sticks. Spicy.

BODY Oily, Creamy, malty.

PALATE Drying.

FINISH Slightly sharp. Provocative.

SCORE **77**

SOME VINTAGE EDITIONS OF GLEN MORAY

GLEN MORAY 1974, Port Wood Aged, Limited Edition, Bottled 1997

COLOUR Full gold.

NOSE Lovely, perfumy complexity.

BODY Far richer than other versions.

PALATE Oily cereal grain. Honey-roast nuts.

FINISH Perfumy again. Sugared almonds. An after-dinner malt of extraordinary delicacy. Beautiful balance of distillery character and port.

SCORE **80**

GLEN MORAY 1973, 43 vol

COLOUR Pale gold, with a tinge of green.

NOSE Very sweet, but still extremely clean.

BODY Very smooth indeed.

PALATE Very complex, with lots of development of sweet (barley, malt and chocolate), delicately spicy notes.

FINISH Light sweetness and light peatiness. Long and lingering, with surges of flavour.

SCORE **78**

GLEN MORAY 1966, 43 vol

COLOUR Solid amber.

NOSE Nutty, juicy, oaky but fresh.

BODY Smooth, soft.

PALATE Nutty dryness, malty sweetness, and a hint of grassy peatiness, beautifully balanced and rounded. A confident, elegant malt.

FINISH Sweetness and dryness, with the latter eventually winning. Touches of sappy oakiness. A curiously spicy lift at the very end.

SCORE **80**

GLEN MORAY 1959, Bottled 1999, 48.4 vol

COLOUR Full amber.

NOSE Rich fruitcake steeped in sherry.

BODY Very creamy indeed.

PALATE Rich. Fruitcake. The dryness of burnt currants. Intensely nutty, almondy, marzipan development.

FINISH Light, nutty dryness. Chewy. Long. Developing a touch of charred oak.

SCORE **79**

GLEN ORD

PRODUCER Diageo
REGION Highlands DISTRICT Northern Highlands
ADDRESS Muir of Ord, Ross-shire, IV6 7UJ TEL 01463 872004
WEBSITE www.discovering-distilleries.com/www.malts.com VC

THE LAUNCH IN 2003 of a 12-year-old "Hidden Malt" from Glen Ord was very welcome, but begged a question. Why was it hidden in the first place? Why has this distillery been obliged to play hide-and-seek over the years? Under different managements, its whisky has occupied endless different positions in the marketing portfolio. It has even sported different names: Glenordie, Ordie, Ord, Muir of Ord.

It is at a village called Muir of Ord ("the moor by the hill"), just to the west and north of Inverness. This is the region where Ferintosh, the first famous whisky, was made (*see also* Ben Wyvis). Glen Ord also has a maltings (of the drum type). The distillery and maltings look over the barley-growing country of the Black Isle.

HOUSE STYLE Flavoursome, rose-like, spicy (cinnamon?),
and malty, with a dry finish. After dinner.

GLEN ORD 12-year-old, Hidden Malt, 43 vol

COLOUR	Full gold.
NOSE	Fresh. Turned earth, daffodil. Resiny. Sultana, malt. Hint of sulphur.
BODY	Medium, firm.
PALATE	Dry grass, warm cinnamon, then toffee. Good punch.
FINISH	Malt and oak.

SCORE **78**

GLEN ORD 1974, 23-year-old, Rare Malts, 60.8 vol

COLOUR Very pale primrose.

NOSE Very fresh, assertive. Leafy, lightly peaty. Fragrant smoke.

BODY Big, soft, slightly syrupy.

PALATE Nutty malt, raisins, ginger, lemon peel, roses.

FINISH Spicy, flowery, peaty.

SCORE **78**

GLEN ORD 28-year-old, Distilled 1975,
Special Release 2003, 58.3 vol

COLOUR Primrose.

NOSE The slightest hint of smokiness. Crusty bread baking.
Sweeter than ordinary bread; brioche, perhaps.

BODY Medium.

PALATE Assertive. Honeyed. Expressive. Spicy. Unusually lively.

FINISH Extraordinary explosion of sweet-and-sour flavours. Spicy. Vanilla.
Flowery. Leafy. Lemon juice.

SCORE **82**

GLEN ORD 1983, Signatory, 58.3 vol

COLOUR Gold.

NOSE Attractive. Meadow grass. Fresh malt. Stewed orange, vanilla.
Toasty wood, cedar.

BODY Silky. Liqueur-like.

PALATE French patisserie. Red fruits. Oranges.

FINISH Grassy.

SCORE **80**

GLEN SCOTIA

PRODUCER Loch Lomond Distillery Co. Ltd
REGION Campbeltown
ADDRESS 12 High Street, Campbeltown, Argyll, PA28 6DS
TEL 01586 552288 *Visits by appointment only*
EMAIL mail@lochlomonddistillery.com

LOVERS OF CAMPBELTOWN MALTS will be pleased to learn that a new bottling of Glen Scotia is envisaged around the middle of this decade, but that is not yet certain. If it materializes, it is likely to be an eight-year-old.

Glen Scotia has been in full production since 1999, after being acquired by the Loch Lomond company. Production had been very sporadic for more than a decade before that. The only official bottling for some years has been a 14-year-old, and there are still stocks available. By now, much of the vatting must comprise older whiskies. This would account for a slightly rounder, less fresh character. Glen Scotia, founded around 1832, is known for more than one manifestation of spirit: it is said to be haunted by the ghost of a former proprietor who drowned himself in Campbeltown Loch.

HOUSE STYLE Fresh, salty. Aperitif, or with salty foods.

GLEN SCOTIA 14-year-old, 40 vol

COLOUR Full, refractive gold.

NOSE Aromatic, waxy, piney.

BODY Seems light on the tongue, then quickly becomes oily and smooth.

PALATE Dry maltiness, coconut, saltiness. Very appetite-arousing.

FINISH Long and robust.

SCORE **86**

INDEPENDENT BOTTLINGS

*Glen Scotia is hard to find, and good casks even more elusive,
judging from the quality of independent bottlings.*

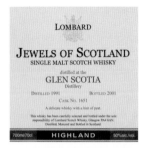

GLEN SCOTIA 1991, Lombard Brands, 50 vol

COLOUR White.

NOSE Harsh, vegetal, sulphury.

BODY Thin.

PALATE Hot with raw edges. Lacks maturity.

FINISH Short.

SCORE **60**

GLEN SCOTIA 1990, Gordon & MacPhail, 40 vol

COLOUR Gold.

NOSE A little metallic. Stewed fruit.

BODY Dry. Drying.

PALATE Malty. Falls apart in the mouth.

FINISH Short.

SCORE **67**

GLEN SCOTIA 1990, Signatory, 43 vol

COLOUR Pale gold.

NOSE A touch of smoke. Intense and zesty.

BODY Light. Dry.

PALATE A raw edge. Lacks substance.

FINISH Short, dry.

SCORE **70**

GLEN SPEY

PRODUCER Diageo
REGION Highlands DISTRICT Speyside (Rothes)
ADDRESS Rothes, Aberlour, Banffshire, AB38 7AU
TEL 01340 882000

A FLORA AND FAUNA BOTTLING launched in 2002 renders this distillery slightly more visible. It is in the heart of Speyside, but not on the river. Glen Spey, dating from the 1880s, is in Rothes. Much of its whisky is destined for the house blend of an aristocratic wine and spirits merchant in St James's, London. (It is coincidence that neighbour Glenrothes follows a parallel path). In the case of Glen Spey, the merchant is Justerini & Brooks, whose house blend is J&B.

Giacomo Justerini was an Italian, from Bologna. He emigrated to Britain in pursuit of an opera singer, Margherita Bellion, in 1749. The romance does not seem to have come to fruition, but Justerini meanwhile worked in Britain as a maker of liqueurs. By 1779, he was already selling Scotch whisky. Brooks was a later partner in the firm. The business was for a time part of Gilbeys, at which point there was for a time a nutty, grassy eight-year-old Glen Spey.

HOUSE STYLE Light, grassy, nutty. Aperitif.

SPEYSIDE
SINGLE MALT
SCOTCH WHISKY

The Scots Pines beside *the ruins of ROTHES CASTLE*, provide an *ideal habitat* for the *GOLDCREST, Britain's smallest bird*, and overlook the

GLEN SPEY

distillery. Founded in 1885, *the distillery was originally* part of the *Mills of Rothes. Water from the DOONIE BURN* is used to produce this *smooth, warming single MALT SCOTCH WHISKY*. A slight sense of *wood smoke* on *the nose* is rewarded with a *spicy, dry* finish.

AGED 12 YEARS

43% vol   Distilled & Bottled in SCOTLAND   70cl
GLEN SPEY DISTILLERY Rothes, Aberlour, Banffshire, Scotland.

GLEN SPEY 12 year-old, Flora and Fauna, 43 vol

COLOUR Full gold.

NOSE Cookie-like maltiness (rich tea biscuit), dusty floor.
Kumquat. Leafy. Garden mint.

BODY Medium. Oily.

PALATE Vivacious. Starts intensely sweet, with light citrus notes,
then becomes dramatically drier.

FINISH Crisp. Lemon zest. Pith.

SCORE **75**

GLEN SPEY 19-year-old, Cadenhead, 57 vol

COLOUR Light gold.

NOSE Very light. Some lime leaf, dry grass, oak, green walnut.

BODY Thin.

PALATE Light residual sweetness but overall dry.

FINISH Cayenne and citrus.

SCORE **70**

Vintage 1974
Single Highland Malt Scotch Whisky
Matured in an oak cask for 26 years
Distilled at Glen Spey Distillery
on 20.5.74   Bottled 8.9.2000
Cask No. 792   Bottle   of 230
*This whisky has been selected,   and bottled in
Scotland for and under the sole responsibility of
Signatory Vintage Scotch Whisky Co. Ltd.
Edinburgh EH6 5PY Scotland*
70cl   NATURAL COLOUR   50.4% vol

GLEN SPEY 1974, 26-year-old, Cask No 792, Signatory, 50.4 vol

COLOUR Straw.

NOSE Corn husks, cream light and grassy. Touch of mint.

BODY Fluffy.

PALATE Tiger nuts, apple sponge, cream, green grapes.

FINISH Sweet and light.

SCORE **75**

GLENALLACHIE

PRODUCER Chivas Brothers
REGION Highlands DISTRICT Speyside
ADDRESS Aberlour, Banffshire, AB38 9LR

TRUE WHISKY LOVERS LIKE TO SAMPLE EVERYTHING, and Glenallachie (pronounced "glen-alec-y") is certainly worth tasting. Although it has only a modest reputation, it is a good example of a subtle, delicate, flowery Speyside malt.

The distillery was built in 1967 primarily to contribute malt to the Mackinlay blends. It was temporarily closed in the late 1980s, then acquired and reopened by Campbell Distillers at the end of the decade.

A dam and a small waterfall soften the exterior of the functional, modern distillery building. It takes its water from a spring on Ben Rinnes, just over the hill from its senior partner, Aberlour. Despite their proximity, their water is different, and so is their whisky: Glenallachie lighter, more acidic, drier, more delicate; Aberlour richer, more luscious, sweeter, maltier.

HOUSE STYLE Clean, subtle, delicate. Aperitif.

GLENALLACHIE 12-year-old, 40 vol

A Mackinlay bottling that is now difficult to find. A graceful pre-dinner companion.

COLOUR Very pale.

NOSE Hint of peat. Fragrant. Lightly malty.

BODY Light but firm.

PALATE Beautifully clean, smooth, and delicate.

FINISH Starts sweet and develops towards a long, perfumy finish.

SCORE **76**

GLENBURGIE

PRODUCER Allied Distillers Ltd
REGION Highlands DISTRICT Speyside (Findhorn)
ADDRESS Forres, Morayshire, IV36 0QX TEL 01343 850258

A RARE RELEASE OF GLENBURGIE as a single malt came in 2002, when proprietors Allied launched their range of Special Distillery Bottlings. These 15-year-olds are primarily for sale at the group's distilleries, but will no doubt find their way farther afield. This example is a long overdue reminder of an enjoyable malt.

A noted admirer of Glenburgie's herbal, fruity whisky was writer Maurice Walsh, whose story *The Quiet Man* was made into a movie starring John Wayne and Maureen O'Hara. Like Robert Burns and Neil Gunn, writer Walsh had a "day job" as an exciseman, in his case at Glenburgie. A less romantic, more technical claim to the noteworthiness of this distillery is its second malt whisky.

The distillery traces its history to 1810, and on its present site to 1829. It is in the watershed of the Findhorn, at Alves, between Forres and Elgin. Glenburgie was extended after the Second World War, at a time when many whiskies were in short supply. At that time, some Allied distilleries were being given additional stills of a different design, to extend their range. These "Lomond" stills, with a column-shaped neck, produced an oilier, fruitier malt. The whisky from Glenburgie's Lomond stills was named after Willie Craig, one of the company's senior managers. Those stills were removed in the early 1980s, but Glencraig can still be found in independent bottlings.

HOUSE STYLE Oily, fruity, herbal. Aperitif.

GLENBURGIE 15 year-old, 46 vol

COLOUR Bright gold.

NOSE Attractive sweetness, fragrant. Praline,

touch of orange peel.

BODY Medium, firm.

PALATE Round, velvety. Assertive. Fruity, toffeeish.

FINISH Dry, leafy. Hint of liquorice.

SCORE **76**

SOME INDEPENDENT BOTTLINGS OF GLENBURGIE
GLENBURGIE 12 year-old, Douglas Laing,
The Old Malt Cask, 50 vol

COLOUR Pale gold.

NOSE Oaky, gingery. Fresh oak, lemon zest.

BODY Oily, medium.

PALATE Smooth, clinging. Fruity. Touch of cinnamon. Walnut.

FINISH Dry, lingering.

SCORE **72**

GLENBURGIE 10-year-old, 40 vol, Gordon & MacPhail

COLOUR Full gold.

NOSE   Touch of sour cream.

BODY Light and smooth.

PALATE Sweet and soft. Buttery fudge.

Fermentation flavours.

FINISH Quick, sweet then oaky.

SCORE **67**

GLENBURGIE 1967, Signatory, 53 vol

COLOUR Bright, sparkling gold.

NOSE Quite complex. Malty and fruity. Beeswax. Citrus touch.

BODY Velvety, oily, firm.

PALATE Rich. Developing fruit and cream. Coating.

Tangy without water.

FINISH Spicy followed by a soothing sweetness.

SCORE **74**

GLENBURGIE 1966, Duncan Taylor, 40.7 vol

COLOUR Light gold.

NOSE Complex, charming. Flowery, honey. Pipe tobacco.
Hint of smoke. Liquorice.

BODY Round, oily.

PALATE Delicate smoothness. Juicy fruitiness, kiwi, pears.
A touch of smoke. Lighthearted sherry.

FINISH Sensuous, lasting. Slow fade to soft spiciness.

SCORE **76**

SOME INDEPENDENT BOTTLINGS OF GLENCRAIG
GLENCRAIG 1981, 21 year-old, Cadenhead, 56.2 vol

COLOUR Full gold.

NOSE Intense. Definitely sherry. Resiny. Strong coffee. Cloves.

BODY Firm, oily.

PALATE Powerful. Smooth to start then develops lively spiciness.

FINISH Very warm, with a slight bitter touch. Seems everlasting.

SCORE **68**

GLENCRAIG 1975, Gordon & MacPhail, 40 vol

COLOUR Deep gold.

NOSE Aromatic elegancy. Leafy. Rich fruit. Apricot. Almonds.

BODY Very oily, round.

PALATE Appetizing spiciness. Rich. Dried fruit. Toffee. Nourishing.

FINISH Warming and fulfilling.

SCORE **73**

GLENCADAM

PRODUCER Angus Dundee Distillers plc
REGION Highlands DISTRICT Eastern Highlands
ADDRESS Brechin, Angus, DD9 7PA TEL 01356 622217

WHEN MERCHANT AND INDEPENDENT bottler Angus Dundee acquired its first distillery, Tomintoul, there were no dramatic changes. The same may be true of this one, its second acquisition. Glencadam's previous owners, Allied, have not aggressively promoted their distilleries, either, though the 15-year-old Glencadam reviewed below was from their series of Special Distillery Bottlings.

Glencadam is a notably creamy malt. Appropriately, much of the distillery's output has over the years gone into "Cream of the Barley", originally blended in Dundee, but popular in Belfast.

The neat little distillery, at Brechin, was founded in 1825 and modernized in 1959. The very soft water is piped an astonishing 48 km (30 miles) from Loch Lee, at the head of Glen Esk. With neighbour North Port now gone, Glencadam is a lonely survivor on this stretch of coastline.

HOUSE STYLE Creamy, with a suggestion of berry fruits.
With dessert, or after dinner.

GLENCADAM 15-year-old, 46 vol

COLOUR Old gold.
NOSE Perfumy. Floral, elegant. Ripe summer fruit. Plum pudding, peach melba.
BODY Full, silky.
PALATE Smooth, mouth-coating. So creamy. Strawberry yogurt. Rounded and appealing.
FINISH A little shy but sweet and satisfying.

SCORE 73

GLENDRONACH

PRODUCER Allied Distillers Ltd
REGION Highlands   DISTRICT Speyside (Deveron)
ADDRESS Forgue, by Huntly, Aberdeenshire, AB5 6DB
TEL 01466 730202   VC

THE BEST NEWS for malt lovers in 2002 was the restarting of production at Glendronach, after six years' silence. At the same time, the distillery's owners took a new interest in making its products available, with plans for a new bottling at 12 years old. This new version will have a light touch of sherry, rounded with a reracking in bourbon barrels. Over the years, Glendronach 12 has appeared in a confusion of styles. At one stage, there was a welcome choice between "The Original" (second-fill, mainly bourbon) and a version labelled "100 per cent matured in sherry casks". These two were then replaced by "Traditional", which attempted to marry their virtues. Stock problems led to this being replaced by a 15-year-old, which is itself now becoming hard to find.

The whiskies are greatly appreciated by malt lovers, but much affection is also felt for the place. Deep in Aberdeenshire's fertile barley-growing country, the glen of the Dronac Burn almost hides the cluster of buildings, but a pagoda is hard to conceal. The floor maltings have not restarted, but there have been suggestions that they might. A flourish of tradition that has been rekindled is the use of coal-fired, direct-flame stills. While steam heats more evenly, flame creates hot spots, which can promote a caramel-ish, toffee-like maltiness.

The distillery has its own small mansion house, flower beds and kitchen garden, as though it were a small estate. (Domaine Dronac?)

The fifth Duke of Gordon, the man behind the legalization of distilling in the Highlands in the 1820s, is credited with having encouraged local farmers to establish this distillery. It was later run by a member of the William Grant (Glenfiddich) family, and in 1960 was acquired to help provide the malty background to the well-known blend Teacher's, now owned by Allied. Teacher's own principal distillery was Ardmore. As that is nearby in Aberdeenshire, and was also coal-fired until recently.

HOUSE STYLE Smooth, big, with a teasing sweet-and-dry maltiness.
Sherry-friendly. After dinner.